ME three
their

The Woman in the White House

THE
WOMAN
IN THE
WHITE HOUSE

The Lives, Times and Influence
of Twelve Notable First Ladies

MARIANNE MEANS

Random House   New York

The following publishers are to be thanked for permission to quote excerpted passages from books and articles. These passages appear in the chapters listed below:

HELEN HERRON TAFT—Dodd, Mead & Company, *Recollections of Full Years* by Helen Herron Taft, 1914.

EDITH BOLLING GALT WILSON—Dodd, Mead & Company, *First Lady Extraordinary* by Alden Hatch, Copyright © 1961 by Alden Hatch. Bobbs-Merrill Company, *My Memoir* by Edith Bolling Wilson, Copyright 1938 by Edith Bolling Wilson.

FLORENCE KLING HARDING—Houghton Mifflin Company, *Forty-two Years in the White House* by Irwin Hood Hoover, 1934.

ANNA ELEANOR ROOSEVELT—Harper & Row, Publishers, Inc., *The Autobiography of Eleanor Roosevelt*, Copyright © 1961 by Anna Eleanor Roosevelt. Harcourt, Brace & World, Inc., *Affectionately, F.D.R.*, by James Roosevelt and Sidney Shallet, 1959. Simon and Schuster, Inc., *The Secret Diary of Harold Ickes* by Harold Ickes, 1954. Article by Arthur Schlesinger, Jr., Copyright by *The New York Times*.

ELIZABETH WALLACE TRUMAN—G. P. Putnam's Sons, *The Man from Missouri* by Alfred Steinberg, 1962; *The Captains and the Kings* by Edith Benham Helm, 1962.

Endpaper photos: Eleanor Roosevelt, permission of Edward Steichen; Bess Truman, permission of U.P.I.; all others, White House Photos.

FIFTH PRINTING

© *Copyright, 1963, by Marianne Means*

All rights reserved under International and Pan-American Copyright Conventions. Published in New York by Random House, Inc., and simultaneously in Toronto, Canada, by Random House of Canada, Limited.

Library of Congress Catalog Card Number: 63-14143

MANUFACTURED IN THE UNITED STATES OF AMERICA BY
The Haddon Craftsmen, Inc., Scranton, Pennsylvania

Design by Tere LoPrete

For my parents—
And for all First Ladies and their parents,
past, present, and future

ACKNOWLEDGMENTS

❀ ❀

Words are ever inadequate, but they are all I have to acknowledge my deep gratitude to the legions of busy and important people who contributed to the preparation of this book.

I especially thank President John F. Kennedy, former President Dwight D. Eisenhower, and former President Harry S Truman for their great help and encouragement. Their co-operation made possible the three chapters on the contemporary First Ladies.

And I wish to acknowledge the co-operation of Tish Baldrige, Pam Turnure, and the present White House staff; friends and former associates of Mrs. Truman and Mrs. Eisenhower who wished to remain anonymous; Mrs. Charles Wrightsman; Mr. David Finley; the staff at the Library of Congress, and Mr. Clark Kinnaird. I am also indebted to my capable friends Mrs. A. Burke Hertz, Mrs. Edmund Hiedenkamp, and Mrs. Betty Lilly.

Finally, I must thank the Hearst newspapers, as personified to me by William Randolph Hearst, Jr., Frank Conniff, Milt Kaplan, and David Sentner, who have put up with more than any one organization should be asked to endure.

CONTENTS

✤✤

INTRODUCTION

❀ ❀

Since President Kennedy's inauguration, I have covered his and Mrs. Kennedy's activities as the White House correspondent for the Hearst newspapers. Before my contact with the White House occupants, I did not suspect that a First Lady's opinions had much effect on the conduct of the presidency. Certainly nothing that I read credited the First Ladies with much more than setting new fashion trends, giving elaborate parties, and being a "good wife and mother"—whatever that sweeping generalization means.

I have watched with fascination the mounting evidence of First Lady Jacqueline Kennedy's impact on the nation and, more subtly, on her husband. Her emphatic endorsement of the highest forms of the performing arts, for example, is helping to enrich the lives of many Americans who never before listened to a concert or visited an art gallery. Mrs. Kennedy has, meanwhile, added a new dimension to the President's life, for he admits he would never sit through a serious concert unless his wife lured him there. An even more tangible effect of Mrs. Kennedy's tastes, interests, and, surprisingly, her administrative ability has been her direction of the restoration of the White House.

I began to wonder what really distinguished roles other First Ladies played as partners to their President-husbands. The Constitution has little to say about the scope of powers and limitations of the presidency. It has even less—in fact, nothing—to say about the duties and privileges of being a First Lady.

Woodrow Wilson said, "The President is at liberty, both in law and conscience, to be as big a man as he can." The same assertion can be applied to the potentialities of the role of the highest-ranking woman in the nation. Of course, the law eliminates her from the administration of government, but what man has not found it expedient to listen to his wife's opinions?

Every day hundreds of proud American mothers look at their new-born sons and reflect on the almost hopeless cliché, "He may grow up to be President." But I will wager that not a mother in history has held her infant daughter and dreamed that some day she might become First Lady. A woman usually marries the man she loves, and what happens to him will determine her life as well. Only three women married men who were Presidents. Other First Ladies married engineers, soldiers, lawyers, and businessmen. In a society where men dominate the professional and business life, men have ample opportunity to prepare themselves for the heavy responsibilities of the presidency. Wives have little opportunity to train themselves for the demands of being a First Lady and those who have met the challenge in unique ways are the subject of this book.

Inspired by Mrs. Kennedy, I have selected eleven other First Ladies who played vital roles in shaping their husbands' lives and, tangentially, their nation's destiny. A few were responsible for prodding their reluctant husbands toward the White House. Our wartime First Ladies gave their husbands the kind of wifely support which made it possible for them to carry out their awesome responsibilities. One became "acting President" during her husband's serious illness and another became her crippled husband's "eyes and ears" during the White House years.

The one person who understands the President's every mood, and who is closest to him personally, is the First Lady. Some First Ladies did not often try to press their opinions on their husbands, especially in the early years of the nation's history when women were expected to be seen but not heard. But many did— and the twelve included in this book are women of strong will and nimble wit, and they made their presence felt.

The Woman in the White House

❋ ❋

Martha Dandridge Custis

WASHINGTON

❀ ❀

Martha Washington outlived her husband by more than two years. But as far as she was concerned, her life really ended with his. Martha Washington had shared her husband with the demands of public service for all but seven of their forty years of married life—and those seven years had been her happiest, for she had little interest in politics and less in fame. Her whole world revolved around her husband; she cared for him, his home, his guests, and during the war she even nursed his sick and wounded soldiers.

George Washington became very ill in December, 1799, just two years after he had refused a third term as President of the United States. Mrs. Washington seldom left his bedside. When the doctors told her that her husband was dead, however, she did not cry. She sighed quietly, "All is over now. I've no more trials to pass through."

Since then, as father and mother of their country, George and Martha Washington have become so idolized as symbols of the American spirit that often they appear more saint than human. Indeed, both had such a strong sense of duty that their public image often overshadowed their very human qualities. They had, however, as many idiosyncrasies as anyone, from quite healthy tempers to a tendency to spoil their children and grandchildren.

When the peace treaty with Britain in 1783 officially ended the Revolutionary War, both General and Mrs. Washington were eager to return to the peaceful life of their plantation. They planned to retire and, as Mrs. Washington put it, "grow old together in solitude and tranquility . . . the first and dearest wish of my heart." Neither suspected that destiny would call upon the tired hero to serve his country once again, in the greatest role of all. Washington was fifty-one; his wife a year older. Mrs. Washington's only son Jackey had died in the revolution; the long war years of neglecting Mount Vernon had left them nearly bankrupt. Mrs. Washington later wrote: "I little thought when the war was finished that any circumstances could possibly happen which would call the General into public life again."

Mrs. Washington's "favorite years" began on Christmas Eve, 1783. That day General Washington resigned his commission as the commander in chief of the American Army. Private citizen and Mrs. Washington rode contentedly home to Mount Vernon, where neighbors and relatives waited to celebrate with them. As the carriage pulled up to the house, the doors swung open in welcome—candles flickered in the windows, fireplaces glowed within, and the slaves began to sing "Merry Christmas."

Those were happy times for Mrs. Washington. They enlarged the house to twice its size, planted formal gardens, and added new walks and driveways. The plantation, with her husband home to manage it, began to prosper once again. Guests came in a constant stream; but both Washingtons liked company, and Mrs. Washington was an excellent hostess. Mount Vernon so continually overflowed with friends that Washington was once driven to complain to his mother that his house sometimes seemed like a hotel. And when he and his wife had dinner at the big table alone one night in June, 1785, it was such a rare occurrence that he recorded it in his diary. He noted: "Dined only with Mrs. Washington, which I believe is the first instance since my retirement from public life."

Most of the visitors were old friends, but frequently the men —especially James Madison and James Monroe—came to see the General with more on their minds than social amenities. The leaders of the new nation were uneasy; they wanted Washington's advice. The Continental Congress had too little power. With the war over, the states no longer felt the strong need for unity and were drifting back into a desire for autonomy. The central government had to be strengthened, a new constitution drawn, a strong leader named.

Martha Washington took no part in these discussions. That was "man talk" and she rarely voiced an opinion on the conduct of her husband's business outside the home, or on his politics She occupied herself with her own duties, which were many. As a child, she had never gone to school—she had merely been "exposed" briefly to reading, writing, and arithmetic by a tutor, since in those times it was not thought necessary to educate women. Social graces were considered more important than book learning, and young Martha had been well trained in those. Her stepmother had also trained her never to be idle: she'd had lessons in sewing, housekeeping, cooking, dancing, and music. She could knit, weave, make pickles, put up jelly, embroider a fancy hem, execute a neat cross-stitch. She mothered everyone: her husband, guests, her two grandchildren (Eleanor Parke and George Washington Parke Custis, whom the Washingtons adopted after the death of Jackey, their father), neighbors, friends.

Neither George nor Martha Washington desired to return to public life. Mrs. Washington overheard her husband frequently protest, during those long serious discussions with the visiting gentlemen, that he would give advice and consultation, but the government did not need his active service. She herself was content to stay forever at Mount Vernon. "I have learned too much of the vanity of human affairs to expect felicity from the scenes of public life," she observed.

Gradually, however, Washington was persuaded to head the Virginia delegation to the Federal Constitutional Convention beginning May, 1787, in Philadelphia. Mrs. Washington supervised the packing of his trunks without protest, but she wished that he would not go away. When she confessed her unhappiness to her mother-in-law, Mary Ball Washington, that strong-willed lady merely told her: "George was always a good boy—he always does his duty."

The convention, with Washington as its president, drew up a stronger constitution. Washington returned to Mount Vernon to wait for the states to ratify it. Upon ratification, the electors met in New York and unanimously elected Washington, the aristocrat who had led the rebels, as the first President. A courier was dispatched to Mount Vernon with the news. He reached there on April 14, 1789, and two days later Washington left for New York, which was then the capital.

Washington left his wife behind to handle the huge task of moving their personal and household belongings to New York. He left a woman who, at fifty-eight, was far from jubilant at the prospect of her new status. The demands of her "new and unwished-for situation" presented a complicated array of problems.

What would her duties be? She supposed her responsibilities as hostess would triple; she did not mind that so much, for she was used to entertaining and had a reputation for social graciousness. But Mrs. Washington was not certain what other things might be expected of a President's wife. And although she liked friendly dinners and get-togethers, her desire for "the innocent gayeties of life" had long since waned.

Where would they live? And how could they pay for their new honor? The government did not provide a residence for its President; however, his salary of $25,000 a year was intended to cover all expenses for rent, furnishings, clothing, and food. Martha was dubious that they could live on this salary in adequate fashion in New York, where, she had heard, it was frightfully expensive to live. The Washingtons had little cash of their own to supplement the salary, for they were "land poor"—although they owned a vast plantation and many slaves, they had accumulated some debts and very little savings.

What sort of pomp and ceremony would be expected of them? Mrs. Washington hoped that she would not have to set the social pattern typical of a European court. But she realized that to obtain respect for the new office they would have to conform to a rigidly dignified public concept of presidential appearance and conduct. There were no precedents for her to follow; she would just have to use her own judgment, based upon the courtly traditions of Southern aristocracy.

Would she be expected to set the fashion? How should she dress? In the past years at quiet Mount Vernon, Grandmother Washington had not worried overly much about the fashionableness of her clothes. Her taste in dress had always been simple; many of her gowns had been worn since before the war. She felt that as the President's wife she must be careful to be neither too modest nor overadorned. Fortunately, her lifelong extravagance had been fancy embroidered slippers, so she knew she would be properly shod. She finally decided to redesign those gowns of the finest imported fabrics. She wished whole-heartedly that this honor had come to her earlier in life, when she was considered beautiful and stylish.

How should she address her husband? And how would she be addressed? She usually called him "Papa," and he called her "Patsy." But "Papa" hardly seemed dignified enough now. During the war she had called him "General," so she assumed this would do once more. As for herself, she could think of no specially appropriate designation. (The expression "First Lady" was not used until 1877, when a magazine writer used it to describe Lucy Hayes at the inauguration of her husband.)

How long would they have to serve? Washington's political friends, seeing how upset his wife was becoming, tried to reassure her that it would be for only a brief period, perhaps two or four years. Mrs. Washington, however, was skeptical and feared they might never be able to return to her beloved Mount Vernon. Finally, since she could do nothing about it, Mrs. Washington accepted the new job dutifully. As she went about the chores of preparing for the move, she tried to be philosophical. "I will not, however, contemplate with too much regret disappointments that were inevitable; though his feelings and my own were in perfect unison with respect to our predilections for private life, yet I cannot blame him for having acted according to his ideas of duty in obeying the voice of his country . . ." she wrote a friend.

Not the least of Mrs. Washington's concern was due to severe doubts about her own adequacy to fill such an exalted position. She worried that her lack of education and her inability to spell competently might embarrass her husband. (Most of the family letters were written by Washington, or dictated by his wife to someone else.) To make matters worse, she had been told that Abigail Adams, the wife of the Vice-President, was exceptionally learned and intelligent for a woman. It made Mrs. Washington uncomfortable to contemplate being continually compared with this paragon. She also did not relish the comparisons with the younger wives of officials, and the envious gossip she knew would be inevitable. "I sometimes think the arrangement is not quite as it ought to have been, that I, who had much rather be at home, should occupy a place with which a great many younger and gayer women would be extremely pleased," she confessed to a friend, Mercy Warren. Mrs. Warren loyally reassured her in the complex and courtly manner of the Colonial era: "Your observation may be true that many younger and gayer ladies consider your situation as enviable; yet I know not one, who, by general consent, would be more likely to obtain the suffrages of the sex, even were they to canvass at election, for this elevated station, than the lady who now holds the first rank in the United States."

Washington was inaugurated in New York on April 30, 1789, and the inaugural ball was held a week later. Because of the difficulty of carriage travel over the rough roads and the time-consuming preparations she had to make at Mount Vernon, Mrs. Washington did not arrive until the end of May, and missed both the inauguration and the ball. She finally set forth with her personal maid and her two grandchilden. They were escorted on horseback by the son of Washington's only sister, Robert Lewis, who would serve the President as a secretary. Mrs. Washington was depressed as they began their long journey. But in every town along the road, people ran out of the houses to wave and cheer the wife of the new President. With her grandchildren excitedly bouncing beside her, Mrs. Washington's spirits rose as the procession continued. Everywhere strangers welcomed her as she passed by—it was reported later that her reception on the road to Philadelphia surpassed that given to Washington when he arrived in New York for the inauguration. At the Pennsylvania border, the governor and a troop of cavalry met her and provided a formal escort into Philadelphia. Mrs. Washington asked to be taken to the home of her friends, Mr. and Mrs. Robert Morris. Morris, one of the wealthiest men in America, was a signer of the Declaration of Independence. As soon as the carriage stopped, a huge cheering crowd gathered around Mrs. Washington. By this time she was exuberant. Impulsively, she stood up in her carriage and thanked the crowd for the overwhelming attentions bestowed upon her. No record was made of what she said, and she never made another public statement.

Mrs. Washington rested a few days with the Morrises, who gave a large reception in her honor. Then she rode to Elizabethtown, New Jersey, where President Washington met her at the home of Governor Livingston. He took her to their new home, Number 10 Cherry Street, at the corner of Pearl and Cherry Streets—a location now in the shadow of the Brooklyn Bridge. The President told her that their home was called the "palace," but when she got there she accused him of teasing her. The "palace" was not only considerably smaller than Mount Vernon; it was grubby, situated in an unfashionable neighborhood, and quite unimpressive.

That first evening at Number 10, Lady Washington (this, it appeared, was to be her title) inspected their "palace" and was dismayed at the overcrowded quarters. The presidential aides, Colonel David Humphreys and Tobias Lear, had organized the establishment with rooms for the secretaries and servants on the third floor, the family bedrooms and drawing room on the second floor, and the first floor divided between executive offices and rooms suitable for entertaining guests. The three-story brick house was five windows wide. The east windows faced toward Long Island. The main dining room would seat only fourteen people. Next to it was a small breakfast room which was later to serve a multitude of purposes, including a schoolroom for the grandchildren. The ceilings were so low that once the ostrich feather in a lady's headdress was ignited by the candles in the chandelier. But Mrs. Washington had to admit the house did have a certain charm. There was a gracefully carved staircase, good wallpaper throughout, and Wilton carpeting. There were deep, cozy window seats, and plenty of fireplaces decorated in blue and white tile. The walls in the hallway were of wainscot. The stable was large enough for sixteen horses. Six matched cream-colored horses with white manes and tails were kept to draw the presidential carriage, a handsome object made in England and painted in the cream-and-red Washington colors. Two white chargers were kept for Washington's daily rides, and the other horses were used to pull two smaller vehicles.

Mrs. Washington inquired immediately about the household organization. She was told that a steward would handle the marketing and dining-room service, so she needn't worry about that. The "palace" had fourteen white servants, a coachman, footman, porter, and houseman, all of whom wore the Washington livery. Mrs. Washington planned to bring a cook, kitchen maids, housemaids, a valet, and seven slaves from Mount Vernon, besides the personal maid who had traveled with her. Obviously, not all of this superabundance of servants could live in.

The President did not give his wife long to collect her wits. He had already sent out invitations to a reception set two days after her arrival. He wanted to present his wife formally to the other government officials and their wives, diplomats, and the city's social elite as soon as possible. Both Washingtons were keenly conscious that they bore the burden of establishing the social customs for all later Presidents to follow. Because they came from the most refined and exclusive circle of the most aristocratic colony, both set great store by manners and courtesy, yet did not indulge in the luxury and excess that sometimes accompanies sudden elevation to power. So the Washingtons planned their first reception carefully, to combine the right blend of simplicity and dignity. The President had hired Colonel Humphreys, his former aide-de-camp, to advise on problems of protocol and etiquette.

Their first reception turned out to be the most elaborate party the Washingtons gave during their eight years in office. In fact, it was much too elaborate for Mrs. Washington's tastes. She herself wore a simple white brocade dress, trimmed only in silver. Her white hair was piled high to add height to her short figure. The President wore a suit of fine fabric which had been woven at Mount Vernon. But the guests who came to Number

10 that night were decked out in finery that would have better belonged in a European court. The ladies, each determined to outdo the other, wore rich satins and velvets and brocades, poked ostrich feathers into artful headdresses, and loaded themselves with pounds of glittering jewelry. Colonel Humphreys presented the guests to the Washingtons by name. When the guests had passed the receiving line, the President then moved informally around the crowded room, chatting just as he would have done at Mount Vernon. Mrs. Washington seated herself on a sofa and conversed quietly with the women, who took turns sitting near her. The servants passed around tea and coffee, with small cakes. The whole affair was modest, and even dull to most of the guests, who had come expecting more frippery—even though to the Washingtons it seemed a bit too stiffly elegant. Promptly at nine o'clock Mrs. Washington rose from her sofa and announced, "The General retires at nine o'clock, and I usually precede him. Good night." She smiled at her guests, but there was no hint of an apology for ending the party so abruptly at a relatively early hour. With a bow, the President and Lady Washington left the room.

Inevitably, this gentle but firm dismissal created an unpleasant stir. But the presidential family had established some important customs: early hours for parties, light and inexpensive refreshments, democratic gatherings where rank did not matter, and dignified but unpretentious dress.

And thus Mrs. Washington entered into what she later called her "lost days." That first year it seemed to her whatever they did by way of entertainment or conduct was cruelly criticized. She was unhappy, and a little angry, too, that people could be so lacking in understanding of the peculiar position of the first presidential family. Both Washingtons enjoyed the theater, and frequently occupied their box at John Street Theater. But whereas some people were delighted that they were bringing respectability to the theater, other prominent citizens loudly disapproved such foolishness. Guests at Mrs. Washington's Friday evening levees, which were patterned after that first reception, complained that they were too democratic and "common." Even Colonel Humphreys and Alexander Hamilton protested that she should institute a little more ceremony. But when she began a series of Thursday dinners for members of Congress she tried to make more lavish preparations, and for her pains was accused of putting on "an awkward imitation of royalty." One of her problems was her own orderliness: she liked events to be well planned and punctual. Invitations to her dinners specified 4:00 P.M., and guests arriving as late as five minutes after the hour would find the company already seated. Despite continued complaints about "arrogance," Mrs. Washington could never be budged on the matter of her unrelenting time schedules. Finally, the President, to smooth the feathers of ruffled guests, took to apologizing gently by saying, "Gentlemen, we are too punctual for you. I have a cook who never asks whether the company has come, but whether the hour of four has arrived."

The Washingtons were constantly hard-pressed for funds to support their concept of presidential appearance and conduct; and although they were wise not to indulge in intemperate high living, in all truth they could not have afforded it anyway. Mrs. Washington continued to be as resourceful about their household expenses as she had at Mount Vernon. She personally supervised every task of her servants. Her great-granddaughter, Mary Custis Lee, wrote: "She was remarkable for inspecting everything daily, giving out with her own hands the meals, going into her dairy, cellar, etc. I have heard my mother say she always wore a white dimity dress on those occasions; that it was spotless and served for a morning dress the whole week." Two dresses which she wore during the "palace" days were entirely homemade, of cotton with silk stripes. The stripes were woven from the ravelings of brown silk stockings and old crimson chair covers.

The President, too, was conscious of the need to pinch pennies in places. He wrote to a friend of his wife: "Mrs. Washington's ideas coincide with my own as to simplicity of dress, and everything which can tend to support propriety of character without partaking of the follies of luxury and ostentation." He had a well-developed temper and was not particularly adept at controlling it. He personally budgeted his $25,000 from the "public funds" and required a weekly accounting on all expenses. When he came across evidence of what he considered an unnecessary expense, his temper would flare. One evening, during a formal dinner, the steward brought to the table a delicately prepared shad, the first of the season. The President eyed it suspiciously. "What fish is this?" he asked. The steward said proudly, "A shad, a very fine shad, the first of the season." Washington demanded to know the price. The steward confessed that the shad had cost three dollars. The President exploded, his fist coming down so hard on the table that he rattled the coffee cups. "Take it away, sir! It shall never be said that my table sets such an example of luxury and extravagance!" he roared. And he complained whenever he felt that tradesmen had overcharged him, without any worry about injuring the presidential dignity. He protested to his tailor that "your charges are most exorbitantly high" and "you have generally sent my clothes too short and sometimes too tight, for which reason I think it necessary again to mention that I am full six feet high." He chastised his carpenters as "an idle set of rascals . . . to make even a chicken coop would employ all of them a week."

Many Americans applauded the new President's conservative tendencies, but just as many thought he did not command enough respect. Mrs. Washington could not make a public move without giving it careful thought. When she drove forth with four horses and two coachmen, critics whispered that she belittled her position and did not know how to behave with proper aplomb. When she drove forth with six horses and four postilions, others accused her of having delusions of grandeur. One observer, Oliver Wolcott, wrote to his wife: "The example of the President and his family will render parade and expense improper and disreputable." But many other observers felt that, to establish the prestige of a baby nation, parade and expense should not be rendered improper.

Those first months provided nothing but a cross current of tension and criticism for Mrs. Washington, and she began to despair of ever doing the right thing. She had never been subjected to such callous scrutiny and gossip; she was homesick for Tidewater Virginia and her friends. She hated going out, and she began refusing to attend functions with Washington. In October, 1789, she wrote dismally to Fanny (Mrs. George Augustine Washington), her niece, who with her husband was managing Mount Vernon in their absence: "I live a very dull life here and know nothing that passes in the town . . . I never goe to any publick place . . . indeed, I think I am more like a state prisoner than anything else, there is certain bounds set for me which I must not depart from . . . and as I cannot doe as I like I am obstinate and stay at home a great deal."

Mrs. Washington, ever the attentive mother, closed her letter on the homey note that "My dear children has very bad colds but thank god they are getting better. . . . Kiss Maria, I send her two little handkerchiefs to wipe her nose."

Not the least of Mrs. Washington's worries was that her new, often oppressive public duties gave her increasingly less time to spend with her grandchildren, who were truly the major interest of her life. She had two grandchildren with her in New York, but she missed the other relatives and their children who had occupied so much of her time at home. In a letter to Mercy Warren that first year in New York, she wrote: "As my grand-children and domestic connections make up a great portion of the felicity which I looked for in this world, I shall hardly be able to find any substitute that will indemnify me for the loss of such endearing society. . . . I have two of my grandchildren with me, who enjoy advantages, in point of education, and who, I trust, by the goodness of Providence, will be a great blessing to me."

Nelly, her little granddaughter, thought of it the other way around—Grandmother Martha was a blessing to her. And when she grew up, she wrote: "I never loved anyone, not even my own children, as I loved my grandmama. Her equal I can never know. Love, admiration, respect, gratitude were all hers. Her judgement, her piety, her fortitude . . . I have never known in an equal degree in anyone. She never praised me in all her life. She feared more than anything to make me vain. When I was right, I looked into her eyes. It never required speech to tell me all I wished to know."

The first winter after the inauguration, Washington became seriously ill. An abcess had formed on his thigh, where his sword had touched for so many years. For a time he was not expected to recover, and as Mrs. Washington cared for him she forgot her own wounds. She had many lonely hours to think while she sat by his bedside. She decided that public criticism was inevitable, and that she would just have to live with it for her husband's sake. She felt ashamed at her own peevishness over the difficulty of their position. He was doing his duty; she must do hers, she resolved. She decided to begin going out in public again, and to try to be more cheerful about the ceremonies she must perform. She expressed her new philosophical attitude in a letter: "I am still determined to be cheerful and happy in whatever situation I may be, for I have also learned from experience that the greater part of our happiness or misery depends on our dispositions and not on our circumstances. We carry the seeds of the one or the other about with us in our minds wherever we go."

The President recovered, and as the months passed they both began to adjust to the new life. In February, 1790, they were able to rent a more spacious home, which helped. Just vacated by the minister of France, the house was owned by a Mr. McComb and was located in a much more fashionable area, on Broadway close to Trinity Church. Washington took the house for an annual rent of $1,000. They lived there only a year, however, for shortly after their move Congress voted to move the seat of government to Philadelphia as of December 1, 1790.

The new executive mansion in Philadelphia was the former home of Mr. and Mrs. Robert Morris, where Mrs. Washington had stood in her carriage to thank the crowd a year and a half before. The Morrises moved to another house next door. The Washingtons' new house was reputed to be the best single dwelling in Philadelphia, but it was nearly as uncomfortable and overcrowded for the Washingtons as Number 10 Cherry Street had been. The Washingtons built some additions, but still they had to live up two flights of stairs and listen to strangers and officials pound past their private quarters to the third-floor office all hours of the day. The executive mansion was wedged between the second Morris house and a hairdressing emporium. In such a situation, the Washingtons had little chance for privacy.

In Philadelphia, however, despite the cramped quarters, life was easier for Mrs. Washington. At last she was surrounded by people she knew. Mrs. Morris was one of her oldest and closest friends, and always stood at her side for the Friday receptions. At these weekly rituals, the ladies sat in a raggedy circle and talked about domestic matters. The President considered himself a guest at these female tête-à-têtes, and usually came into the drawing room to greet each woman in turn.

He held his own stag receptions on Tuesdays. They were more stately affairs, and the President always wore his dress sword. He offered his hand to no one, and the guests were not permitted to sit down. All strangers, old friends, and ambassadors who wished to pay their respects but had no pressing business of state to conduct were expected to visit the President during this weekly reception hour.

As the years passed and Mrs. Washington grew fully accustomed to her high station, she became a great help to her husband, a bulwark of quiet strength upon which he could lean. She never concerned herself with affairs of state, but concentrated on employing public tact and politeness in order to relieve Washington of irksome duties of hospitality when he had other things on his mind. The President was growing increasingly aloof to his contemporaries; a developing deafness was in part responsible. He had never been a loquacious man, and he used his words ever more sparsely. His end of a conversation frequently consisted of no more than a nod or a gesture of his hand. He preferred writing to speaking, and composed daily extensive, wordy, flowing reports and letters.

Archibald Robertson, a portrait painter, described Lady Washington's manner as "easy polished and familiar gayety and ceaseless cheerfulness." William S. Johnston wrote: "I have just left the President's . . . we had some excellent champagne; and, after it, I had the honor of drinking coffee with his Lady, a most amiable woman. If I live much longer, I believe I shall become reconciled to the company of old women, for her sake, a circumstance which I once thought impossible . . . I now really believe there are some good old women."

Mrs. Washington's grandson, George Washington Parke Custis, was equally lavish in his praise: "Mrs. Washington was remarkable for her affable and dignified manners, and her courteous and kindly demeanor to all who approached her. Again, it is notorious that the politicians and statesmen of both parties were equally well and kindly received at the presidential mansion . . . In the whole period of the first presidency, I never heard Mrs. Washington engage in any political controversy, or, indeed, touch on the subject of politics at all."

George Custis was particularly outraged at an anecdote

which depicted Mrs. Washington as having a sharp, and partisan, tongue. The story reported that she had entered the parlor just as a gentleman exited through another door. She asked Nelly, her granddaughter, who the caller was, but Nelly did not know. Mrs. Washington looked around the room and noticed a spot on the wall just above the settee. "Ah, that was no Federalist," she reportedly said. "None but a filthy democrat would mark a place with his good-for-nothing head in that manner!" Custis insisted that such a remark would be out of character for his grandmother.

One aspect of that story was totally in character, however. Mrs. Washington was a meticulous housekeeper and paid close attention to the condition of her house. She would have noticed a spot immediately, and probably been irritated at its appearance. Washington himself kept all the records and did the accounting. But his orders were generally given after consultation with his wife. Letters he wrote to Lear, one of his aides, regarding the selection of a new coachman, for example, show that he and his wife disagreed on whom to hire. "Mrs. Washington's predilection for Jacob is as strong as my prejudices and fears are great," he wrote. Later letters indicate who won—Jacob was hired, and Jacob's wife as laundrywoman as well.

Although Washington demanded a strict accounting of finances, he did not want to be stingy where his wife was concerned, for he knew from long experience that she was not extravagant herself. "Furnish Mrs. Washington with what money she may want—and from time to time—ask her if she does want, as she is not fond of applying," he instructed Lear.

Mrs. Washington's memory on household matters was also better than her husband's. He asked an agent in 1795 to sell the tobacco in his warehouses at Alexandria and Georgetown, admitting that it "rarely occurs to me, except when I am reminded of it by Mrs. Washington."

Mrs. Washington's tactfulness and gentle, motherly way were helpful to her husband in an indirect but unexpectedly important fashion that he could not fully appreciate. For Martha Washington became a very good friend of the sophisticated Abigail Adams, who was so unlike her. Their genuine affection for each other sprang up at their very first meeting, when Mrs.

Adams was "received with the greatest ease and politeness" by Lady Washington, and endured until the latter's death on May 22, 1802. Their friendship did much to keep the relationship between the President and Vice-President smooth and satisfactory. John Adams had been among the first to declare that George Washington was the only possible choice as the first President, but he had an enormous ego and was easily irritated. Washington had no small temper of his own, and political discussions between them often grew testy. But through their own friendship and their influence upon their husbands, Martha Washington and Abigail Adams were always able to keep the two men working more or less peacefully together.

For the eight years of their two terms, Mrs. Washington was occupied in what she called "scenes more busy, tho' not more happy, than the tranquil employment of rural life. . . ." Both she and her husband were relieved when the second term was over. They were both past sixty-five. In his farewell address, March 4, 1797, Washington said: "This is the last time I shall drink your health as a public man. I do it with sincerity, wishing you all possible happiness."

Mrs. Washington's delight in being home again was reflected in a letter to Lucy Knox, wife of General Henry Knox, the first Secretary of War: "I cannot tell you, my dear friend, how much I enjoy home after having been deprived of one so long, for our dwelling in New York and Philadelphia was not home, only a sojourning. The General and I feel like children just released from school or from a hard taskmaster . . . the twilight is gathering around our lives. I am again fairly settled down to the pleasant duties of an old-fashioned Virginia house-keeper, steady as a clock, busy as a bee, and cheerful as a cricket."

Their lives had come full circle; they were content to end their days quietly at Mount Vernon, where they had first come as newlyweds in the winter of 1759. They were surrounded by the countryside and friendly neighbors they had known since childhood, although Martha complained "the changes which have taken place in this country [since the beginning of the war] are, in one word, total."

Martha Washington was born June 21, 1731, the eldest daughter of Colonel John D. Dandridge, a wealthy planter and the county clerk of New Kent County—a position of considerable prominence in Colonial Tidewater Virginia. The Dandridge plantation, "Chestnut Grove," was sprawled along the south bank of the Pamunkey River, a tributary of the Chesapeake Bay. It was twenty-five miles from Williamsburg, the capital of the colony, the center of society, and the gayest city on the American continent.

Martha—or Patsy, as she was called by her family—was a third-generation Virginian, born with the best social credentials into the most tightly held, elite aristocracy in the Colonies. But this did not mean young Patsy was a prig; actually, she was something of a tomboy. She liked to ride her horse beside her father's to the plantation wharf, to watch the ships arrive with supplies from Europe, or canter alone through the fields and woodlands. Once she rode her horse up the stairs and onto the veranda of her Uncle William's house. When her stepmother tried to reprimand Martha, her father defended her: "Let Patsy alone . . . she's not harmed William's staircase. And, by heavens, how she can ride!"

There were no schools for young ladies in Tidewater Virginia, as there were in the colony of Massachusetts and some other areas. Dandridge hired a tutor to instruct her three younger brothers, but Martha and her two sisters were only "exposed" to book learning, as was then the custom. Throughout her life, Martha never learned to spell, although her letters reveal a well-ordered mind. The "school" that Martha attended was her stepmother's daily training in the social graces and the art of homemaking.

When she was fifteen, Martha was presented to Williamsburg society. She was short and slender, with light brown hair and rather prominent hazel eyes. She was considered pretty, in a vivacious, rosy-cheeked fashion, rather than a classic beauty. She knew how to manage a house, play the spinet, do the minuet; and it was time for Martha to meet an eligible young man to marry.

Two years later, at seventeen, Martha Dandridge became Mrs. Daniel Parke Custis. Her husband was in his mid-thirties, and the only son of the wealthiest man in all the Tidewater country. The couple lived at "the White House," a plantation, during the summers and in an impressive Williamsburg town house, "Six Chimneys," during the winter social season. They had four children: Daniel, Frances, another Martha-called-Patsy, and John Parke. The two oldest children died in infancy. In August, 1757, after only eight years of marriage, Daniel Custis died—and Martha Dandridge Custis, at the age of twenty-five, became a widow with two children, and one of the wealthiest women in Virginia.

Martha Custis inherited a plantation of about 1,500 acres, a smaller plantation, the Williamsburg house and property, and some two hundred slaves. The family solicitor advised her to hire a manager to operate her farmland, but she wanted to try to manage the business affairs of the estate herself. After a year, however, she had to admit to herself that production was falling and the field hands did not respond to her control as the house servants did.

Then in May, 1758, Colonel and Mrs. Richard Chamberlayne invited the widowed Martha Custis to visit their plantation for a few days. The first evening of her visit, Colonel Chamberlayne wandered alone down to the river to watch the activity at a public crossing nearby on the route to Williamsburg. He recognized the tall, agile figure of Colonel George Washington, at twenty-six commander in chief of the Virginia militia and the state's greatest hero, and he called to him. Washington told Chamberlayne that he was on his way to confer with the governor in Williamsburg about military affairs. Chamberlayne invited him to stay for dinner, but Washington protested that he was in a great hurry. Then the wily Chamberlayne added some magic words: he would introduce Washington, he promised, to Virginia's prettiest and wealthiest widow. Washington decided that his hurry was not so great after all.

The dinner was a success. It was well after the candles had been lit before Washington stirred himself to depart. (The fashionable dinner hour was 3:00 P.M.) Chamberlayne observed that "no guest of mine leaves after sunset," and Washington was easily persuaded to spend the night. Martha Custis and George Washington were more than casually interested in each other by the time he left the next morning, and she invited him to stop at "the White House" on his return trip. Four days later the tall soldier came to call; shortly thereafter their engagement was announced.

Martha Custis was not Washington's first love. He had proposed to Mary Philpse of Yonkers, who was even richer than Martha; but that young lady had rejected him. Romanticists would like to believe that George and Martha fell in love at first sight. Indeed, from the day he was married until he died, George wore a miniature portrait of Martha on a gold chain around his neck. But chances are the young couple based their reasons for marriage more on practical than on romantic grounds. Young widows were expected to remarry after a few months of mourning, and the Widow Custis had remained in lonely seclusion longer than custom required. She was having trouble managing her property; she needed a husband to take care of the business while she ran the household. The young colonel already had a state-wide reputation for bravery, and he was eminently acceptable in her own social circle. And her two small children immediately adored him. As for Washington, he had very little money of his own, and the Widow Custis' vast holdings must have looked very good to him. That Washington took this into consideration in the selection of a bride was evidenced later in his advice to a granddaughter about to marry: "Love is a mighty pretty thing . . . but too dainty a food to live upon alone, and should not be considered rather than a necessary ingredient for the matrimonial happiness which results from a combination of causes; none of which are greater than the subject on whom it is placed should possess good sense, good disposition and the means of supporting you in the way you have been brought up. . . ."

The fact that Washington acquired most of his holdings through marriage was an irritant to his pride in later life, however. Once, after his retirement from the presidency, Washington rode over to visit David Burns, who owned a farm near Georgetown, the new "federal city" then being laid out. The present White House now stands on land that was part of Burns' farm. Washington tried to persuade Burns to donate a larger portion of his land to the public, so that what is now Lafayette Square could be developed. Burns didn't want to give away any more land, however. Washington, failing to persuade him, lost his temper. "Had not the federal city been laid out here, you would have died a poor tobacco planter," he thundered. "Aye, mon," retorted Burns, in an agitated, thick Scotish brogue, "an' had ye nae married the Widow Custis, wi' a' her nagurs, you would hae been a land surveyor today, and a mighty poor ane at that." Washington stalked away, grumbling that Burns was nothing but an obstinate old man.

Before she died, Martha Washington threw all her love letters from her husband into a fireplace, because she thought they were too intimate to be exposed to curious public eyes. The few letters that escaped were messages scribbled hastily from a battlefield, containing more advice about his whereabouts than ardent expressions of love.

Two weeks after their engagement Colonel Washington was ordered to return to the upper Ohio Valley, to attack Fort Duquesne, held by French forces. In July she got her first "love letter" from her fiancé, a rather formal, courtly communication. "We have just begun our march for the Ohio," Washington wrote. "A courier is starting for Williamsburg, and I embrace the opportunity to send a few words to one whose life is now inseparable from mine. Since that happy hour when we made our pledges to each other, my thoughts have been continually going to you as to another self. That an all-powerful Providence may keep us both in safety is the prayer of your ever faithful and affectionate friend, G. Washington."

Colonel Washington's mission was successful, and the hero returned safely to Virginia to marry Martha Custis and become a farmer. He resigned his military commission, and they were married on January 6, 1759, at "the White House." One of the guests was Sally Cary Fairfax, the beautiful young wife of a Mount Vernon neighbor, George Fairfax—for whom, it was common gossip, Washington had once suffered unrequited love. On her wedding day Martha wore entwined in her hair the pearls Daniel Custis had given her as a wedding present.

While Washington was still fighting at Fort Duquesne, his friends had managed his campaign for a seat in the House of Burgesses representing Frederick County. He won; and so their honeymoon was combined with the meeting of the Assembly in Williamsburg. Although Washington was to become much more stoical as the years passed, even now, as a very young man, he had no flair for oratory. His first day in the Chamber, the House leader, John Robinson, rose to welcome the hero. "On behalf of the members, I wish to thank Colonel Washington for his brave and steady behavior . . ." Robinson poured forth an extravagant tribute. The Chamber applauded, and looked to Washington for a reply. But Washington could not think of what to say; embarrassed, he tried to mumble a few words. "Sit down, Mr. Washington. Your modesty is equal to your valor; and that surpasses the power of any language I possess," Robinson said, coming to his rescue.

In the spring of 1759, the Assembly adjourned and the newlyweds moved to Mount Vernon. Washington had inherited the plantation from his half brother, Lawrence, and was in the midst of remodeling the house when he took his bride there. He was such a forgetful bridegroom that he nearly carried Martha across a dusty threshold. Halfway to Mount Vernon, his bride asked him if he had warned his servants to prepare the house for their arrival; and, of course, he had not. So he had to dispatch a hasty letter ordering the house cleaned, the staircase polished "to make it look well," and beds set up. Mount Vernon was then a square two-story house, with four rooms on each floor—not very imposing, and a little shabby from having a non-resident owner for so many years.

Washington controlled their finances and the management of their estate completely. In fact, he took upon himself the responsibilities of the Widow Custis' vast holdings immediately, and in no uncertain terms. Within twenty-four hours of their marriage, he notified his wife's banker that he was now in charge. And within a week he put her on an allowance of her own money. All this, of course, Martha approved; she had no head for figures, anyway.

The Washingtons never had any children. But he treated Patsy and Jackey as though they were his own. He never referred to them as "stepchildren" or "your children"; they were "the children" always. If anything, he spoiled them. He once sent to England for two dozen Christmas presents for each child.

Although life at Mount Vernon for the young couple was peaceful and prosperous, throughout the Colonies a growing unrest was changing from rebellion into revolution. On March 5,

1770, a mob of men and boys in Boston stoned British soldiers; the soldiers fired back and seven colonists were killed. In the fall of 1771 the newly appointed Virginia governer decided he could do without the Assembly, and declared it closed until the spring of 1772. The angry delegates thereupon walked across the street to the Raleigh Tavern, held their own assembly, and agreed the colony would import no more goods from England, in protest of taxation without representation. Martha put away her tea canister, although she wished there was an easier way to show one's patriotism than by giving up English tea. In April, 1773, the British Parliament passed the Tea Act, remitting all British duties on tea while retaining tax on tea exported to America. The resulting monopoly of the East India Company all but ruined Colonial merchants, and led to the Boston Tea Party. England retaliated for the destruction of the tea cargo by closing the port of Boston. Washington, although an aristocrat, was in the vanguard of the rebels. His wife fully agreed. She chided a relative who bewailed the "folly" of the rising cry for independence, while admitting that she foresaw dark days ahead—perhaps even war. "But what are all these evils when compared with the fate of which the Port Bill may be only a threat? My mind is made up; my heart is in the cause," she said.

The angry Colonies organized the first Continental Congress, which met September 5, 1774. The Virginia delegation included Patrick Henry, a young backwoods attorney, and Edmond Pendleton, who stopped overnight at Mount Vernon before continuing onward to Philadelphia with Washington. Pendleton recalled after their visit: "I was much impressed with Mrs. Washington and her spirit. She seemed ready to make any sacrifice and was cheerful, though I know she felt anxious. She talked like a Spartan mother to her son on going to battle. 'I hope you will all stand firm—I know George will,' she said. The dear little woman was busy from morning until night with her domestic duties, but she gave us much time in conversation and affording us entertainment. When we set off in the morning, she stood in the door and cheered us with the good words, 'God be with you, gentlemen.'"

The Washingtons had been at Mount Vernon for sixteen years. Their children were gone—Patsy had died of consumption, and Jackey had married Nelly Calvert of Mount Airy, Maryland. His mother did not attend their wedding, because Patsy had died only a short time before—she felt that "a wedding is no place for tears." But she sent a note by her husband to her new daughter-in-law: "God took from me a daughter when June roses were blooming—He has now given me another daughter, about her age when winter winds are blowing, to warm my heart again. I am as happy as one so afflicted and so blest can be. Pray receive my benediction . . . your affectionate mother."

After the Congress, Washington returned home to form a militia company; he ordered a new uniform in buff and blue, the colors of Fairfax County. Conversation at Mount Vernon was filled with ominous references to war. Then in April, 1775, the first shots of the Revolutionary War were fired at Lexington, Massachusetts. In May the second Continental Congress assembled to draft a constitution. And on June 15, George Washington was made the supreme commander of the Continental Army. He insisted that he would accept no pay for his services. Three days later he wrote to his wife about the appointment, urging her to "summon your whole fortitude, and pass your time as agreeably as possible." He enclosed his will, assuring her that "I should enjoy more real happiness in one month with you at home than I have the most distant prospect of finding abroad." He had not wanted to command the defense of the American cause, but he felt that he could not honorably decline the duty. He was filled with "inexpressible concern," which he added was "greatly aggravated and increased when I reflect upon the uneasiness I know it will give you . . . I shall feel no pain from the toil or the danger of the campaign; my unhappiness will flow from the uneasiness you will feel from being left alone."

Washington went immediately to Cambridge, to assume command of troops laying siege to Boston. Mrs. Washington, left alone in the big house with only the servants, made her own war preparations. She acquired sixteen more spinning wheels, trained slaves to operate them, and began storing away cloth for uniforms and bandages. She stirred her household to redoubled effort—twice as many hams and sausages were cured and hung in the smokehouse; more potatoes, yams, and turnips went into the kilns; fruits and vegetables were dried in the sun and put into the vast storehouse; jars and jars of jellies and preserves were put up. When Mrs. Washington sat down to rest, her hands stayed busy, knitting socks and scarves and sweaters for the soldiers.

In October, while General Washington was still in Boston, Mrs. Washington was warned by alarmed friends in Alexandria that Lord Dunmore and a British crew were on their way up the Potomac to burn Mount Vernon and capture the commander in chief's wife. But she refused to leave. When a neighbor, George Mason, came to lead her to safety, she insisted, "No, I will not desert my post." But when the British ship was reported in sight of the Mount Vernon landing, she was finally persuaded to flee. Mason wrote Washington later: "She finally did so with reluctance, rode only a few miles, and plucky little woman as she is, stayed away only one night." When Mrs. Washington returned, she found Mount Vernon intact and the British gone; for some reason Dunmore had changed his mind.

In every letter Martha Washington had begged her husband to let her join him at the battlefront; and after this scare he decided that she would be safer with him. It was now midwinter, but the General sent a courier to escort her to Cambridge. She loaded several pack horses with food and cloth she had stored, and took Jackey and Nelly with her in the carriage. Reunion with her husband was not the only reason for her trip: the British had spread a rumor that she was loyal to the Crown, in defiance of her husband. And so couriers rode ahead of her carriage to spread the word to the towns along her route that the General's Lady was on her way to join him at headquarters. Crowds lined the road and families stood in their doorways to wave at her. Mrs. Washington frequently stopped the carriage to touch the outstretched hands and exchange words of encouragement and hope. The face that peered out, smiling, at the worried Colonists was rosy-cheeked, round-faced, and friendly. She wore no furbelows or finery, only a plain-stitched homespun gown. Her carriage was serviceable but far from luxurious—in fact, it had been borrowed hastily from her mother-in-law, Mary Ball Washington, for the trip, and the senior Mrs. Washington had admonished her to return it as quickly as possible. Martha Washington arrived at headquarters in time to spend Christmas with her husband, and to parcel out her foodstuffs to brighten the soldiers' holiday.

Throughout the war Martha Washington joined her husband after every campaign and stayed with the army until the next campaign began. During the battles she retreated to Philadelphia, or Mount Vernon, to await the messenger from the General who would escort her back to camp. She was proud to be at Washington's side; she often said, later, that she had heard the first cannon opening nearly all the campaigns of the war. But she was also frightened. "I confess I shudder every time I hear the sound of a gun. . . . To me, that never see anything of war, the preparations are very terrible indeed, but I endeavor to keep my fears to myself as well as I can," she admitted to a friend.

In the first visits to camp Martha Washington found she did not have much to do. So she took upon herself the task of mending the General's wardrobe and the coats of other officers, and she rarely sat down without her knitting. She volunteered to make copies of the General's routine orders, although she hated to write and her penmanship was distressingly individualistic.

But as the war dragged on, the poor Colonial army struggled not only with the British but with the enemies of starvation, inadequate shelter, lack of warm clothing, and a shameful lack of medical care. Mrs. Washington took charge of administering to their needs as efficiently as she had administered to the needs of her guests at Mount Vernon. She organized nurses and ordered clean bedding, soap and water, medicines for the hospitals. She formed knitting and sewing groups among the women of Morristown. She tried to keep up her own spirits, and the morale of the men. Her letters to friends while with the army at Valley Forge note that the army "is as well as can be expected," and their own quarters were "small, but better than they were in the beginning."

Mrs. Washington spent nearly every morning with the sick and wounded. A female resident of Valley Forge recalled: "I never in my life knew a woman so busy from early morning until late at night as was Lady Washington, providing comforts for the sick soldiers. Every day, excepting Sunday, the wives of officers in camp, and sometimes other women, were invited to Mr. Pott's to assist her in knitting socks, patching garments, and making shirts for the poor soldiers, when materials could be procured. Every fair day she might be seen, with basket in hand, and with a single attendant, going among the huts seeking the keenest and most needy sufferer, and giving all the comforts to him in her power."

Mrs. Washington tried to inspire the other wives in camp, and the women of the neighborhood, by her own example and by stirring, sincere little talks to the groups that called upon her in the General's apartments. She always urged that "whilst our husbands and brothers are examples of patriotism, we [the women] must be patterns of industry." She believed deeply that it was important for the women of the Colonies to become accustomed to being independent of England, and learning to do without what they could not make themselves. She was scornful of those who longed for the comforts once imported from England, while around them men and boys were dying for freedom's sake.

One of the women thus inspired by Mrs. Washington confessed later that she had expected to meet the wealthy wife of the great General attired in elegant fashion and surrounded by comforts. But Mrs. Washington met her wearing a plain brown habit—in such a contrast to the visitor's dress that she felt rebuked. Nevertheless, this visitor felt that Mrs. Washington was gracious and cheerful, very wise in experience and kind-hearted: "She talked much of the sufferings of the poor soldiers, especially of the sick ones. Her heart seemed to be full of compassion for them."

Then, finally, it was 1783, and the war was won. The Washingtons prepared to return home: they had fulfilled their duty, or so they thought.

Through the war, as through the peace, Mrs. Washington had been her husband's greatest comfort—devoted, dutiful, providing him the gentle relief of her care. And Washington, always the faithful husband, never let her down. "I have always considered marriage as the most interesting event of one's life, the foundation of happiness or misery," he said.

Abigail Smith

ADAMS

❀ ❀

It was more than slightly frustrating to be a woman in America in the eighteenth century. At least it was to a woman with a deep knowledge of the political realities and a firm philosophy for the conduct of mankind—a woman whose intelligence far surpassed that of most men she knew. Abigail Adams was such a woman. If she had been born a man, the Colonies would have had still another hero. And no less a student of history than former President Truman said, "She would have made a better President than her husband."

Of all our First Ladies, Abigail Adams was the most uniquely qualified for the job. Yet she lived in an era when women were not supposed to have opinions about their government or the exciting events around them; or, in any case, if they had opinions, they weren't supposed to express them. Abigail Adams, self-taught, outspoken, incredibly brilliant, chafed all her life under the arbitrary limitations put upon her by her femaleness. She was the wife of a President and the mother of one, but she could not even vote. And the law did not permit her to hold public office, or become President herself (something she would have dearly loved, had she dared confess such an outrageous notion).

Women were generally treated like some kind of adult children, and Mrs. Adams' most gratifying compliment from a man of affairs was that "many acknowledge her to be superior to her sex." Yet rarely in history has a wife so completely shared government secrets and understood so well the complicated and brutal mechanics of politics. Abigail Adams contributed, through her own stimulating mind, an inestimable amount to the success of her husband and son.

Abigail Adams had plenty of ideas the Founding Fathers would have done well to adopt. She freely proffered advice to her husband at the Continental Congress, where he was helping to draw up the first code of laws. She prodded him to "remember the ladies and be more generous and favorable to them than your ancestors . . . . Do not put such unlimited power into the hands of the husbands. . . . Remember all men would be tyrants if they could." Besides advocating votes for women, the trailblazing Mrs. Adams suggested doing away with slavery, a vastly expanded program of education for the young, and an excise tax on liquor "as too frequent use of spirits endangers the well-being of society." There was scarcely a subject on which Mrs. Adams did not have a reasonably well-informed opinion. Fortunately, one of the few men whose views she respected above her own happened to be her husband. Their continuous lively exchange over the years benefited them both greatly.

As First Lady, Mrs. Adams was privy to nearly everything that went on in the government. So much so, in fact, that she became a campaign issue. One of the charges which helped to defeat John Adams in his 1800 bid for re-election was that Mrs. Adams had "a degree of influence over the public conduct of her husband."

In the drawing rooms, Mrs. Adams insisted upon taking her place among the men, discussing political affairs and current events. She was careful not to express an opinion which would reflect upon her husband, but she refused to take refuge in the meaningless small talk relied upon by most fashionable ladies in the company of men. This is not to imply that Abigail Adams was unfeminine; indeed, she had strict ideas about womanly conduct and manners.

By the time she became the wife of the President, Abigail Adams was a sophisticated world traveler; she had no qualms about her abilities to act as the nation's leading hostess. She maintained the stiff, courtly social life established by the Washingtons; she did so well that the Adamses' ceremonious style was the one aspect of their administration which escaped criticism. This part of her public role, however, Mrs. Adams did only because she felt it her duty. Her real taste, as her daughter put it, was for "a dish of politics." She could not resist political intrigue, although in her letters she constantly claimed to feel shocked at the perfidy and folly of men in government.

Politics was the spice that made life bearable during the long years of separation from her husband: when he became a delegate to the Continental Congress, then a commissioner, and later, our ambassador to France and England. While apart they both filled up the hours of loneliness with letter writing, a habit Mrs. Adams never abandoned even during the busy days as First Lady. She wrote in great detail, with a consciousness of posterity, as though she were recording for future historians almost as much as for her husband. She was so conscientious even about writing to family and to friends that the President was once driven to complain it did him no good to be with her—she spent so much time at her writing table she had little time left for him.

Abigail Adams had the letter-writing habit even as a young girl in her father's house. She was always observant but shy, and she spent hours setting down her thoughts for her girlish confidantes. The daughter of a parson, after all, does not have much chance to be in gay society or participate in other diversions which might prove more exciting than scribbling.

Abigail, born November 11, 1744, was the daughter of Parson and Mrs. William Smith of Weymouth, Massachusetts. It was a miracle that she lived at all, for she was born into the middle of a raging "throat distemper" epidemic. The usual medication of snail water (concocted of roasted garden snails, scoured earthworms, and salt) was not noticeably effective on infants. Abigail survived, however, for the Smiths were of strong New England stock.

Abigail grew up socially secure, rigidly moralistic and painfully serious-minded. From her father she acquired a pious, righteous attitude which she was never able to shake. Her health was never robust, so she was not allowed to attend a school. But Abigail found the atmosphere of a parsonage, steeped in church and parish matters, highly conducive to self-study. And frequently Abigail visited her Grandfather and Grandmother Quincy, in the township of Braintree by the sea. Her grandfather was prosperous, and lived in a spacious, comfortable home filled with books. He was Speaker of the Massachusetts House of Respresentatives, and his home was a gathering place for the state's leading men. Night after night a shivering Abigail sat hunched on a small stool, inconspicuous in a corner, listening with absorption to heated discussions on the problems of the Colonies. From early childhood Abigail learned about the importance of freedom and the course of the fast-moving fight by the Colonies for power to control their own destiny.

This double environment—the one with its stern moral standards, the other with its open-minded, intellectual approach to life—produced a young lady who made most young men uncomfortable. On the one hand she was so bright, and on the other so strait-laced, that poor Abigail had a frightful time finding proper beaus. The fact that she was not a beauty didn't help her plight, either. At eighteen, Abigail was well on the road toward spinsterhood; most of her girlhood friends were married, some already mothers. She complained that she had absolutely no "sparks," but resignedly admitted that "they'd never been plenty as herrings anyway."

One day, however, her sister Mary's fiancé, Richard Cranch, brought a companion to the parsonage. John Adams, a young lawyer, had squired some of Abigail's cousins but had never before paid much attention to her. They found that first day they enjoyed talking together; after that, Adams came often to the parsonage. He was not exactly the best catch in town: he was high-minded, egotistical, brilliant, haughty, and often chillingly withdrawn. To make matters worse, he was poor and just beginning his career in a profession considered only slightly more respectable than sweeping chimneys. The aristocratic parson did not approve of young Adams.

Abigail, however, liked Adams very much—and she had attracted no other suitors. The parson did his best to interfere with the match, but finally, after three irksome years of courting and delay, John Adams and Abigail Smith were married on October 25, 1764. The parson was grudging to the end, unkindly taking for his tender marriage text, "For John came neither eating bread nor drinking wine, yet ye say he hath a devil."

Both Adamses were shy, but in each other's company they gained courage. Mrs. Adams was very impressed by her Harvard-educated husband, who could discuss law, philosophy, or books with authority. And Adams in turn was affected by his wife's quick wit, good sense, perception, and genial optimism. Both were as demanding of themselves as they were of others, but the wife sometimes felt that the husband overdid it. During their courtship she complained that "I think you are too severe, and that you do not make quite so many allowances as human nature requires . . ." Adams protested somewhat feebly that he did indeed possess a warm heart: "My affection for a certain lady (you know who, my dear) quickens my affection for everybody else that does not deserve my hatred." This same stiffness that irked Abigail Adams was to annoy others throughout John Adams' career, and contributed in no small measure to his unpopularity while in office. His impatience and periods of deep depression and self-doubt often made him ill-mannered and short-tempered.

The newlyweds moved to a small homestead in Braintree, which at that time numbered about two thousand souls. Abigail was quickly assimilated into the Adams family: across the road lived her husband's widowed mother and his two brothers, and Abigail's only servant was a colored slave on temporary loan from her mother-in-law. The couple was poor, but both enjoyed working with their hands. Abigail cooked and sewed, and shelled peas while she argued about the conduct of foreign and domestic affairs with the men who came to see her husband. Adams cleared his land, cut firewood, milked the cow—physical labor gave him as much joy as exercising what he called "that great gland, the brain."

Abigail soon proved more capable at the management of their
domestic economy than Adams. He began bringing his leather
pouch full of fees directly home to empty in his wife's lap, and
she budgeted it out carefully. Farm life was not expensive—
turkeys, geese and squab were abundant; salted or smoked fish,
pork, mutton and beef were cheap and plentiful; breads of corn
and rye were also cheap, although flour was sometimes difficult
to obtain; milk was a penny a quart, if one didn't get enough
from one's cow; vegetables grew easily in the rich Massachusetts
soil, as did herbs, berries and fruits. Most hard to come by were
the "luxuries" (which were fast becoming necessities as Colonial
living became more urbane), since they were all imported—
fabrics, glass, china, shoes, paper, needles and pins, sugar, salt,
pepper, coffee, and tea.

In the first ten years of life in their little cottage Mrs. Adams
bore five children: Abigail II, John Quincy, Charles, Thomas,
and a girl who died in infancy. At the age of twenty, Adams had
envisioned that soon "the great seat of empire" would be transferred to America, and the "only way to keep us from setting up
for ourselves is to disunite us." The men who frequently visited
the bustling Adams fireside all shared this vision of freedom and
independence for the Colonies. Mrs. Adams' patriotic fervor
matched her husband's: she scornfully called her Tory neighbors
"those poisonous talkers" who go about "sowing seeds of mis-
chief."

This group of young firebrands around Adams led the fight
against the increasing British stubbornness in dealing with the
Colonies. It was Adams who led a boycott against the Stamp Act
in 1765. This was so successful that the governor of Massachusetts
in retaliation closed all law courts and public offices, which
deprived Adams and other lawyers of their jobs. He bleakly predicted the doom of his career and the starvation of his children,
but his wife cheered him in her blunt fashion. "Tush," said she,
"show the king how wrong-headed he is, and there'll be plenty
of work for everyone."

Before long, the British Parliament nullified the Stamp Act,
and Adams was able to work again. But the rebellion and
resentment continued to grow, and in the Adams household a
typical day went like this: "Mr. Hayward dined; town politics

the subject. Doctor Tufs here in the afternoon; American politics the subject." Mrs. Adams was a full partner in all these heated discussions. Later Adams praised her: "Your sentiments of the duties we owe to our country are such as become the best of women and the best of men. Among all the disappointments and perplexities which have fallen to my share in life, nothing has contributed so much to support my mind as the choice blessing of a wife whose capacity enabled her to comprehend, and whose pure virtue obliged her to approve, the views of her husband."

In the spring of 1768 the Adams family moved to a house which, like the early home of George and Martha Washington, was aptly called "the White House," in Brattle Square, Boston. From its windows Abigail Adams watched the first seven hundred British Redcoats march into the city—a show of strength by the British to teach the Colonists, who were increasingly restless under new taxation, obedience.

Being a patriot in those days of trouble was a difficult business. One day Mrs. Adams was alone with the children, peacefully warming her feet by the fire, when, near the Adams home, rash British soldiers killed five Boston citizens and wounded eight more in the infamous "Boston Massacre." She raced to the window, then upstairs to soothe her frightened children, who had also heard the shots and screams. By the time John Adams reached home, she was pale and somber, but in control of herself: "I fear not for myself, or even for the little ones. . . . I fear—I know not what I fear—for our country."

Boston was the center of the mounting rebellion in the Colonies, and Adams was rapidly becoming the leading spokesman for the Colonists. In the winter of 1773 the King decided to test the Colonies' loyalty by trying to force them to pay their overdue taxes on tea. Mountains of tea were piled in English warehouses because of the stubborn American boycott against paying the tax, but it was decided to ship some tea to the Colonies willy-nilly.

The Colonial leaders protested, to no avail; so they began casting about for other ways to keep the tea from landing. There is no doubt that Adams was one of the plotters of the Boston Tea Party, and that his wife knew all about it. Adams' diary reads: "Twenty-eight chests of tea arrived yesterday, which are to make an infusion in water at seven o'clock this evening." And Abigail, writing to her friend Mercy Warren on December 5, eleven days before the Tea Party, commented breathlessly: "Tea, that baneful weed, is arrived. Great and I hope effectual opposition has been made to the landing of it. . . . I tremble when I think what may be the direful consequences."

Adams was, supposedly, out of town riding his circuit on the night a riotous mob roughly disguised in soot, paint, and blankets as "Indians" marched to the ships in Boston Harbor and threw the tea overboard. But he had secretly pledged the ringleaders that he would defend anyone accused by the angry governor. His comment after the deed: "It was magnificent!"

An angry England closed the port and moved the seat of government to Salem. Abigail Adams was now back in Weymouth, under her mother's care, recuperating from influenza and recurrent migraines resulting from the painful birth of her fifth child. Adams reported to his wife that the city of Boston, with its commerce strangled, was dying. He added gloomily, "Our principal consolation is that it dies in a noble cause . . . let me know what is best for us to do."

Mrs. Adams thought the best thing was to move promptly back to Boston and her husband, which she did. She was there to share the excitement when the Massachusetts House of Representatives passed a resolution to send a delegation to Philadelphia for the first gathering of all the Colonies in a Continental Congress. Of course Adams was one of the delegates—and so his wife packed up her brood and went back to Braintree to begin a dreary period of long separations from her husband.

Left alone, Mrs. Adams struggled to manage the farm and educate her children. Her letters now were different. She had always, from the days of their courtship, addressed Adams as "my dearest friend"; but now they were signed "your most affectionate AA," not the coy "Diana" or "Portia" of gayer, lighter years. Her letters are filled with concern for "My country, for you and for our family"—but country comes first, and each letter is a patriotic political document.

She seldom complained about her problems at home, although they were many. Each letter was aimed at lifting the spirits of a husband she knew well would be plagued by paroxysms of self-doubt in his important role. "Uncertainty and expectation leave the mind great scope. Did ever any kingdom or state regain its liberty when once it was invaded, without bloodshed? . . . I long impatiently to have you upon the stage of action. . . . I wish you every public as well as private blessing, and that wisdom which is profitable both for instruction and edification, to conduct you in this difficult day. . . ." she wrote.

Adams showed his wife's letters to his fellow delegates at the Congress, as trustworthy, clear-eyed chronicles of developing events back in the hotbed of the rebellion. Mrs. Adams wrote about the preparations for war, and that the powder supply had to be moved. She wrote that the Negro slaves were suspected of a conspiracy against the Colonists, in return for their freedom. She could not, however, resist some sympathy for the slaves: "I wish most sincerely there was not a slave in the province. It always seemed a most iniquitous scheme to me to fight ourselves for what we are robbing the Negroes of, who have as good a right to freedom as we have." There were few in the Colonies, however, to share *that* progressive viewpoint.

After ten weeks Adams came home, discouraged and disappointed. His efforts to draw up provisions for an American legislature had been voted down, and the Congress had done little but draft a weak bill of rights. But after the first shots of the revolution at Lexington and Concord, a second Congress was called in May, 1775. Adams left his wife alone once again, with the cheerful admonition: "In case of real danger, of which you cannot fail to have previous intimations, fly to the woods with our children."

Abigail Adams busied herself playing reporter, and fed her husband with her own ideas as well as with her observations. Once the war was begun, she took a practical viewpoint of the nasty business. "Courage, I know we have in abundance; conduct, I hope we shall not want; but powder, where shall we get a sufficient supply?" She met General Washington, who was camped with his ragged troops near Cambridge, and was very favorably impressed. She reported that the soldiers' morale was low, that the army was near starvation; she proffered her opinions of the various revolutionary officers; she described conditions in beleaguered Boston. Meanwhile she was finding it difficult to provide for four children, even on a farm outside the center of battle, for ordinary goods were scarce—"not one pin to be purchased for love or money."

Even now, with the war initiated, few Congress delegates were ready for full independence. They clung to the hope that negotiations with the king might yet bring more rights. John Adams, his wife, and his cousin Sam, however, were boldly talking—almost alone—of complete freedom from England. Mrs. Adams was much more impatient with the lukewarm Congress than her husband: "A people may let a king fall, yet still remain a people; but if a king let his people slip from him, he is no longer a king. And as this is most certainly our case, why not proclaim to the world, in decisive terms, your own importance?" Adams, for his part, continually urged that the basic steps toward a new government be taken, and admonished her: "As to declarations of independency, be patient!"

Adams sometimes grew exasperated with his wife's constant advice, and once replied sarcastically, "I think you shine as a stateswoman of late, as well as a farmeress. Pray, where do you get your maxims of state? They are very apropos."

Undaunted, Abigail taunted him: "Whilst you are proclaiming peace and good-will to men, emancipating all nations, you insist on retaining an absolute power over wives."

"I cannot but laugh, you are so saucy," Adams commented tolerantly to her suggestions of equal rights for women.

Mrs. Adams resented just a bit that her husband was in the middle of all the action while she coped with children's illnesses, her own loneliness, the problems of running a manless farm, fears for the safety of her husband and country and—last but not least—the single-handed education of her children. She liked to call the wives of other delegates "sister delegates," on the not entirely facetious grounds that wives deserved their husband's titles since they had given up their last names for them. As she struggled to teach her children, she constantly felt the lack of her own education, as exceptional as it had been for the times. She hoped the delegates would provide a liberal plan of education for women, for "It is very certain that a well-informed woman, conscious of her nature and dignity, is more capable of performing the relative duties of life, and of engaging and retaining the

affections of a man of understanding, than one whose intellectual
endowments rise not above the common level."

Adams became president of the Board of War—in today's
terms, a sort of Secretary of Defense. He ordered an assistant to
take his wife a map to show her the present theater of war, and
sent her faithful reports on its progress so that she could follow
it on the map. Usually he was dependent on her letters and her
advice: "I want a better communication. I want to hear you think
or see your thoughts," he frequently demanded.

And all the while, as the war continued, John and Abigail
Adams played their fascinating game of nation-building. They
discussed the form and principles of a new government when
few men even dared think of full independence. Adams was the
public instrument; it was his voice and his pen which outlined
in 1775 the principles underlying the constitutions of the thirteen states that became, after the war ended in 1783, the basis
for the new national constitution in 1787. And Abigail was his
sounding board, a woman often ill, burdened with farm and
family, but the one person to whom Adams turned for advice and
support on politics, religion, government. Adams had few con-
fidants among his male contemporaries—during his whole career
he was extremely unpopular because of his uncomfortable habit
of telling the truth and rejecting compromise.

And now a new role descended upon Adams. He became a
foreign representative for the new Confederation, one of three
commissioners appointed to represent the American states in
negotiations with France. He was in Paris for a year, and socially
he conducted himself very much like an angry bull in a china
shop. But what he lacked in personal charm he made up for in
official salesmanship. He began laying the foundation for future
dealings with foreign nations, and established the dignity of
a new country as yet little more than an intangible collection of
ideas.

Next Adams moved on to England, to attempt a treaty of
commerce. He believed, as did his wife, that the independent
states could, and should, be self-sustaining, and should make no
treaties of alliance, only treaties of commerce. In one of her letters
Mrs. Adams observed that she was amazed at Britain's short-
sightedness in compelling the Confederation to become a manu-

facturing nation by its unfair trade tax levies and harassments. Thirty years later President Madison was to voice the same wonderment—that a "seller" nation should seek to destroy a great and growing market for its goods.

From 1778, with only a three-month rest at home, until 1784, John Adams was in Europe. Mrs. Adams, in Braintree, kept her farm running, paid her bills, and dabbled in politics as the war drew to a close. Educating her children, she particularly labored to develop the abundant natural talents of her son John Quincy, who joined his father in Europe for part of his stay. She confessed to friends that she and her husband had marked John Quincy for leadership "in the Cabinet or the field . . . a guardian of his country's laws and liberties." She continued to prod and inspire him throughout his career. Once, during one of the periods of despondency from which he frequently suffered, as did his father, she told him: "These are times in which a genius would wish to live. It is not in the still calm of life, or the repose of a pacific station, the great characters are formed. Would Cicero have shone so distinguished an orator if he had not been roused, kindled and inflamed by the tyranny of Cataline, Verres, and Mark Antony? The habits of a vigorous mind are formed in contending with difficulties . . . great necessities call out great virtues."

Thus the influence that Mrs. Adams exerted over two future Presidents was unobtrusive, often at long distance, but omnipresent. Vulgar, public domination of the fishwife variety was beneath her; yet her opinions and thoughts were set forth in full anticipation of their acceptance and adoption, at least in part. She tried to practice dutifully the self-improvement she preached to both her Johns; she was not given to frivolity or the esthetic pleasures. She preferred, for example, to have her children sing Dr. Watts' "Moral Songs for Children" rather than gay ditties like "Little Jack Horner." She quoted freely from Shakespeare, Pope, eighteenth-century poets and essayists, Molière, even the classics, down to the relatively unknown Polybius. She made little Johnny study ancient history and learn Latin, which she first had to teach herself.

That Adams considered his wife an intellectual equal is a tribute to them both, but mostly to Mrs. Adams. For a man of

Adams' ego to accept advice from a woman was a remarkable thing indeed. He was not always delighted with her outspoken ideas, of course. Sometimes his praise was faint, and was heavily flavored with sarcasm. And he could tease. He wrote from France, after she complained that his letters were dull: "I must not write a word to you about politics, because you are a woman. What an offence I have committed! A woman! I shall soon make it up. I think women better than men, in general, and I know that you can keep a secret as well as any man whatever. But the world don't know this. Therefore if I were to write my sentiments to you and the letter should be caught and hitched into a newspaper, the world would say I was not to be trusted with a secret."

Mrs. Adams kept the family hand in the political world by throwing her energies into the first state campaign in Massachusetts. She experienced her first political disappointment when John Hancock, president of the first Continental Congress, was elected governor. "Low, mean arts," she grumped. "I could tell you many, yet nothing that would surprise you, for you know every avenue of his vain heart." She complained, too, that because she was a woman she could not vote. "If I cannot be a voter upon this occasion, I will be a writer of votes. I can do something in that way," she protested to Adams. Then she sighed to herself: "What a politican you have made me. . . ."

The new nation made Adams its ambassador, first to France, then to England. And, at last, in 1784, Adams felt that it would be safe for Mrs. Adams to join him. She was now forty; she had never been more than forty miles in any direction from her home. Her children were nearly grown, and she was proud of them— but they did make her feel "exceedingly matronly."

All reports of Adams' achievements in his role as ambassador, however, give the high-principled New England matron a great deal of the credit. She exhibited enough charm and tact to cover up her husband's frequent shows of irritation in countries which considered Americans barely more than bumpkins. She was forced to remind Adams almost daily that he must bear the British snobbery and criticism with "silent contempt."

By 1788 Adams was restless. England was cold and damp; he had not been able to negotiate a favorable treaty of trade with England. Back home the new postwar government was foundering in the face of rising inflation. And now, Abigail Adams, working behind the scenes as women have done since time immemorial, made a notable contribution to history. It was her opinion that a new loan from Holland, which had already given the new nation one loan, could tide over the Confederation's finances until the new treasury could collect taxes and reach a stable basis. Adams, however, pooh-poohed the idea—he did not want to beg a second time from Holland, and he still hoped that England would eventually sign a treaty. Mrs. Adams was so convinced that she was right she resorted to a little scheming. She wrote to their friend Thomas Jefferson, who was then in Paris, urging him to persuade her husband that a loan from Holland was the only answer. Jefferson was convinced by her letter, and did as she suggested. He was so persistent that he finally persuaded Adams to negotiate the loan. The Confederation's credit was thereby preserved for two years, and the nation saved from bankruptcy. Only later did Adams discover his wife's role, and he was not overly pleased: "It is all your own intrigue which has forced me to this loan. I suppose you will boast of it as a great public service," he wrote.

By 1789 the new nation was ready to elect its first President, under the new Constitution. The electors unanimously named George Washington as President, and selected John Adams as Vice-President. Mrs. Adams said, when she heard the news, "Sweetly do the birds sing!"

At first Mrs. Adams did not become too involved in her new political environment. "I am fearful of touching upon political subjects; yet, perhaps, there is no person who feels more interested in them," she complained. Adams, who as Vice-President presided over the Senate, came home to her each night with the details of the day's events. She wrote in detail to her sister of the intrigues and storms in the capital, predicting with a good deal of accuracy their outcome. She frequently rode to the House (the public, not even the Vice-President's wife, was never admitted to the Senate chambers) to hear the debates. Adams showed her each public statement and speech before he delivered it. It became more and more difficult for her to contain her own opinions; she was much more of a Federalist partisan than her husband, who thought of country, not party. (So much

so, in fact, that Albert Gallatin called her "Mrs. President not
of the United States, but of a faction," after Adams became the
second President.)

Abigail Adams discovered a good friend in Martha Washington. They enjoyed each other's company, despite their dis-
similar backgrounds; and frequently, together, they were able
to smooth over arguments between the President and Vice-President. Mrs. Washington, accustomed to the isolation of rural
Virginia, leaned heavily upon Mrs. Adams. "Madame makes very
few visits but those of ceremony when she does not request my
ladyship to accompany her, and I have several appointments of
that kind on hand now," Abigail recorded. "We live in a most
friendly intercourse," she added.

Time was taking its toll of the energetic Abigail Adams,
however. The "rumatick" was troublesome and recurring. For
long periods she was so ill that she avoided much of the social
life, in both New York and Philadelphia. Often, when bothered
by her "rumatick," she retreated to the peace of their farm,
from whence she peppered the Vice-President with the same
sort of advice-filled letters she had always written when he was
less important. Adams, for his part, continued to praise her
soundness of thought: "Yours [letters] give me more entertainment than all the speeches I hear. There are more good thoughts,
fine strokes, and mother wit in them than I hear in the whole
week."

After eight years Adams was elected to succeed Washington.
He barely made it, despite his long apprenticeship: Alexander
Hamilton put on such a concerted undercover campaign on behalf of Thomas Jefferson that Adams won by only three votes.
Even his inauguration, which his wife did not attend, was hardly
a glorious tribute from the people. Instead of cheering for the
new President, the crowds wept—in sorrow at bidding farewell
to their hero, George Washington.

The government was in a terrible state in 1797—the executive
branch was divided on every issue; the Vice-President, Jefferson,
was openly hostile to the President; the Cabinet was filled with
leftover Washington appointees who soon proved disloyal to their
new leader; and Hamilton, the strong man of Adams' party, the
Federalists, hated Adams because he could not control him. Mrs.

Adams began to have doubts, for the first time, about her prominence. The press was unmercifully critical of the President and even occasionally criticized his wife. Mrs. Adams reflected sadly: "It requires courage and firmness, wisdom and temperance, patience and forbearance to stand in such a conspicuous, such an elevated station."

The Adamses moved into the Philadelphia house just vacated by the Washingtons, since the new capital at Washington was still a muddy, fever-ridden swamp. Mrs. Adams conscientiously continued the stately "court" pattern established by Martha Washington, but her social events were not so ostentatious, primarily because the Adamses had virtually no private funds and simply could not afford it. Her parties were more relaxed, however, for the Washingtons were so deeply revered that their dinners had tended to be a bit stuffy. Guests went away with the impression that Mrs. Adams "continues the same pleasant attentive person as at Quincy." Although she dressed somewhat modestly for the times, she was always conscious of the importance of dressing appropriately for her dignified position. She liked rich fabrics, heavy lace, and bright colors. She usually wore modish high-heeled shoes, a short cloak, black bonnet, a quilted petticoat. Her hair was done in a mass of curls decorated with ribbons, beads, bugles or bands—and sometimes with all four. She kept so well within the current fashion that her only innovation was to make silk dresses popular. Muslin, because it was easy to clean, was the most common winter dress material; but Abigail disliked it so much she generally wore silk instead.

It was an exciting, trying time; politics was developing faster than policies. Party lines were forming. Adams believed in a neutral America, free of foreign entanglements; he stood for a national government strong in credit, court, army and economy. These principles had been forged primarily by Hamilton, who now sought to destroy them in his efforts to gain personal power. Jefferson, at the head of the Republicans, had long since parted philosophic company with the Adamses. His program was based on state and individual rights, with emphasis upon expansion westward. Government limped along, at best. Severe yellow fever epidemics in Philadelphia and New York—in one year 2,086 out of New York City's population of 50,000 people died—forced the

President and Congress to flee the city during the summer months when the hazard was at its worst.

To maintain their social schedule, the Adamses had thirty servants. Mrs. Adams nonetheless put in a full day. She still handled the family budget and expenses—so completely that she once made a loan to her sister, with the warning that the President was not to know about it. She arose at 5:00 A.M., read, wrote letters, and planned her entertainments until 8:00 A.M., when she was served breakfast. Then, until 11:00 A.M., she supervised household matters and gave the servants their instructions for the day. At eleven she began to dress for her afternoon "at homes," when she received visitors from noon until three. The family usually dined at three, and in the late afternoon Mrs. Adams rode out to make her public appearances, return calls, and so forth.

She took her responsibilities as the wife of the President very seriously. "I shall esteem myself peculiarly fortunate, if at the cost of my public life, I can retire esteemed, beloved and equally respected with my predecessor," she said. And, later, she wrote: "I would hope that I have not lived in vain. . . ." After her husband's defeat for re-election Abigail was not unsatisfied with the job they had done: "I [not "we!"] leave to posterity to reflect upon the times past; and I leave them characters to contemplate."

The nation was aware that Abigail Adams was no ordinary housewife. The press, in its crude infancy, complained about her influence over her husband. The Bache newspapers referred to the President and Mrs. Adams irreverently as Darby and Joan. Abigail Adams didn't understand the reference, but she told her sister she'd take it as a compliment anyway. (John Darby and his wife Joan, who died circa 1730, are often cited as types of conjugal felicity.) And although it was considered ungentlemanly to mention the name of any lady in a rough-and-tumble public forum, Mrs. Adams' views were so widely known that a merchant quoted her to back up his own argument during a town meeting political debate. When she heard about it, she was incensed; she insisted upon her right to express her views equally with men, but she also had a high sense of her prerogatives as a woman. "I could not believe that any gentleman would have had so little delicacy or so small a sense of propriety as to have written a vague opinion and that of a lady, too, to be read in a publick assembly as an authority. The man must have lost his senses," she wrote. "I cannot say that I did not utter the expression . . . but little did I think of having my name quoted. . . . I shall always consider it as a wan [lack] of delicacy in him, and a real breach of confidence to make use of my name." She added wryly: "It will, however, serve as a lesson to me to be upon my guard."

Abigail Adams could get equally angry at newspaper criticisms of the President, which were consistently harsh. The pro-Jefferson Bache paper, she noted in 1798, called the President "old, querulous, bald, blind, crippled, toothless." It also, "among other impudence," reported that Mrs. Adams attended a play and cried during the performance. "That was a lie," she sputtered. She never cried. "Let the vipers cease to hiss. They will be destroyed in their own poison." And still another time Mrs. Adams pleaded with her sister to furnish "the truth" to the Massachusetts *Mercury,* a pro-Adams newspaper, in order to refute some current Bache story.

Meanwhile there was increasing unrest over deteriorating relations with France and England. Pro-British, anti-French sentiment was rampant. Britain was at war with France, and popular opinion held that America should jump in to aid Britain. Adams felt that a war would weaken the new nation and determined upon the unpopular course of neutrality. Later he said that avoiding war with France was the most satisfactory deed of his life, and he asked that his gravestone be inscribed simply: "Here lies John Adams, who took upon himself the responsibility of the peace with France in 1800." His wife didn't see it that way. She was strongly pro-British and believed the enmity toward France had gone so far it could only be solved by war. She argued with the President about it endlessly; but much of the time during this period she was ill and back at Braintree, where her influence was somewhat diluted by distance. She grumbled to friends, "We are all but at war anyway. Intercourse with France is forbidden, and the treaties are declared void and no longer obligatory— three frigates are already at sea. All we need is a declaration of war, and one ought to have been made. . . . Great Britain is fighting for all the other powers." Adams, less of a firebrand than his wife, persisted in his patient course; he appointed William

Vans Murray as envoy to France, with a secret mission to make
one last try to smooth things over. Mrs. Adams protested from
her sickbed, and there were powerful elements of the government who agreed with her. Adams wrote to her sarcastically: "O
how they lament Mrs. Adams's absence! She is a good counsellor!
If she had been here, Murray would never have been named
nor his mission instituted. This ought to gratify your vanity
enough to cure you. . . ." It is doubtful that Mrs. Adams really
could have persuaded the President to go to war, but her voice,
had she been with him, combined with the overwhelming popular sentiment for war, might have weakened his resolve. In any
event, life would have been pretty unbearable for the poor
President. In the end he had his way. Murray went to France
and miraculously a final-hour settlement was made which avoided
war.

Adams desired a second term, but as election time approached he found himself with no organized party behind him.
Hamilton, in his hate for Adams, had split the Federalist party
irreparably. Jefferson rode into the breach, and he and Aaron
Burr received an equal number of votes. The House of Representatives then voted Jefferson as President and Burr as Vice-
President. Mrs. Adams was appalled at the campaign, and bitter
against Jefferson: "I have heard so many lies and falsehoods
propagated to answer electioneering purposes that I am disgusted with the world." She completely grasped the political
situation, and knew that the returns from South Carolina would
be decisive in the close election. She wrote her son Thomas afterward: "South Carolina has behaved as your father always said
she would." Then, rightfully regarding herself as sharing her
husband's career, she added sadly: "The consequence to us personally is that we retire from public life."

But for the Adamses defeat carried a double blow. They
were obliged to move into the new capital city of Washington
when Congress reconvened there in the fall, although they would
occupy the new executive mansion for only a few months. Ten
years before, the Congress had ordered the creation of a brand-
new city to be the permanent home of the federal government.
It decreed that the government would officially move there from
Philadelphia in the winter of 1800, but no one foresaw that in-

terminable delays and financing problems would plague the city's development. Consequently, the Adamses moved into a muddy, ugly village, barely habitable. The great house of white sandstone which was to be their home was unfinished and stood in the midst of rough fields. Scattered about its grounds were stacks of rubbish, shacks to house the workmen, pits for storing supplies, and old brick kilns. Only a half-dozen rooms were livable. There was no plumbing; the main stairway was not finished; the only source of heat was open log fires, but logs were hard to find.

Adams went to inspect the city during the summer, to quicken the normally leisurely pace of its construction. He supervised the moving of the one hundred and thirty-six federal employees into the few habitable buildings. In the fall, in advance of his wife, Adams moved into the executive mansion, becoming the first President to live in the federal city. Mrs. Adams was not feeling well, and for a time she considered staying at home while Adams finished out his lame-duck term alone. The President, however, wanted her at his side. "It is fitting and proper that you and I should retire together, and not one before the other," he argued. During the campaign Mrs. Adams had a foreboding that her husband would not be re-elected, and so that summer she had supervised the construction of a new wing on their farmhouse, to house her husband's papers. She also decided, on her own, to catalogue and ship his papers and books there from Philadelphia to be preserved for posterity.

Finally, in November, Abigail Adams set off for Washington by coach with the final household goods she could not send ahead by vessel. She was fifty-six years old, and she dreaded the journey for personal as well as political reasons. She stopped in New York to visit her son Charles. Unable to live up to the brilliant records set by his father and brother, and deeply in debt, Charles had become an alcoholic. The President had rejected him; but his mother could not. She found him fatally ill; as she left him to continue her ride to the capital, she knew she would never see him again and her heart was heavy with grief. Three weeks later Charles was dead.

At the end of her tortuous journey, Mrs. Adams found matters as bad as she had feared. "As I expected to find it a new country, with houses scattered over a space of ten miles, and trees and stumpes in plenty, with a castle of a house . . . and so I found it. . . . [Georgetown] is the very dirtyest hole I ever saw for a place of any trade, or respectability of inhabitants. It is . . . a quagmire after every rain." The so-called city contained just two finished government buildings. Only the north wing of the Capitol was completed. Pennsylvania Avenue, which was to lead from the executive mansion to the Capitol, was a narrow dirt road heavily skirted by brush. Four or five hundred residences were visible on the swampy landscape.

Mrs. Adams was well aware of the historical importance of the new mansion, but she was impatient with the problems of being its first resident. "I had much reather [sic] live in the house at Philadelphia. Not one room or chamber is finished of the whole," she wrote. She kept thirteen fires going daily in a vain attempt to dry out the damp walls. She worried about the cost of maintaining such a huge house on the President's meager salary. She could find no handymen to chop wood for her, and, besides, the roads were almost impossible for hauling wood anyway. She had to shout for her servants, because no bells had been installed. Georgetown, the nearest market area, "affords nothing." She had "no looking-glasses but dwarfs," and no matter how many lamps she set up, the house was never light enough to suit her. Much of her china and glass was lost, stolen or broken en route, and the trunks bringing her clothes were delayed. And—most inconvenient of all—there was no place to hang laundry. So, with New England practicality, the President's wife hung her wash in the great unfinished audience room.

But even in her gloom Mrs. Adams had to admit that the house was substantially built. And it did have a magnificent view —overlooking the Potomac.

Mrs. Adams considered her few months' duty in Washington primarily as a responsibility for setting up a dignified social salon. Although her health suffered from the dampness of the house, she earnestly tried to transplant to the capital her ideas of courtly customs. She set up her weekly "drawing room," and organized the first full-dress social fete in the new mansion. To maintain her important social obligations was often plain hard work: to return one visit was the project of a whole day, for some of her visitors came three and four miles, and the roads were little more than muddy paths.

She had not intended to stay through February, but she stayed in the city for the Jefferson-Burr contest. She held both men in equal disrepute, but she was merely angry at Jefferson for betraying her husband, while she really feared for the country if Burr was elected. On February 13 the House met and balloted every hour for a whole day, coming up each time with a tie. Finally, on the thirty-sixth ballot, Representative James Bayard of Delaware deposited a blank ballot, which gave the election to Jefferson. Then, the excitement over, Mrs. Adams went back to Massachusetts, leaving the President to wind up the loose ends before the March inauguration of his foe.

During their retirement period, Abigail Adams did one more thing worthy of historical note. In 1804 Jefferson's daughter Mary, whom Mrs. Adams had cared for as a child, died. Without telling her husband, she penned Jefferson a note of sympathy, stifling her animosity toward him. Thus began an unusual correspondence, for Jefferson promptly replied in an attempt to heal the breach between them. He expressed his regret that "circumstances should have arisen which have seemed to draw a line of separation between us." He proceeded to blame all their squabbles on the influence of others and mentioned a few actions of Adams which had piqued him. Mrs. Adams rose to her husband's defense and shot back a crisp list of her own grudges against Jefferson. "Often I have wished to have seen a different course pursued by you," she noted politely. Jefferson was obliged to defend himself, which in turn called for another letter of attack from Mrs. Adams.

During the whole exchange she clearly had the best of it, commenting not only upon his personal acts but upon the philosophy of his party and expounding clearer logic than Jefferson. With courtesy, she pointed out that he was avoiding the issue, corrected him as to the powers of the executive under law, and politely closed the correspondence. It was not until a month later that she showed the correspondence to Adams, who carefully filed the letters away. He noted upon the blue-ribboned packet, "I have no remarks to make upon it."

The retired Adamses lived quietly on their farm, "picking

a political bone" or two with friends who came to visit. Mrs. Adams lived for eighteen more years, until she was seventy-four. Her husband survived her by eight years, dying, ironically, on the same day as Jefferson. Occupying the White House that year was the sixth President, a gentleman named John Quincy Adams.

For many years Adams had been alone in Paris and London, surrounded by the sophisticated, beautiful women of a glittering, gay society; but he longed only for his wife to join him as soon as it was considered safe to sail the seas. He was not of an amorous nature; a weakness for women was not among his vices. Once, at the age of seventy-six, in a reflective mood, he insisted: "Among all the errors, follies, failings, vices and crimes which have been so plentifully imputed to me, I cannot recollect a single insinuation against me of any amorous intrigue, or irregular or immoral connection with women, single or married, myself a bachelor or a married man." And Mrs. Adams, for her part, never looked at any man but her husband; every letter poured forth her devotion and loneliness.

In his diary Adams wrote: "On the 25th day of October I was married to Miss Smith, second daughter of the Rev. William Smith . . . a connection which has been the source of all my felicity, although a sense of duty, which forced me away from her and my children for so many years produced all the griefs of my heart." When his wife died, Adams told his son sorrowfully that in all the vicissitudes of fortune his wife had been his help and comfort, and without her he could not have endured —or even survived.

Dorothea Payne Todd

MADISON

❀ ❀

The humorist Will Rogers once noted that "more Presidents are elected between sundown and sunup than sunup and sundown." Actually, his words are truer than most politicians would care to admit—the late-night smoke-filled back room and the official-studded cocktail party have played indisputable roles in political activities.

It was Dolley Madison, the exuberant wife of our fourth President, James Madison, who brought Washington activities after sundown into their own, and provided a vigorous social life which she thought was necessary to complement the increasingly important official life. The standard of manners and refinements set by Mrs. Madison served as a civilizing influence throughout a still primitive young nation, where women were struggling to bring the little graces of life into rough, male-dominated communities. She felt that social, as well as governmental, leadership should come from the White House—and besides, she thoroughly enjoyed parties.

Mrs. Madison never did anything halfway; her parties, and she held them with breathless frequency, were always sensational, extravagant, and overcrowded. One of her best efforts was the massive reception at the executive mansion on New Year's Day, 1814. Gentlemen in lace and women in flowers, feathers, gloves, and teetering headdresses waltzed in the great audience room, nibbled ice cream, drank Madeira, and tried to worm their way close enough for a word or two with their elegant host and hostess. The First Lady, beaming and bobbing, was wearing a new gown from France, soft pink satin trimmed in ermine. She had on a new turban, fashionably done in white satin and velvet, topped with ostrich plumes. By her side, bowing to the guests, stood the diminutive Madison—a good three inches shorter than his wife, several pounds lighter, seventeen years older, formal, reserved, and enveloped in an air of abstraction. Generally he enjoyed his wife's parties; but lately he had found it difficult to be light-hearted, before or after sundown. For over two years the United States had been at war with England—"Madison's war," his enemies called it. The war had gasped on fitfully, depressingly, with most of the victories on the British side, except for a small naval skirmish or two on the Great Lakes. The President was burdened with weak Secretaries in the War and Navy Departments, who seemed unable to meet the British challenge. But Madison did not believe that the British would dare to attack the capital city itself; and since there was no threat of personal danger, his wife had seen no reason to discontinue her gay parties. She believed that fabulous goings-on at the executive mansion bolstered the morale of the people and presented an air of normalcy to the disturbed nation. The entertainments went on unabated, although Mrs. Madison did complain that it was terribly difficult now to get the lavish gowns she wanted from France.

The threat to Washington itself did not become apparent until six months later. Everyone, including the President, found it hard to believe at first—except the Reverend Mr. Breckinridge, a Federalist preacher. He thundered every Sunday from the pulpit against Madison and his war, and proved to be an unhappy prophet. He was particularly disturbed that Sabbath observance was being broken by "dinner parties given at the White House," and he predicted wrathfully that "It is the government that will be punished, and, as with Nineveh of old, it will not be the habitations of the people, but your temples and your palaces that will be burned to the ground."

In July, President Madison ordered defense plans to be hastily prepared for the supposedly safe government "temples and palaces." British ships were poised at the mouth of the Patuxent, and the Cabinet held secret, worried sessions far into the night. The Secretary of War insisted that the British would attack Baltimore, not Washington, and that fortifications around the capital would only frighten the residents. Unhappily, Madison agreed—until it was too late and the British troops were already advancing across Maryland. The few American troops they encountered were quickly routed, and by Monday, August 22, the British were within sixteen miles of the capital. People fled the city, helter-skelter. Men rode through the streets, warning their neighbors: "The enemy is advancing, our own troops are giving away on all sides . . . go, for God's sake, go!"

Such had been Dolley Madison's aplomb throughout this month of frightened chaos that she kept up her pretense of hospitality as usual, although it was difficult to guide table conversation off the gloomy subject of war. She put forth extra effort to make the evenings lively respites from worry, with special songs around the grand piano; or extra servings after dessert, such as almonds, raisins, apples, and pears; or handy conversation props like a popular book, carried opened to a page from which she could quote a provocative passage.

Mrs. Madison's parties were such command performances for all of Washington, that on August 23, Mrs. E. Jones sent a regretful note to decline Dolley's gracious invitation to dine at the mansion that evening. "I imagine it will be more convenient," Mrs. Jones wrote politely, "to dispense with the enjoyment of your hospitality today, and therefore pray you to admit this as an excuse for Mr. Jones, Lucy and myself." Mrs. Jones explained that Mr. Jones was engaged in dispatching the Marines and attending to other public duties relative to the defense of the city, while she and her daughter were busily preparing for a hurried departure, for "there appears to be rather serious cause for apprehension." Mrs. Jones's letter stands today as a classic of understatement. The President, the very day she sent her message, had already left Washington, galloping away to assume command personally of Commodore Joshua Barney's battery, stationed a half-mile north of Bladensburg, Maryland, and entrusted with the final defense of the city. The guard of one hundred men which the President had ordered stationed around the White House for his wife's protection had disappeared—some to join the militia elsewhere, some to seek a more healthy climate. She was alone in the big house with a few terrified servants and her faithful steward, Jean Pierre Sioussant. When the President left he had admonished her to take care of herself and the Cabinet papers. Mrs. Madison, with surprising calm, replied quietly that she "had no fear but for him, and the success of our army."

To keep away tears and fears, Dolley Madison spent the day of the now-canceled party packing the national insignia, the original draft of the Constitution, the Declaration of Independence, and all the other government papers (which were entrusted to the safekeeping of the President, since there was no national archive) into one small trunk which could if necessary be wedged into her carriage. She hopefully collected into other barrels and boxes her silver plate, the yellow velvet curtains, and the best pieces and trinkets of her lavish wardrobe, on the chance she could find a way to escape with some personal belongings. She entrusted her pet macaw to Sioussant, who promised to carry it to a safer house (he did, and the bird survived the invasion).

Sioussant was the only protector who remained, and he offered to spike the cannon at the gate and lay a train of powder which would blow up the British if they tried to enter the house. Mrs. Madison, however, could not bring herself to let him do it. And so, waiting for word from her husband, as carriages and wagons crowded with frightened families and their belongings rumbled past her window, she sat down alone to write a remarkable historic document to her sister Lucy. Coolly she recorded the only time an American President was forced to flee the nation's capital.

"Dear Sister," she began. "My husband left me yesterday

morning to join General Winder. He inquired anxiously whether I had courage, or firmness to remain in the President's House until his return, on the morrow or succeeding day. . . . He desires I should be ready at a moment's warning to enter my carriage and leave the city. . . . I am determined not to go myself until I see Mr. Madison safe, so that he can accompany me, as I hear of much hostility towards him. Disaffection stalks around us. My friends and acquaintances are all gone. . . ."

The next day, August 24, Mrs. Madison climbed to the White House roof and watched through a spyglass the scene of chaos around her; she saw hundreds of fleeing, defeated American soldiers wandering in all directions, but she could not locate her husband anywhere. That morning she had cheerfully hoped he would return victorious from battle with a group of gay officers for dinner; she had even ordered the servants to set the table for a banquet and be prepared to serve a dinner party on short notice. As the day passed, her hopes faded, and at 3:00 P.M. she wrote again to Lucy: "Here I am still, within sound of the cannon. Mr. Madison comes not. May God protect us! Two messengers, covered with dust, come to bid me fly; but here I mean to wait for him. . . ." She was interrupted by an old friend, Charles Carroll, who insisted that the President's wife stop her foolish dallying and flee with him. Reluctantly she was persuaded, but not until she took time to record that Carroll was in "a very bad humor with me." She delayed further to see that the Stuart-Winstanley portrait of George Washington, which she remembered at the last minute, was removed from the wall and given to two strangers passing by, who promised to carry it to safety. Mrs. Madison later explained her action: "I acted thus because of my respect for General Washington—not that I felt a desire to gain laurels." Thanks to Dolley Madison the Washington portrait is the only object in the White House today which belonged in the original President's House. With the portrait safe, and the valuable documents packed in her waiting carriage, she concluded her letter to Lucy: "And now, dear sister, I must leave this house, or the retreating army will make me a prisoner in it, by filling up the road I am directed to take. When I shall again write to you, or where I shall be tomorrow, I cannot tell!"

As Dolley Madison's carriage rolled toward the safe Virginia countryside, the British were already in the city, burning the public buildings—the Capitol, government office buildings, and the Navy Yard were monstrous orange bonfires. That evening British soldiers strolled into the White House, ransacked the empty mansion for souvenirs, piled up the elegant tables and chairs in the drawing room—and set the place on fire. The mansion was soon a sheet of flames, and all night the skies over Washington were bright as day with reflected light from the burning public buildings. Mrs. Madison and her Negro maid Sukey reached the protection of the soldiers' encampment north of Georgetown, where they spent an uneasy night. On the way they had stopped at a roadside tavern to rest. The tavern mistress welcomed them until she discovered Mrs. Madison's identity. Then she flew into a rage and chased the President's wife back into her carriage, screaming, "Your husband has got mine out fighting, and damn you, you shan't stay in my house!" Dolley Madison drove on, without food or water.

Thursday morning, nature added her vengeance to that of the British. A storm described as "the most tremendous hurricane ever remembered by the inhabitants" blew down houses, tore up trees, and spread new terror in the streets. But it also put out the fires. The White House, which had burned all night, was a blackened, steaming shell. Nothing remained but the walls.

The Madisons returned to the desolated city three days later, after the British withdrew. Mrs. Madison was horrified: "I cannot tell you what I felt on re-entering it—such destruction, such confusion. The fleet full in view and in the act of robbing Alexandria. The citizens expecting another visit—and at night the rockets were seen flying near us."

It was necessary to start all over again. The city of Philadelphia sent a beguiling invitation to move the national government back there. Madison, discouraged, gave the offer serious consideration. Here Mrs. Madison, however, made a historic decision. She felt deeply that the capital should remain where the Founding Fathers had decreed it should be, that her husband had no historical right to move it. She persuaded Madison to reject the Philadelphia offer—and he began the weary task of rebuilding in Washington. The Madisons found temporary shelter in Octagon House, which had just been vacated by the French minister and was considered the most impressive house in the area. They lived there for a year, then finished out their administration in a larger house on Lafayette Square. They never did return to the White House, for its restoration was not completed until James Monroe was President.

The anti-Madison newspapers expressed the hope that now, in such dire times, the endless parties, receptions, and dinners given by the President and his wife would cease, since they were "the resort of the idle and the encouragers of spies and traitors." Mrs. Madison ignored this, of course, and by fall was once more enmeshed in her usual round of hospitalities. Despite the war, she continued to be the focal point of fashionable gossip and envy. Her dresses were obtained at great effort and expense from France. Her parties drew such crowds in their now-smaller quarters that Margaret Bayard Smith, a social chronicler of the day, called them "Mrs. Madison's squeezes."

Mrs. Madison was now middle-aged, but her spirits showed no sign of flagging, and she still maintained a strenuous social schedule. She rarely let a day pass without riding out to return calls, or hostessing some sort of social event herself. The writer Washington Irving described Mrs. Madison after one of her parties as a "fine, portly, buxom dame who has a smile and a pleasant word for everybody." He was less kind with President Madison, whom he dismissed with "as to Jeemy Madison, ah, poor Jeemy . . . he is but a withered little apple-John." A female visitor gushed, "It is not her form, 'tis not her face, it is the woman altogether whom I should wish you to see." The incomparable Dolley Madison was not beautiful; it was her great personality, her love and friendship for people of all sexes, ages, and stations, her exceptional tact in avoiding controversy and gossip, political or otherwise, that give her a unique place in American history. And yet her direct influence upon her husband was negligible. She was a legend in her own time, as the first truly American counterpart of the European *grande dame*.

When peace was finally concluded, the whole city of Washington celebrated on February 15, 1815. It was reported that Dolley Madison was the most popular person in all America that night: she celebrated the only way she knew how, by giving a huge party. The President was not there, for he was closeted with his Cabinet in a night session. Mrs. Madison presided alone, in full glory. A guest recalled: "The most conspicuous object in the room, observed of all observers, was Mrs. Madison herself, then in the meridian of life and queenly beauty . . . with a grace all her own, to her visitors she reciprocated heartfelt congratulations upon the glorious and happy change in the aspect of public affairs."

After the treaty had been signed, but before word could travel to him, General Andrew Jackson had won a spectacular victory in New Orleans. He was the hero of the war, and when he paid a visit to Washington the following fall Mrs. Madison outdid herself to welcome him. Her reception was criticized as "barbarous grandeur" and "an Egyptian display," and there was considerable justification for such complaints. She invited so many guests they could barely jam into her house, and she spread a wastefully lavish table. She placed Negro servants holding lighted candles or torches in front of each window. Her reasoning was that these eerie human candles would provide more light for her dark drawing room by which the guests could see her hero.

At her last reception as the President's wife, before the inauguration of the Monroes, she wore a gown of rose-colored satin with a white velvet train that swept the floor for several yards. She festooned this with a golden girdle, gold necklace and bracelets, a white velvet turban trimmed with white ostrich tips, and a gold-embroidered crown. She was a plump, middle-aged matron. But the new British minister, very impressed, said, "She looked every inch a queen."

Mrs. Madison wasn't born that way. In fact, she was possibly the least likely candidate for queenly material produced in the Colonies. She was one of nine children—born, on May 20, 1768 (although later she herself deducted four years off her age), to John and Mary Coles Payne, devout members of a Quaker settlement at New Garden Meeting, North Carolina. John Payne was a convert, and as is often the case with those who adopt a faith instead of being born into it, he interpreted its "Book of Discipline" more rigidly than many Quakers. Young Dolley grew up on a small plantation at Cedar Creek Meeting in Virginia, learned to read and write from Quaker gospel, attended quiet prayer meetings faithfully, and played only with other Quaker children. She wore the plain gray cloth Quaker bonnet and gown, was taught to regard fictional literature, dancing and other frivolities as "sinful," and colorful clothes as "vanity." The only person in Dolley's young life who was not Quaker was her Grandmother Payne. It was her grandmother who first responded to Dolley's un-Quakerlike desire for pretty trinkets and personal adornment. She secretly gave Dolley a small brooch. Dolley was delighted, but she knew that her parents would take it away from her if she wore the glittering trinket in public. So she hung it around her neck on a ribbon, inside her gown, where she could slip it out for admiring peeks. One day, however, the ribbon broke and the brooch was lost. Dolley cried all day as she searched the dusty road between her home and the meeting house where she attended school. Her father would have scolded her, had he known, and said losing the brooch was just retribution for submitting to the folly of vanity. But Dolley was not born with a Quaker's gentle, humble philosophy; she was so upset at losing the one pretty thing in her life that she never forgot this incident.

Dolley was always concerned about her appearance. For instance, she wore a sheer gauze mask to protect her complexion from the ravages of the sun, grime, and dust on the long walk to school. In permitting Dolley this extravagance, Mrs. Payne was indulging in wishful thinking, for her daughter was not destined to grow up a fragile, magnolia-type beauty, gauze or no gauze. She was never the dainty, petite type, either. Rather, Dolley Payne was blessed with a clear, healthy, blooming complexion —and a clear, healthy, blooming personality to go with it. She was big-framed and handsome; full-busted and broad-shouldered, with a soft oval face, an impish, turned-up mouth, widely set-apart blue eyes, dark hair brushed forward over a high, smooth brow.

In 1782 Virginia passed a law which permitted owners to free their slaves if they desired. John Payne, with his strong Quaker conscience, was one of the first to do so; as a consequence, the Paynes, unable to pay the wages for hired hands, sold their land and moved to Philadelphia, the city of Brotherly Love, where Payne expected to find a proper religious atmosphere in which to rear his large brood. Dolley was then fifteen. The Paynes moved into a two-story frame house and set up a small business making and selling laundry starch in the first-floor front room. But times were hard, and starch was a luxury that hard-pressed people found they could do without. Payne's business failed; when his debts became staggering, the Quaker society, according to its custom, publicly disowned him. Payne, at forty-nine a broken and disgraced man, shut himself up in his second-floor bedroom and seldom emerged during the remaining three years of his life.

Dolley's mother, penniless, took in boarders to support the family. But her father's disgrace seemed to have little effect upon Dolley's personal status, for she continued to attend the young people's meetings with other Quaker teen-agers and have a great number of beaus. She could not attend school, for there were none for young women in Philadelphia; but she did not mind, for she was never inclined much to studies, anyway. Dolley's most persistent suitor was a young Quaker lawyer, John Todd, Jr. She kept him dangling for years; but after her father's failure left the family destitute, Dolley found the security of marriage more appealing. She accepted John Todd, and on January 7, 1790, they were married. Dolley was twenty-one; her husband was twenty-six. The Congress was now sitting in Philadelphia, and life was good for a promising lawyer. The Todds lived quietly, as conforming Friends, and confined their outside activities mainly to the Quaker meeting house. They had two sons, John Payne and William Temple. But the summer of 1793 brought a vicious yellow fever epidemic to Philadelphia. Todd took Dolley, still weak from childbirth, from the city, where people were dying by the hundreds, to the healthful countryside. Then Todd returned to Philadelphia—where he soon caught the fever and died. Dolley Todd herself was very sick, and her infant son William died from the fever.

After the epidemic abated, the young Widow Todd reopened her house on South Fourth Street. Because of her husband's investments, she was moderately well-off. Her youngest sister Anna moved in with her and John Payne. Dolley continued to dress in the plain Quaker garb, but at twenty-five she was too radiant, too full of smiles and dimples not to attract male attention. Elizabeth Collins, Dolley's best friend, was so embarrassed by all the admiring glances thrown Dolley's way that she once took her to task: "Really, Dolley, thou must hide thy face, there are so many staring at thee." Dolley adhered strictly to the firm Quaker morality, but she was not shy. It did not send her into frightened, modest simperings to think that her looks pleased a man. Her favorite route for shopping excursions took her in front of the Indian Queen, Philadelphia's finest hotel. She liked to look at the fine ladies and gentlemen on the porch—and be looked at, and admired, in return, from a discreet distance. One day a short, shy, little bachelor with a reputation already far bigger than his actual personage noted the shapely Quaker girl as she passed his hotel. James Madison promptly arranged an introduction through his political enemy Aaron Burr, the senator from New York, who had been a boarder at Mrs. Payne's and an early confidant of young Dolley.

When Burr and Madison came to call upon her, Dolley Todd and Elizabeth Collins were waiting in their finest Quaker gowns. It would not have been proper for Dolley to receive Madison alone, so she had appealed to Elizabeth: "Thou must come to me. Aaron Burr says that the great little Madison has asked to be brought to see me this evening." The courtship was conducted demurely and quietly, but it was so unusual for Madison to pay attention to any one woman that gossip quickly spread. Eventually the talk reached President and Mrs. George Washington, who were extremely interested. The President thought very highly of Madison's statesmanship, and both Washingtons had long been friends of Madison. Motherly Mrs. Washington felt that Madison, who was over forty, needed the comfort and companionship of a wife. So she summoned Dolley Todd to the President's House for tea and to offer advice. Martha Washington was Dolley's distant cousin by marriage, so she approved of her as Madison's choice. "Are you engaged to James Madison?" the President's wife inquired, raising a private courtship to the level of a question of state. "No—I think not," stammered Dolley, who had not yet made up her mind. "He will make thee a good husband, and all the better for being so much older. We both approve of it; the esteem and friendship existing between Mr. Madison and my husband is very great, and we would wish thee to be happy," Mrs. Washington advised kindly.

Thus prodded from no less a personage than the President's

wife, Dolley Todd fled to the solitude of the Virginia countryside
to mull over her future. There is no indication that either Madison or Dolley felt much passion or romantic inclination. Her
deliberations on his proposal seem based entirely on practical
considerations, and she took all summer to decide. For his part,
Madison never once mentioned his fancy for the Widow Todd in
his writings or recorded remarks to friends during the whole
period of their courtship. And when she did accept his hand,
after keeping him on tenterhooks all summer, he took three days
to get around to answering her letter. There is no question but
that Dolley was full of doubts right up to her wedding day. She
was so distraught that she penned a letter to a friend after the
ceremony—and dated it wrong. She did not even know her own
wedding date! In the letter Dolley carefully explained that she
had just given her hand "to the man who of all others I most
admire" and that her little Payne would have a "generous and
tender protector." She signed the note as Dolley Todd, with a sad
little postscript: "Evening—Dolley Madison! Alas!"

Dolley Madison, the reluctant bride, was promptly overwhelmed by a strange new world, a world of politics and public
responsibility. As a peace-loving Quaker, she had little of the fire
in her veins which drove most of the patriots who had fought
for independence. Her life had been totally secluded from the
intricacies and intrigues of the formation of a new republic,
matters which were Madison's whole life. If she did not at first
realize the difficulties of her new position, they were immediately
borne home to her. Madison's friends greeted her coolly, for
they were afraid that a happy marriage would slow up the middle-aged patriot's ambitious drive. Jefferson wrote a long letter,
upon hearing of the wedding, pleading with Madison not to
retire to Montpelier, his family home in Virginia. Another friend,
Charles Pinckney, confessed he feared Madison would become
a victim of "petticoat government." (Years later he was pleased
to comment that he had heard nothing but good things of Mrs.
Madison.) The Quaker sodality dismissed Mrs. Madison from
membership. The old ties were cut and Dolley Madison was embarked upon a new life much more to her liking.

The Madisons settled in Philadelphia, where Madison was
embroiled in what his wife called "public business." Dolley

Madison began her social apprenticeship. Under the eyes of her horrified former Quaker friends, she studied fashionable dress and copied it; formal entertainment patterns, and copied them; customs and manners of top-drawer society, and copied them. She looked upon this as her job, and she worked hard at it; just as "public business" was her husband's job, and he worked hard at that. From the beginning Dolley Madison arranged her dinners and receptions with total disregard for political differences. She developed, and practiced, small artifices and chatty gambits to guide the conversation whenever it steered toward a disrupting political argument. Madison himself hated a narrow partisan social atmosphere and encouraged her to invite his political enemies, the Federalists, as well as members of his own Republican party. Federalist Vice-President John Adams, never a social charmer, dined and came away with the impression that "Mrs. Madison is a fine woman." The President and Mrs. Washington were frequent visitors, as well as Thomas Jefferson, who considered Madison his protégé. Madison was comfortably fixed, but not wealthy; he strained his purse so that his wife and her sister Anna could dress elegantly and entertain as lavishly as the rest of Philadelphia society. Dolley Madison blossomed out in resplendent colors and gown stuffs, all in the latest fashion. Only one outward sign remained of her plain Quaker background: in the mornings, as she worked at home, she always wore the plain gray gown and white apron of a good Quaker housewife.

When Jefferson was elected President, one of his first actions was to appoint James Madison as his Secretary of State. The social scene in Washington was pretty dismal; the city was so new and so raw that few women had homes suitable for proper entertaining. Jefferson, a widower, brought no feminine relief to the society-starved city; his two daughters were retiring and had no desire to take on the staggering hostess duties. The Vice-President, Aaron Burr, was also a widower; besides, he was so disgruntled at losing the election to his enemy Jefferson that he did not show up in the capital for an entire year after Jefferson's inauguration. As the wife of the Secretary of State, Dolley Madison thus became overnight the foremost hostess in Washington. Now a mature thirty-three, Dolley had lived seven years with the aristocratic little Madison, surrounded by gay society and the aura of politics; she was ready to accept the mantle. Jefferson turned to her as a sort of substitute First Lady; at virtually every presidential dinner or reception she acted as his hostess. She had served part of her social apprenticeship under the courtly tute-lege of Martha Washington and Abigail Adams, and she learned to combine their ideas of social dignity and elegance with Jef-ferson's own concept of informal democracy.

From the early days of the Jefferson administration, Dolley Madison was the big social arbiter of the federal city. Fortu-nately, she took her responsibilities seriously: a visitor at Jeffer-son's dinner table recalled she was full of "good humour and sprightliness, united to the most affable and agreeable manners." Dolley Madison also became the undisputed fashion leader. There were no such things as fashion magazines or an organized fashion industry in the nation. "What Mrs. Madison wore" was the fashion of the moment in Washington for sixteen years. William Dunlap, the painter, described her as "the leader of everything fashionable in Washington." When it was discovered that Mrs. Madison's ladylike white fingers were tobacco-stained from habitually taking snuff, it became chic for Washington ladies to take snuff also. When Mrs. Madison purchased a macaw, it became popular for every household to own a macaw. When she wore an emerald necklace, emerald necklaces suddenly be-came fashionable.

Dolley Madison was well aware of her one-woman rule over fashion, and she took great trouble with her attire. She dressed ornately and colorfully, and she liked to display her neck and arms—but she was careful never to go so far as to be scandalous or distasteful. She reserved white for state occasions. She always wore a great deal of jewelry, preferably sparkling green emeralds and red rubies, or warm pearls. She took an almost naïve pleasure in carefully matching accessories; ordered all her gowns from France, sparing no expense; and owned a dozen pairs of gold, silver, and beaded slippers (the average lady of her class would have owned three pairs). She was never without a small ornate snuffbox, which she carried as much for a conversation piece as an object of personal necessity. Whenever conversation dragged, Mrs. Madison pulled out her snuffbox (both men and women used snuff, although men had begun to smoke cigars).

Only her old friend Burr found her snuff habit offensive. "Mrs. Madison is still pretty, but oh, that unfortunate propensity to snuff-taking!" he deplored.

Jefferson, the great democrat, possessed an unerring instinct for simplicity; and Mrs. Madison, whether from her Quaker training or her easy compatibility, was perfectly matched as his hostess. Both at the President's House and at her own parties, she set the proper tone to elicit both friendship and respect from her guests. The women who were her White House intimates treated her with full respect: they called her "Mrs. Madison," or, after her husband became President, "her majesty," or "Lady Presidentess." She insisted upon proper forms and procedures. She mixed enemies freely, but under her roof she expected them to behave like civilized citizens. "I confess I do not admire contention in any form, either political or civil. I would rather fight with my hands than my tongue" she said. She rarely turned down an invitation, and she paid return calls on all who called upon her. She practiced animated, friendly small talk until a guest could say, "She talks a great deal and in such quick, beautiful tones." She was a good diplomat, and often advanced her husband's political aims by offering a key person the seat of honor next to her, or by playing up to his wife. She conversed brightly, a little, on every subject, emulating the fashionable Parisian salon ladies, who knew a little about everything but not much about anything. And she never lost her temper publicly. Once the snobbish wife of the new British minister, Anthony Merry, grumbled about the lack of protocol in Washington and dismissed Mrs. Madison's table as "more like a harvest home supper than the entertainment of a Secretary of State." Her reply, with typical diplomacy, is a classic. "The profusion of my table so repugnant to foreign customs arises from the happy circumstance of abundance and prosperity in our country," she said sweetly.

Mrs. Madison's task was the proper conduct of society, and she held herself within the same rules she set for others. She was as kindly and gracious to bores as to fascinating war heroes. There is no record of jealousy or antagonism toward Mrs. Madison from any of her guests—with one accord, they simply liked her. Her self-control was remarkable. She never commented upon the course of politics. "I am learning to hold my tongue well," she remarked with satisfaction. She refrained amazingly well from common gossip. Even after Aaron Burr shot Alexander Hamilton in the infamous duel, an event which shocked the nation, Dolley Madison had no comment to make about it. Her private letters to her sister mention only that she supposes her sister had heard about the duel.

For his second term Jefferson chose to run with elderly George Clinton as the vice-presidential candidate; Clinton would obviously never make a presidential contender and Jefferson would be free to pick his successor. It was between Madison and James Monroe, whom Jefferson called his "two pillars." But in the end Jefferson backed Madison—and the one and only Dolley became the President's hostess in her own right.

The new First Lady moved into the White House on March 4, 1809, at the peak of her social success, the only real, full-time, devoted public hostess the nation was ever to have. She had come to accept her prominence as her due, and she still enjoyed the constant, daily round of entertaining. She never failed to "amuse myself with the mob." Prospects were not as bright for the new President, however. The threat of war hovered over the country. The rival blockades of warring Britain and France were terrific obstacles to economic advancement. The nation was indignant at the frequent seizure of United States ships; the people were weary of British bullying.

Dolley Madison was never her husband's political confidante as Mrs. Adams had been, nor the fireside homebody that Mrs. Washington was. Although the President did much of his work at home, she absorbed little more than the rudiments of political issues. "You know I am not much of a politician," she confessed once in a moment of self-analysis. "I believe you would not desire your wife to be the active partisan, nor will there be the slightest danger while she is conscious of her want of talents." But her husband kept her informed, in general terms, of major events such as the progress of the approaching war with Britain. He advised her, for example, to remember that technically the power of deciding war rests with Congress not with the President. This was "always our answer to newspapers," he explained, and could be her answer to curious guests, too. Dolley Madison was more interested in the personalities who created the issues than in the nuances of the issues themselves. When she felt her private opinion might inadvertently slip out, she simply avoided a subject altogether—she never once publicly mentioned Burr's name during the whole scandal over his attempt to overthrow the government and his subsequent trial for treason.

The years together had brought, from all outward appearances, a mutual devotion to the couple who had married without love. Around her neck Mrs. Madison wore a locket of intermingled locks of hair set in gold. She called the President "my darling little husband," and he called her "my beloved." They wrote ardent, flowery love letters when they were separated. Madison was proud of his wife's great social success; and he often said that a visit to his wife in her sitting room, where he was sure of a bright story and a good laugh, was as refreshing as a long walk. She could always make him relax and take his mind off problems of state.

Dolley Madison began her sojourn in the White House in fitting splendor; she instituted the first inaugural ball, which starred, of course, herself. It seemed to her that an event of such magnitude as the inauguration of her husband should be accompanied by a social celebration equally as tremendous. Outgoing President Jefferson paid her the tribute of attending the ball, although he confessed that he didn't know how to behave—it had been forty years since he had been to a ball. And even in her moment of triumph she displayed the diplomatic tact for which she was famous. She sat between the ministers of warring England and France, and so carefully did she divide her attention between them, they went away feeling she had been "equally gracious" to both.

The White House soon became the center of all activity in Washington. Mrs. Madison's weekly "drawing rooms" drew young people looking for flirtations and a good time; ambitious officials looking for new appointments; social dowagers looking for the latest fashion and gossip; politicians hoping to make a deal quietly for some Capitol Hill maneuver; out-of-town visitors hoping to speak with scholars and officials. No invitations were issued—the city's old family aristocrats, congressmen, diplomats, top government officials, and special visiting dignitaries came as a matter of course. It was not considered etiquette, however, for a female to appear until she had first been "presented to her majesty" in private. Dolley Madison was a friend to all, but she never allowed her guests to use her to intervene with her husband. Washington Irving tried this, with notable lack of success. He wanted an appointment as secretary to the Paris embassy, and was hopeful of his chances because "Mrs. Madison is a sworn friend of mine." He did not, however, get the job.

Mrs. Madison customarily presided at the White House table, with President Madison seated with the guests. This was his own idea; it relieved him of directing the conversation. In contrast, Mrs. Madison as hostess, like a good actress, was always completely self-possessed. A guest once commented: "We remarked on the ease with which she glided into the stream of conversation. . . ." She had also acquired a social asset her husband had not: she never forgot a face or a name. And in her ready small talk and cheerful patter, she was careful to comment on people and things without personal emotion. This air of detachment was one key to her popularity. "It is one of my sources of happiness never to desire a knowledge of other people's business," she once said. This was a big help in avoiding political enemies, which her husband had enough of anyway.

Her political dinners were well timed and well served. She spared no effort to make her parties go smoothly; being a successful hostess on such a grand scale was oftentimes just plain hard work. It took planning, and organization, and attention to details. Mrs. Madison had bells installed in every room in the White House in order to improve the service. She more than doubled the number of Jefferson's servants from fourteen to thirty. She hired additional slave waiters from neighboring plantations, at thirty-five cents each, for big dinner parties, so there would be one waiter for every guest. She served refreshments to all callers, regardless of their business. She surprised the British minister, for example, by interrupting his angry conference with the President over the war by sending in a Negro servant with glasses of punch and seed cake. (She didn't stop the war this way, but she at least put them both in a better mood.) And she redecorated the White House at a cost of about $11,000, which the government paid. She bought a piano, a guitar, china, silver, mirrors—and lots

of yellow cloth, satin for the drawing room and damask for drap-
eries.

The mood of the nation increasingly favored war; in the
election of 1810 the pacifists lost more than half of their Congressional seats to young pro-war Westerners dubbed War Hawks.
Their leader was Henry Clay, and he was promptly elected
Speaker of the House. Mrs. Madison, warned of their political importance by her husband, increased the number of socials to a
degree that was tedious even for her. The War Hawks were her
honored guests and Clay was her special favorite. She accorded
him the rare privilege of taking snuff from her box.

Mrs. Madison's role in bringing the President around to
Clay's point of view is not clear, but years later the election
analyst James Blaine gave her so much credit that he said, "Mrs.
Madison saved the administration of her husband, held him back
from the extremes of Jeffersonianism, and enabled him to escape
from the terrible dilemma of the war of 1812. But for her, DeWitt
Clinton would have been chosen in 1812." At any rate, it was she
who first made a friend of Clay, and she believed in the necessity
of war to assure Madison's re-election long before Madison did.
As the election approached, Madison and Clay agreed that there
would have to be a war; in return, Clay agreed to support Madison
for re-election. And the West—the War Hawks—won the election
for Madison by voting solidly for him.

After the formal declaration of war, things went badly. In
every battle Americans were getting the worst of it. Morale was
low in the capital, and Mrs. Madison realized the importance of
dramatizing the minor victories that did occur. One of her social
lions was Oliver Hazard Perry, who directed the only big naval
victory, on Lake Erie. Another favorite of Mrs. Madison's was
General William Henry Harrison, who defeated a British contin-
gent near Detroit in the fall of 1812. Shortly after his victory General Harrison went to the capital to consult with the President.
After their talks Madison ordered him to return to his post. Later
that evening, however, Mrs. Madison announced that General
Harrison would be at her party. The President protested: "General Harrison should be thirty or forty miles on his way west by
now." She dismissed this with a wave of her hand: "I laid my
command on him and he is too gallant a man to disobey me." "We

shall soon see whose orders he obeys," grumbled the President. The lady won. That night General Harrison danced at Mrs. Madison's party.

Mrs. Madison's personal popularity was much higher than that of her husband, who was being blamed for the defeats of the war. A friend complimented her: "You give and have given universal satisfaction to all friends and visitors, which is indeed a very difficult matter, that of pleasing everybody. You, however, were always so good, and possessed such an amiable temper. . . ." There is no indication, however, that Dolley Madison was ever embittered because fickle people who enjoyed her hospitality, and were glad to eat her food, whispered unkind things about the President. She tried to follow the example of her philosophical husband, who had warned: "Be always on your guard that you become not the slave of the public nor the martyr to your friends."

The burning of the capital miraculously marked the beginning of the end of "Madison's war." Peace commissioners began negotiating with the British at Ghent, Belgium, in August, 1814, about the time of the attack on Washington. With the commissioners had gone Mrs. Madison's son Payne. He was handsome, well educated, tutored in French, and elegant-mannered. He was so popular, he was called "the American Prince." But Payne did not have his mother's self-control; his easy social success went straight to his head and no worthwhile thought entered it thereafter. He drank to excess, dallied with the ladies, went on wild sprees. He refused to come home, and stayed overlong in Paris, where he was already slipping into the irresponsible, careless life which would bring his mother so much grief. Mrs. Madison spoiled her son, and never seemed able to discipline him. In her overindulgence she stressed her pleasure at his "popularity," which she apparently prized over any serious efforts at earning a living. She lavished love and money on him. She was continually trying to arrange a suitable marriage, in hopes that he would settle down. But he never married and he never settled down. He indulged himself selfishly all his aimless life. He squandered his inheritance and totally disregarded his mother's feelings unless he needed money from her. He was finally imprisoned in Philadelphia for failure to pay debts, and in 1852, at sixty-one, he died in a broken-down hotel, without friends or human dignity. One

solitary, unnamed mourner followed his coffin to the Congressional Cemetery in Washington.

Only one specific example has come to light in which Mrs.
Madison interfered directly with her husband's duties as President. It was a minor instance, typical of her warm heart. During
the war a young conscientious objector, a Quaker, refused military
service and was put in prison. He was the son of Debbie Pleasants,
a childhood friend of Mrs. Madison's from the Quaker meeting
house. He languished in prison until she heard about it. She immediately interceded with the President, who arranged the young
man's freedom.

After the war ended, the nation entered upon an era of good
feeling and peace, and Madison's popularity suddenly increased
to the level of his wife's. They ended their administration happily;
both had met what they considered their responsibility, and they
were satisfied. Mrs. Madison's old friend, Elizabeth Lee, wrote on
the day of Monroe's inauguration: "Talents such as yours were
never intended to remain inactive . . . as you retire you will carry
with you principles and manners not be be put off with the robe
of state. . . ."

Dolley Madison never did put off the robe of state. For
twenty years, until Madison's death, she lived at Montpelier,
dispensing the same lavish, unstinting hospitality she had shown
in the White House. They seldom were without house guests, and
ninety people for dinner was not unusual. One guest, seeing Mrs.
Madison after ten years, said, "She looks young and she says she
feels so. I can believe her, nor do I think she will ever look or
feel like an old woman." When Madison died, in 1835, a female
writer took the occasion to pay tribute to his widow: "She is
celebrated throughout the country for . . . grace and dignity . . .
she administered the hospitalities of the White House with such
discretion, impartiality, and kindliness. . . . She is a strong-minded
woman, fully capable of entering into her husband's occupations
and cares; and there is little doubt that he owed much to her intellectual companionship, as well as to her ability in sustaining
the outward dignity of his office." Left alone (Payne refused to
live with his mother, rarely bothered even to write to her), Dolley
Madison moved back to Washington. Now "the venerable Mrs.
Madison," she once more took over as queen of that element for

which history has provided her no peer—official capital society. The widowed President Van Buren relied upon her for social advice, and she quickly produced one of her own relatives, Angelica Singleton, whom she married off to Van Buren's son Abraham. The daughter-in-law of widowed President Tyler, overwhelmed by her social responsibilities, reserved a seat in the Tyler carriage on all official occasions for Mrs. Madison. President Polk paid one of his three social visits his first year in the White House to her. Despite a bothersome eye affliction, she played whist regularly with ex-President John Quincy Adams. Wherever she went she was accorded reverence and a place of honor. Congress gave her the highest accolade ever given a President's widow, voting her a lifetime seat on the floor of the House. In her late seventies, despite pressing poverty, she was still indulging herself by giving parties, although they were less frequent than in the old days. When she attended her last White House reception, given by President and Mrs. Polk in February, 1849, she was resplendent as ever in a white satin gown with fringed turban. Her gown was youthfully low-cut, and ecstatic eyewitnesses recorded that her arms and shoulders were still beautiful at eighty-two. At any rate, she still had the same old energy: President Polk reported later in his diary that he and Mrs. Madison had strolled through the crowded rooms till nearly midnight.

The incredible Dolley Madison died on July 12, 1849. President Taylor led the notables at her funeral services, which were as elaborate as for any President.

Sarah Childress

POLK

President James K. Polk once remarked that if he had remained clerk of the Tennessee state legislature his wife would never have consented to marry him.

That she did consent proved to be a lucky development. For certainly the eleventh President of the United States brought with him to the White House a woman just as politically astute, hard-working, serious-minded, and ambitious as himself. And as another asset, she was a stunning beauty.

Sarah Childress Polk, a Spanish-type raven-haired woman, was forty-one when her husband was inaugurated in 1845. Polk himself was only forty-nine, the youngest President yet elected at that time. Polk was as slender, dark-haired, youthful, and gentle-featured as his wife. Together they made as handsome a couple as the present occupants of the White House.

Polk's administration did not begin auspiciously. In fact, the inauguration was a dismal failure. The "short man with a long program," who was to preside over the beginning of a new era in which the United States would become a continental power, shouted his address into a driving rain which drowned out nearly every word. Only a few bedraggled, cold, and sneezing officials, huddled under umbrellas, braved the storm to hear the new President. Sarah stood behind him on the platform, bare-headed in the downpour, clutching a useless ivory fan which featured elegantly carved stickers and a silken spread imprinted with portraits of the eleven Presidents.

It was the Polks themselves, however, who helped spoil the inaugural ball later that night. The First Lady, it was reported, looked lovely in an expensive blue velvet dress with deeply fringed cape; but when they arrived at the ball they ordered that the dancing be stopped. They stayed for two hours, long enough to greet every guest, and only when they left did the dancing resume.

On this sober note began a sober four years. Polk is not one of the best-remembered Presidents, yet historians rate him as one of the near-great, the best of the second-ranking Presidents. His wife saw his work as her work, and left most of the social and household chores to others in order to be his private secretary. They looked upon the so-called worldly pleasures as wasteful indulgence, and they regularly worked twelve hours a day on government problems. Polk announced that he would not seek a second term because he wanted to be free to make his decisions for the good of the country, not for the good of his own popularity.

Sarah Polk, who was deeply religious, took her responsibilities very seriously, because she believed that God had determined this as her destiny. One scorchingly hot day in midsummer she and the President were writing at their desks in his big office. She laid down her pen and wandered to the window. Outside, some young Negroes were at work in the garden, the sweat on their backs glistening in the sun. Every few minutes one straightened up and wiped his brow with the back of his hand or a dirty piece of cloth. "The writers of the Declaration of Independence were mistaken when they affirmed that all men are created equal," Mrs. Polk said. The President, without bothering to look up from his labors, crossly grumbled that she was having "foolish fancies." Persisting, his wife pulled him to the window.

"There are those men toiling in the heat of the sun, while you are writing, and I am standing here fanning myself, in this house as airy and delightful as a palace, surrounded with every comfort. Those men did not choose such a lot in life, neither did we ask for ours; we are created for these places," she told him gently.

The Polks were not really unsociable, although most people in Washington thought they were. It was just that they felt they were, as Polk put it, "hired to work," and each reception and party meant hours lost from working. Often, after a party, both Polks sat up far into the night working on projects they felt they should have done while they were carrying out their duties as host and hostess.

Polk paid only three visits his entire first year in office; Sarah refused to return any calls. They reduced entertaining to only those events which were so entrenched as to have become established custom—the state dinners and the twice-weekly public receptions. Since the Polks did not play cards, dance, or drink, they forbade these activities in the White House. Mrs. Polk's receptions were so staid that a gentleman once commented wryly: "Madam, you have a very genteel assemblage tonight."

Mrs. Polk seemed horrified. "Sir," she replied spiritedly, "I have never seen it otherwise!"

Guests at the White House were not overwhelmingly pleased at the new sedateness. Many complained outright that Mrs. Polk's affairs were just plain dull. There was nothing to do but promenade up and down the East Room and chat with other promenaders. She was so strict that she not only banished drinking—even punch—she refused to serve food, too.

In spite of this, however, the Polks, who were witty and friendly, were liked personally. Mrs. Polk, because she was so handsome, gained a national reputation for goodness and stability, which in an older, dumpier woman might have been called simply stuffiness.

When she was asked why she did not permit dancing in the White House, she replied: "To dance in these rooms would be undignified, and it would be respectful neither to the house nor to the office. How indecorous it would seem for dancing to be going on in one apartment, while in another we were conversing with dignitaries of the republic or ministers of the gospel. This unseemly juxtaposition would be likely to occur at any time, were such amusements permitted."

Mrs. Polk was behaving in accordance with her own Calvinistic conscience, but she was also reflecting the genteel, moralistic mood of her times. Newspapers generally applauded. Said the Nashville (Tennessee) *Union:* "The example of Mrs. Polk can hardly fail of exerting a salutary influence. . . . However politicians may differ in regard to the merit of Mr. Polk's administration, there can be no difference as respects that of his lady, in her department of the presidential mansion."

If anything, the President was even less inclined toward amusements and recreation than his wife. Once he reported in his diary that she had given permission for a juggler to entertain after dinner, a rare event. He was called from his desk to watch, and reported it "innocent in itself but time unprofitably spent." And as for those dinners and receptions which he could not avoid —a contemporary chronicler noted: "It was known he was in the habit of cutting off from his sleep the hours lost [after a party] to make up the amount of time which he felt belonged to the nation."

To give Mrs. Polk credit, she was generally tolerant of those who did not share her own ideas of propriety. Or perhaps she was just too much of a politician. In any case, whenever people remarked about her formality, she always responded mildly, "You were not brought up in so strict a school as I was."

While Polk was a congressman, his wife was invited to attend the races with the wife of a Cabinet member. She did not wish to offend the influential woman, but she declined. Mrs. Polk had never been to a horse race in her life, and did not wish to start. "Well," the woman said, "that is a reflection upon me."

"No, not at all," Mrs. Polk said. "You are in the habit of going I am not."

The White House had been without a bona-fide mistress since the time of John Quincy Adams, so Washington society had grown accustomed to a lack of social gaiety. President Tyler had married his child-bride Julia only a few months before his term was over, so she had not had time to revive White House festivities. The other Presidents had been without wives.

At her parties, Mrs. Polk's austere nature was reflected in

her proud style of receiving. She was personally much admired, for her quick tongue and her impeccable courtesy as well as for her appearance. She always dressed elegantly, in simple, chaste styles of rich fabrics. As *Godey's Ladies Book* prescribed, she wore bell-shaped crinoline gowns which swept the street, swaying over their hoops; beribboned bonnets, and heelless cloth slippers. Even the memoir of an obviously suffering guest indicates the respect which the austere Mrs. Polk commanded. He recorded: "Such scraping, such curtsying, such jabbering of foreign compliments and violent efforts of some of our people to do the polite in uncouth tongues . . . such a wild clamor of conversation rages."

The Polks ran a Spartan household, and were proud of it. She managed most of the finances and insisted that they live within the presidential salary of $25,000 a year. They had a sizable private income, but they preserved that for their retirement. They were not so eager to save money that they would accept expensive gifts, however. Mrs. Polk even refused bouquets grown in the federal conservatory attached to the Patent Office, rather than seem to receive special privileges. No doubt the money saved was a factor in her absolute refusal to serve refreshments of any kind at her receptions.

Mrs. Polk's weakness, if it could be called that, was her lack of interest in household details. The Polks never had any children, and their home was always neat and well-appointed. But she left the problems of accomplishing this strictly up to the servants, overseeing carefully only the expenses. She rarely interfered in or directed, or arranged, the details of her White House dinners. Once a guest remarked that there were no napkins on the table. Mrs. Polk hadn't even noticed. The only thing to which she paid attention at her own parties was the conversation. Often she would get so animated that she forgot to eat, and the steward took to saving dishes she particularly liked so that she could nibble after the guests had left.

During Polk's presidential campaign, an old lady who supported his opponent, Henry Clay, had sought out Mrs. Polk. She expressed the opinion, with the audacity of old age, that Mrs. Clay would make a better First Lady because she was such a good housekeeper. Besides, the old lady added, Mrs. Clay made such excellent butter. Sarah replied coldly that if her husband were elected she would live within the public salary and not have to make her own butter to do it, either.

Sarah's concept of ladylike propriety forbade her to speak out in public. She took great pains to inform herself on abstruse and complicated political questions, but she discussed her own views upon them only with her husband in private. Whenever she discussed government issues in public, she habitually prefaced every comment with "Mr. Polk believes . . ." Much later, as an eighty-year-old widow, having lived alone in retirement for decades, Sarah would sigh that although age somewhat "toned down my ardor," she still took a "deep interest in state and national affairs." Franklin Pierce, who was later President himself, is recorded as saying that he much preferred to talk politics with Mrs. Polk than with anyone else, including her husband.

She preferred to discuss the meaty topics of the day with the gentlemen, rather than engage in simpering social gossip with the ladies. Consequently, more than one female guest at her parties complained that the First Lady would never stay in the sitting room with the ladies, but was "always in the parlor with Mr. Polk" and the other male guests.

Mrs. Polk found no conflict between her interest in government affairs and her ladylike manners. The big factor about "perfect ladies" (which was her highest compliment for other females) was that, in the 1840's, they stayed demurely in the background, never bossed their husbands in public, and never displayed themselves in so unseemly a way as to draw attention. And that is why there is so little of Sarah Polk's interpretation of her First Lady role on record today. To avoid personal prominence, she gave her husband credit for everything. And for the same reason she refused to accompany the President on his political campaign jaunts. As an old woman she reminisced about the difference in generations of women: "Opinions and manners are now quite different. . . . In those days, it was not thought suitable or dignified for them [women] to be thus prominent and conspicuous."

Polk's letters to his wife indicate that he told her everything and that he expected her comments in return. Indeed, she was a good listener and funneled every bit of new information to the President. In a letter written during the summer of 1848, she complained to him that "I saw Mr. Buchanan [then Secretary of State; later President] last evening; he was full of the foreign news, but I learned nothing very specific."

A New York newspaper called Mrs. Polk "a most auspicious domestic influence" and the President's "guardian angel." The President himself once said, "None but Sarah knew so intimately my private affairs." He frequently paid public tribute to her "wisdom." And he relied upon her help and advice as he did on no other person. He never assembled, as did Jackson, a "kitchen cabinet"; he had no national party committee or trusted personal advisers; he frequently complained that he could not— and would not—rely upon his Cabinet for much advice. He distrusted his Cabinet because he felt the members wasted too much time on frivolities and vacations. "I have conducted the government without their aid," he recorded wearily in his diary. "It is only occasionally that a great measure or a new question arises upon which I need the aid and advice of my Cabinet." Clearly, as much as any leader in American history, President Polk was a man who worked alone—with the exception of his only constant confidante and co-worker, his wife.

Both Polk and his wife had good reason to maintain secrecy about the continuous influence which she exerted, through her husband, on the conduct of government. They had seen too clearly how much pain can be inflicted upon a couple when the wife's name becomes a matter of public gossip. Both the President and Mrs. Polk had been friends of General Andrew Jackson since their youth, and young Polk for many years was Jackson's favorite political protégé. They visited often at the Hermitage, and Sarah Polk was very close to Rachael, Jackson's wife. She watched Rachael turn into a near-recluse, suffering under the cruel gossip of Jackson's political enemies. She knew Jackson had once killed a man who insulted his wife's honor. She sympathized helplessly as slurs against Rachael's character were smeared across the country as a campaign issue when Jackson sought the presidency. She shared Jackson's smoldering hatred for the scandalmongers, and his bitter belief that the agony and tension of the whispering campaign was the real cause of his wife's death. Even as Jackson took the oath of office, leaving behind the fresh grave of his Rachael, the whole nation was repeating awful words about her. (Tragically, Rachael has since been exonerated. She was not a wanton, sinful woman at all. She married Jackson believing that her first husband had obtained a divorce in another state. The Jacksons later discovered that her husband had deceived her, that she was not actually divorced. They continued to live together, anyway, until a divorce was finally obtained, whereupon Jackson and Rachael remarried legally.)

Polk had encouraged his wife's advice from the first days of their marriage. In fact, it was his idea that she help out as his secretary. Mrs. Polk recalled that he liked to keep her busy. She would walk into his study, day after day, and find him poring over papers. "You work so much," she said sympathetically at first. Polk looked up only long enough to hold out a paper filled with a fine scrawl, and mumble, "Sarah, here is something I wish you to read . . ." or, "Would you find . . ."

And so, Mrs. Polk remembered, "He set me to work too."

Polk was even too busy to scan newspapers, although they were rapidly multiplying and becoming increasingly influential. He felt that papers were essential reflectors of public opinion, however, and after he became President he relied upon them heavily as indicators of reaction to his administration. All the newspapers, therefore, were delivered to his wife. She began selecting articles which she felt he should read during his terms in Congress, and she continued the duty in the White House. She carefully marked each pertinent article, folded the papers with the marked sections on the outside, and piled them beside his chair.

Sarah Polk was interested in all the things that were happening in America, and she made an extra effort to read the current books as well as the newspapers. One morning a White House guest came upon her reading a new novel. He expressed surprise that Mrs. Polk had the time. "I have many books presented to me by writers, and I try to read them all," she said and smiled. Then, confidentially, she admitted, "At present that is impossible; but this evening the author of this book dines with the President, and I could not be so unkind as to appear wholly ignorant and unmindful of his gift." Since the Polks would not accept large gifts, they were swamped with presents of books. The flood prompted the President to suggest that they build the White House addition his wife desired out of books instead of bricks.

In his four years in the White House, Polk was so conscientious about his duties that he almost worked himself to death. The rapid growth of the nation had multiplied the number of government offices of all types, and westward expansion made it necessary to increase the size of the army, thereby creating thousands of applications for commissions. Further, transportation was so improved that most people could travel to Washington easily. Polk felt the people had a right to see their President, and so he spent tiresome hours every day receiving everyone who called on him. The beggars seeking favors and the men seeking jobs, both civil and military, were like locusts swarming into his office. He was given little or no relief, for he preferred to do his own work rather than delegate authority to his officials. He rarely took a day off, never had a long vacation during his whole presidency, and after two years had traveled no farther than three miles from his office.

Mrs. Polk matched her hours to his. The toll was visible on them both. She was very ill several times during their White House years. Polk was too stubborn to admit his exhaustion, but after four years in office he was thin to the point of emaciation and too weak to walk without a cane. Deep lines were etched in his face, his skin was a constant ashy pallor—he looked like an aged grandfather of the energetic young man who had once been called "Young Hickory" and made his inaugural address to a few umbrellas bent against a downpour.

Mrs. Polk's illnesses did not affect her beauty. She remained a slim, graceful figure, favoring dark silk or velvet gowns, with a kerchief of muslin and lace around her shoulders and folded across her bosom. Prim curls framed her patrician face with its clear creamy-olive complexion. An impressed English visitor at the White House recalled: "Mrs. Polk is a very handsome woman . . . she is well-read, has much talent for conversation, and is highly popular. Her excellent taste in dress . . . characterizes the lady."

Back in Nashville, Tennessee, the *Union* honored her as few women were honored in those days: "The country will owe a debt of gratitude to Mrs. Polk for introducing a system of Republican simplicity to the presidential mansion, to which it has hitherto been a stranger."

There was one thing about Mrs. Polk's "Republican simplicity"—it made her, despite her polite manner, terribly partisan. She had the emotional involvement in politics which has always prevented the majority of women from being very good, or very interested, in the profession. She could not separate personality from political philosophy; she never quite learned how to keep a personal friendship intact despite an honest political difference. She so resented former President Van Buren, who had opposed Polk for the nomination, that she refused to invite him to the White House even though the Polks and the Van Burens had once been friendly. Several times President Polk urged his wife to invite Van Buren, and even tried to add Van Buren's name to a dinner list without her knowledge. Mrs. Polk learned about Polk's trick, however, and threw the prepared invitation angrily into the fireplace.

When Mrs. Polk discussed current Senate debates, she would tick off the names of those who voted against the President's program, and excitedly vow: "I never will forgive him." Mrs. Polk could arise to any occasion, however, if she felt she had to. She managed to be perfectly cordial to Henry Clay when he returned to Washington in 1848, although she never forgot the bitterness of his campaign against her husband. The Polks chatted amiably with Clay for half an hour, and as Clay left he gallantly remarked that whatever difference of opinion he might have heard about her husband's administration, he had heard only praise for Mrs. Polk's administration. She, for her part, replied gracefully: "If a political opponent of my husband is to succeed him, I have always said I prefer you, Mr. Clay, and in that event I shall be most happy to surrender the White House to you." Polk recorded in his diary that Clay left with a hearty laugh, "in an excellent humor."

Both the President and his wife greatly missed their champion and leader, former President Jackson. It was Jackson who had launched Polk's career, and it was Jackson who virtually alone had made Polk a presidential nominee. The Polks had relied heavily on Jackson's sage advice and were saddened by his death three months after Polk's inauguration. The last letter Jackson wrote went to the new President, expressing his affection and proffering advice on several questions of national importance. Jackson had been their closest and truest friend. Had he not written to Mrs. Polk shortly before the national convention in 1844: "Daughter, I will put you in the White House if it costs me my life"?

Because of his close identification with "Old Hickory," it was inevitable that Polk should be nicknamed "Young Hickory." There were those who suspected Polk would falter without Jackson; but he soon made it clear that he was no rubber stamp. He had campaigned on a promise to annex Texas, and by December of his first year had completed all the legal details of the annexation. Then Polk began to eye the disputed southern boundary of Texas and all the Mexican territory lying between Texas and the Pacific Ocean. He felt that the great mission of his presidency was to complete the continental expansion of the United States, on the grounds that she had clear title to her "natural frontiers," everything between California and Alaska.

Polk steered a bold course: he was ready to negotiate a peace treaty with Mexico to settle the disputed border, but in the meantime he girded for war. He put warships in the Gulf of Mexico and he sent troop reinforcements to the border. He sent secret orders to the commander of our Pacific fleet to seize San Francisco and blockade the California coast in the event of war. Mexican and American troops faced each other across the Rio Grande: soon there was, predictably, a shooting skirmish which both sides blamed upon the other, and the war with Mexico was on.

Polk took full responsibility for the war and insisted upon managing personally all the psychological, diplomatic, economic, and military details of the campaign. He complained in his diary that General Zachary Taylor, in charge of the border troops, did not send him sufficiently detailed field information on which to base his next campaign moves. Meanwhile Polk rammed through a treaty with Britain resolving the squabble over the Oregon border, thus eliminating the threat of war from that quarter.

The latest news from the battlefront was a regular feature of the White House weekly levees—sometimes Mrs. Polk hushed all conversation for a report from some young injured officer on leave; sometimes the President read the report himself. All this time Polk was having trouble with Secretary of State Buchanan. He suspected that Buchanan had presidential ambitions, and was disturbed at Buchanan's hesitancy to put himself on record regarding any aspect of the war. Buchanan also opposed the finally negotiated treaty, which alienated a large number of voters who favored conquering all of Mexico. The only wartime confidante the President could trust, as always, was his wife.

The treaty with Mexico was ratified in the Senate on March 10, 1848. Under its provisions Polk added 525,000 square miles of territory, which was later to become the states of California, Nevada, Utah, most of Arizona, New Mexico, Colorado, and Wyoming. In addition, he accumulated 275,000 square miles through the Oregon settlement. And the war with Mexico had brought to public attention the next President, General Taylor, and given combat experience to at least four young men who would be prominent in the Civil War—Stonewall Jackson, Ulysses S. Grant, William Sherman, and Robert E. Lee.

In more ways than one, the new era was crowding in on the old. Gold was discovered in California in January, 1848; the following December the Secretary of War brought several nuggets to a Cabinet meeting. A month later Polk called a special Cabinet meeting to discuss the problems brought on by the pell-mell, lawless rush to California. His term was drawing to a close, but he sensed the sudden pressures for statehood. The final days of his administration were embroiled in a great furor over the question of statehood for California. Polk was strongly in favor of California's admission, largely because he feared the vast territory would set itself up as an independent nation if not admitted promptly. But it remained a problem for President-elect Taylor, whom Polk considered of "very ordinary capacity," to resolve.

Mrs. Polk shared her husband's belief in the great potential of continental America, and she helped by acting as sounding board, personal secretary, and clipping service. She was the first President's wife to have the background of a formal education, and she was the first to serve as an official member of her husband's staff. She seemed to consider it her personal mission in life to insure her husband a secure place in history: while he was President she tried to cut down his workload by doing some of it herself; and after his death, she devoted her energies to perpetuating his memory. A visitor to the Widow Polk in 1880 reported that "she loses herself in her admiration of all that Mr. Polk did that was noble." She refused to discuss her own part in White House affairs, but the same visitor observed the old lady retained "such a clear mind, such choice, chaste language; the rapid flow of thought, the vivacity of expression . . . her knowledge of the times, her recollections of the past, how accurate."

As long as she lived Sarah Polk believed that she and her husband "belonged to the nation." When they moved out of the White House on March 3, 1849, President Polk left a clear desk for his successor, and Mrs. Polk left a spotless house. She also left behind a symbol of the changing age—gas illumination in the White House living quarters. Because of its beauty, she had not, however, removed the elegant candlelit chandelier in the reception hall. (The decision proved to be wiser than she anticipated, for the first night the gas lights were used at a reception, the jets mysteriously vanished and left the party in darkness. Only Mrs. Polk's chandelier, with its candles, provided light. The next day's newspapers waxed eloquent on the subject of Mrs. Polk's "sagacity.")

Both Polks retired with satisfaction: they considered their work well done, and they knew they would not miss the public adulation, the pomp and circumstance, and the privileges they had never really wanted. She said it felt "like Christmas," and Polk, ailing and feeble, was relieved to shift his crushing duties to fresh shoulders. The Polks had been married for twenty-seven years, and all of these years were devoted to public service. They had purchased a home, which they named Polk Place, in Nashville, Tennessee, that was to be their retirement haven. And they took with them from Washington trunkfuls of mementos designed to make Polk Place a private museum.

The long journey home to Tennessee, however, was tiring; and the President, sick and exhausted, lived but a few weeks in his new house. Mrs. Polk had urged him for two decades to join a church, and on his deathbed he finally did so. She was at his bedside when he died. His last words have been recorded as "I love you, Sarah, for all eternity, I love you." Mrs. Polk, still youthful at forty-six, wept blindly. "And life was then a blank," she said.

The Widow Polk, although in good health, handsome, and

reasonably well-to-do, never accepted a single invitation after the President's death. She ventured outside her house only to attend church. She opened her home, however, to any and all visitors who wished to pay their respects and view the collected memorabilia from the White House. She did not lack for company, for both strangers and friends came regularly. She talked freely to all callers about her husband, who was buried under a simple marble marker on the front lawn.

Years later, during the Civil War, Nashville was occupied by Union generals. Mrs. Polk, who owned a large plantation in Mississippi as well as the Nashville house, was a slaveholder and, privately, sympathetic to the South. But throughout the war she conducted herself not as a Southerner but as a former First Lady —the only opinion about the war she allowed herself to express out loud was that she wished the awful thing would end. The Union generals respected her unique position, and called upon her with all the formality deserving of her former position. They ordered that Polk Place be left untouched, and even stored other historic valuables there for safekeeping. Polk's will had recommended that his widow free their slaves, but although she outlived him by forty years Mrs. Polk never did so: eventually, of course, the Civil War freed them. During the trying period after the war she still refrained from a personal comment, except to say when asked about slavery, "The war settled all that."

Mrs. Polk did, however, have considerable to say in her old age about the dawning emancipation of another class of citizens —women. She herself had been too schooled in the tradition of ladylike propriety and acquiescence to male dominance to be much of a feminist. In 1848, while Sarah Polk was First Lady, Lucretia Mott, Elizabeth Stanton, and other bold women had met at Seneca Falls, New York, to demand equal rights with men and propose the incredible idea that women should be allowed to vote. A few women were being accepted in the 1840's as well qualified in their fields, but the majority of women preferred the comfortable, genteel nothingness to which they had become accustomed. For the most part Mrs. Polk had ignored their struggle, although there were infrequent occasions when she expressed sympathy with these first stirrings of female independence. Once she invited to the White House a highly respected woman who, with her husband, operated a prominent school. The woman confessed that it was her first visit there, and Mrs. Polk was dismayed —though not overly surprised. "Though a woman of culture and high character, her occupation of school-teacher barred her from social equality," she explained later.

In her eighties Mrs. Polk looked upon the growing movement of women into the workaday world with approval. "It is beautiful to see how women are supporting themselves, and how those who go forward independently in various callings are respected and admired for their energy and industry. It is now considered proper for young ladies, when they leave school, to teach or to do something else for themselves. It was not so in my young days," she said.

Sarah Polk died just before her eighty-eighth birthday, on August 14, 1891. The nation in 1891 was a far different place from the pioneer country into which she had been born in 1803. Murfreesboro, her home town, with 7,000 citizens, was one of Tennessee's largest communities. Tennessee itself had become a state less than ten years before. Captain Joel Childress, her father, was a successful merchant of substantial means. Sarah was his eldest daughter, and he had a son, Anderson, and a second daughter, Susan.

In middle Tennessee in the early 1800's it was not considered necessary to send girls to school, but Mrs. Childress persuaded the headmaster of Anderson's private boys' school to give Sarah and Susan private instruction after the daily classes. In their early teens the girls were sent to Nashville, which was a big enough city to possess a school for girls. They lived in the home of their father's friend, a Colonel Butler, a staff officer of General Andrew Jackson. When Sarah was fifteen she was allowed to attend Salem Female Academy in Salem, North Carolina, but her studies were interrupted by her father's death. In 1820 Sarah returned home to live with her widowed mother.

James Knox Polk, by contrast, was not so fortunate in his education and did not attend a formal school until he was seventeen. His father, Samuel Polk, a farmer, had considered him too frail and sickly. He attempted to direct his son's education at home. His efforts were so inadequate, however, that when James, at fourteen, underwent an operation for gallstones, the doctor noted on his medical record: "uncouth and uneducated."

Eventually Samuel realized that farming was too strenuous for his son, and that he must have an education so he could enter a profession. Despite his late start James Polk was such an apt and eager pupil that he graduated from the University of North Carolina in 1818 as salutatorian. Polk, twenty-six, promptly opened his own law office. Through his friendship with a former congressman and local political boss, Felix Grundy, a friend of General Jackson's, Polk secured an appointment as chief clerk of the Tennessee House of Representatives.

In 1821 the legislature was meeting in Murfreesboro. At the first governor's reception there, Polk spotted a slender, dark-haired girl with General Jackson. Before he could reach them, she had disappeared; he did not find her again in the crowd the rest of the evening. But as he was leaving, Polk was offered a ride home by his former schoolmate, Anderson Childress. Waiting inside the carriage was the girl Polk had failed to meet, his friend's sister. From that night on, Polk became a frequent visitor at the Childress home, and he didn't come to see Anderson. Before long Polk proposed, and Sarah accepted. First, though, she suggested that he should run for the legislature.

Polk was appalled. He was too young, too poor, and too inexperienced. Sarah dismissed all these factors with an airy wave of the hand; in her opinion, General Jackson was so popular that anyone known as a friend of Jackson's could win an election. And she figured Jackson would approve of Polk's candidacy. So a meeting between Polk and Jackson was arranged, and Jackson did approve.

Polk as a candidate made up for his short stature (he was five feet, seven inches) by his earnestness, and he was soon dubbed "the Napoleon of the Stump." His engagement to Sarah was announced before the campaign, but Sarah delayed the marriage until after the election. They were wed on January 1, 1824, and moved into a two-room log house in Columbia, with a kitchen in the back yard and slave quarters nearby. Sarah reportedly remarked, upon seeing her newlyweds' cottage for the first time, that it was perfect—because it was small enough never to be a burden and she would be free to travel back and forth to Washington with James. The story goes that up until that moment the thought of going to Washington had not occurred to Polk.

Regardless whose idea, the summer of 1825, hardly more

than a year after his marriage, found Polk on the stump again, campaigning for a seat in the United States House of Representatives. Once again Polk was elected on the coattails of Jackson. In the national election of 1824, Jackson, the hero of New Orleans, had tied with John Quincy Adams for the presidency; the House of Representatives, to break the tie, gave the election to Adams. Jackson had returned home to Tennessee, charging "bargain, intrigue, and corruption," and Polk wisely campaigned with a promise to defend his friend Jackson's name in the capital, where the man from Tennessee had been cheated of the presidency.

Polk did not take his wife with him to Washington the first year. The city was still little more than a few buildings scattered through a swamp, and the only paved street was cobblestoned Pennsylvania Avenue. The Polks also thought it best to save their money. At home Mrs. Polk read and digested the local newspapers and filed lengthy reports to her husband on what was happening in his district. In 1826 Sarah returned with Congressman Polk to Washington.

The Polks partook of the official social life, but they were not swept up in it. Sarah refused to attend a party unless her husband accompanied her, or unless he expressly wished her to go for political reasons. She usually begged off by saying, "I wouldn't have a good time without Jim, so there's no use going."

Polk applied himself to his Congressional duties with the same diligence he would later apply in the White House. He worked late hours and on weekends, and eventually his friends took to dropping in on Sunday morning as the best time to discuss political strategy without interruption. Mrs. Polk never objected to her husband's working, but she drew the line at Sunday morning. She would take no excuse for not attending church. As the church bells tolled, therefore, she entered the parlor every Sunday, hatted and gloved, carrying her husband's hat, gloves, and cane. If other gentlemen were huddled in the room with Polk, Mrs. Polk would smile sweetly at the group. "If we don't hurry, we will all be late for church," she would announce. "Do come with us," she added innocently to the visitors. It soon became known that unless one wanted to hear a sermon at the First Presbyterian Church, it was more prudent to call upon James Polk some other time.

In 1828 Jackson was elected President, and Polk became one of the administration's chief spokesmen in the House. Besides his close ties with the President, his own drive for perfection and endless capacity for detail was earning for him a formidable reputation. One of Jackson's major legislative battles was to prevent the recharter of the privately owned Bank of the United States. He entrusted to Polk the House campaign on this issue. Polk's campaign advocated the exclusive use of gold or silver as a medium of exchange, to prevent the banks from continuing their irresponsible issuance of paper currency.

Sarah Polk was her husband's biggest political booster, but she was never persuaded of the wisdom of this particular issue. During one of their long, arduous journeys from Tennessee to Washington, Polk asked his wife to "get some money out of the trunk. I haven't enough in my pocket to pay expenses during the day."

She unlocked a trunk, dug in all four corners futilely, and was halfway through a second trunk before she found the bags of coins. Annoyed, she protested: "Don't you see how troublesome it is to carry around gold and silver? This is enough to show you how useful banks are."

But Polk, who hadn't been the one who searched for the coins, merely laughed. "Sarah, you've turned your politics, I see," he teased.

Mrs. Polk felt so strongly that her husband was being impractical, that this was the only subject on which she is recorded as publicly disagreeing with him. Frequently, talking with friends, she argued: "Why, if we must use gold and silver all the time, a lady can scarcely carry enough money with her." Despite her persistence, she never budged him.

Polk served in Congress for fourteen years, with two terms as Speaker. Mrs. Polk was fascinated by the prerogatives and the power of the Speakership. Long after Polk's death she observed to another former Speaker, Samuel Randall, that a Speaker can have "even more power and influence over legislation and in directing the policy of parties than the President or any other public officer."

But Polk was not content with the power of the Speakership. He wanted to be President. Jackson persuaded Polk that his best stepping stone would be the Tennessee governorship, and so Polk returned home to run for governor. As Polk gave his farewell address to the House, Whig Senator Henry Clay, already twice defeated for the presidency and destined to be defeated three more times, stood in the back of the visitors' gallery and shouted: "Go home, damn you! Go home where you belong!"

Polk was easily elected governor, at a yearly salary of $2,000. They continued to avoid a full social life, declining most dinner invitations. Polk said, "I cannot lose half a day just to go and dine," and his wife would not go without him. They were seldom separated: whenever Polk went to other parts of the state on business, he insisted that his wife travel with him. At first she demurred, thinking it unseemly. But Polk replied, "Why stay home? To take care of the house? If the house burns down, we can live without it." And so she went.

And then the Polk political magic failed. He ran for re-election and was defeated. After two years of obscurity he ran again, and was defeated again. At home, with nothing else to do, Polk and his wife began to plot a try for the vice-presidential nomination at the 1844 convention. They still had one big political trump: in the background there yet lurked the ailing but powerful figure of the shrewd former President Jackson.

Jackson, the sage of his party, was dying. He wrote shaky notes from the Hermitage, but his was still the single most influential voice. He had supported President Van Buren once, and he was prepared to do so again in 1844. Van Buren was the favored candidate for the nomination at the Democratic convention; he and Polk had sounded each other out about the vice-presidency.

President Tyler, who had succeeded to the presidency after the death of Harrison, was not popular and had little chance of winning re-election. Clay, the Whig candidate, and Van Buren, however, feared Tyler might attain new popularity at their expense by seizing upon the annexation of Texas, recently become independent from Mexico, as a campaign issue. Tyler, supported by Jackson, favored annexation. Both Clay and Van Buren opposed it, because it would mean extending slavery. They knew that the Texas question was explosive: the slave issue was always loaded with political dynamite. So Clay and Van Buren made a pact not to debate the Texas problem during their campaign, and issued mild Tweedledum-and-Tweedledee statements opposing the treaty for immediate annexation.

Jackson read Van Buren's statement and could not believe it. He himself had long sought expansion of the states, and his political sense told him that "no man can be President who opposes annexation." Not only had Van Buren crossed him, but Van Buren had made a political blunder that Jackson felt would cost him the election. Jackson, trembling with fury, called for Polk. It was only two weeks before the convention.

The next day Polk announced his candidacy for the presidential nomination. The Democratic party was astounded. Most of those outside Tennessee had never even heard of him because of his long absence from Washington. He was, in all truth, the first successful "dark horse."

Jackson went to work. At the convention the Democrats were deeply split. They could not decide between Van Buren and General Lewis Cass; wearily, prodded by Jackson's strategists, they settled upon Polk as a compromise.

Polk was a hard campaigner, and he made the annexation of Texas his chief issue. During the entire campaign Jackson wrote letters steadily, giving sound political advice to party chieftains all over the country. He was "joyful," he said, at Polk's nomination. Clay started out as the favorite, being a popular figure who had narrowly missed the prize so often before. But he was handicapped by the annexation issue: at the end of the campaign Clay began to waver in his firm opposition to it, and this cost him just enough votes to lose the election.

The underdog had done it. And he owed it primarily to two people, his wife and Andrew Jackson.

Mary Todd

LINCOLN

❀ ❀

A special train of the Wabash Railroad, spouting smoke and scattering cinders, rumbled across northeastern United States in February of 1861, at thirty miles an hour. Thousands assembled at the roadbed to watch it go by; and at every little town huge crowds gathered around red, white, and blue bunting-draped train stations to cheer its arrival. At each stop, the train's chief occupant appeared briefly on the back platform to bow and say a few words to the crowd. Only once did he introduce his five-foot, three-inch wife, saying he had decided to show the folks "the long and the short of it." Otherwise he appeared alone; when the crowds called for his wife, he told them he didn't believe he could induce her to come out—in fact, he could say that he never succeeded very well in getting her to do anything she didn't want to do.

Abraham Lincoln, fifty-two, was on his way to Washington,

to be inaugurated as the nation's sixteenth President—and its greatest and most tragic figure. The Northern crowds which roared their approval and support beside the tracks provided the only enthusiastic welcome the President-elect and his wife were to have. For the capital city which awaited them was an uneasy caldron of seething hatred, a city of enemies and North-South tensions. Washington was primarily a Southern city, filled with Southern aristocracy; and throughout the South men were shouting, "Resistance to Lincoln is obedience to God!" That very month five states had joined rebellious South Carolina to form the Confederate States of America, declaring themselves "separate and independent states." Abraham Lincoln, who said, "I believe this government cannot endure permanently half slave and half free," represented a menace to the very survival of a society based upon the forced labor of some three million slaves. Convulsed with a fear of extinction, the South was in no mood to listen when Lincoln said, "I hold that the union of these states is perpetual," and promised no action against Southern "property, peace and security."

The plain man of the people became the focus of all Southern resentment—and his wife, born a Southerner herself, was a handy target for its malice. A plot to assassinate the President-elect in Baltimore, en route to Washington, was discovered; so Lincoln was spirited through the unfriendly city secretly by night, his wife and sons following on the special train the next day. At Washington's Willard Hotel, where the Lincolns were to stay before the inaugural, several threatening letters greeted them. One warned: "If you don't resign we are going to put a spider in your dumpling and play the devil with you." At a pre-inaugural dinner party, Mary Lincoln overheard a gentleman at the next table grumble, "How can he, with any honor, fill the presidential chair? His Western gaucherie will disgrace the nation." General Winfield Scott received over three hundred letters threatening the President and his family, so he took the unusual precaution of stationing green-coated sharpshooters on the roofs of buildings along the inaugural parade route and placing armed guards at every corner and at regular intervals. In the crowd that watched the President ride toward the Capitol could be heard unhappy mutterings.

"There goes that Illinois ape, the cursed Abolitionist," a male voice growled distinctly. "But he will never come back alive."

The First Lady who stepped into the center of this tense atmosphere—certainly enough to give nightmares to the calmest wife, was a high-strung, excitable, erratic little woman who was neither physically nor mentally well. Her world, until now, had been limited to two small Western towns; she was not prepared by background or by temperament to cope with her new situation. She was subject to excruciating headaches, which periodically sent her to bed for days at a time. Her temper was notoriously uncontrollable; a neighbor once claimed she chased Lincoln into the yard, brandishing a kitchen knife. Another witness contended he had seen her throw herself on the floor and refuse to budge until her husband promised when he got to Washington he would appoint a certain friend to a federal post. She was so terrified of thunderstorms that Lincoln left his office at the first sign of rain so he could go home to comfort her. She was so neurotically afraid that something might harm her children, that when an emergency did arise she was totally helpless. When her sons Tad and Willie caught the measles, a cousin had to be called in to care for them. She wrote later: "The mother, always over-anxious and worried about the boys and withal not a skillful nurse, was totally unfitted for caring for them."

Yet for all this, Mary Lincoln was an affectionate, gentle woman who idolized her husband and adored her children. Lincoln, for his part, seemed to love her despite her weaknesses. When others frowned at her tantrums, he would say only, "Mrs. Lincoln is not well today." If her hysterical screams grew unbearable, he would simply gather up the boys and take a long walk; inevitably, by the time he returned his wife would be contrite and calm again. He called her, appropriately, his "child-wife." At a reception, a guest remarked to Lincoln that he looked often at his wife. Lincoln laughed and said, "My wife is as handsome as when she was a girl, and I, a poor nobody then, fell in love with her; and what is more, I have never fallen out."

Some historians hold to the theory that Lincoln's great patience, which enabled him to bear the incredibly trying burdens of the Civil War, was developed in self-defense over long years of tongue-lashings from his wife. Others contend that his deep compassion for humanity was an extension of the personal sorrow he felt in an unhappy marriage. There is considerable evidence, however, that Abraham Lincoln possessed both these traits long before he married Miss Mary Todd and that the Lincolns got along better, on the whole, than several other couples who have occupied the White House.

Mary Lincoln came from a proud, prosperous family that was so social-conscious Lincoln joshed her, "One 'd' is good enough for God, but not for the Todds." Her family looked down on her for marrying a backwoods, penniless lawyer who was not even handsome or well-mannered, and she longed desperately to regain in the East the social position she had lost in the West when she became Mrs. Lincoln. But social customs in the East and South were not at all the same as those practiced in the more primitive West, and the sophisticated ladies of Washington society were quick to point out her mistakes. Mary Lincoln knew they gossiped that she was ignorant, vulgar, and rude; her answer was to try to outdress them. She developed a psychopathic passion for extravagant gowns, hoping to impress the other ladies with her finery. "I must dress in costly materials," she told a Negro modiste, Elizabeth Keckley. "The people scrutinize every article that I wear with critical curiosity. The very fact of having grown up in the West subjects me to more searching observation."

Eventually Mary Lincoln realized that her wild spending for fancy dresses could not win the admiration of the Southern enemies who were all about her—it only gave them something to criticize. This did not stop her shopping, but she did say, "I have been the victim of evil counselors." The aristocratic wives of officeholders and army officers, who secretly sympathized with the South, accepted her White House invitations but privately ridiculed her "attempts at Southern hospitality." A friend of hers wrote disgustedly: "Women who knew the wire-pulling at Washington, whose toilet arts and social pretensions, society-lobbying and opportunity-seeking taught them to lie in wait and rise in the social scale by intimacy at the White House, these basely laughed at the credulous woman who took counsel from them. . . . Some said to her, 'They say you are a Western woman, and that brilliant life is unknown to you. Prove by your style and splendor that to be Western is not to be a boor.'"

On March 8, the new President and First Lady held their initial reception at the White House. Mrs. Lincoln was so nervous that she was in tears by the time Mrs. Keckley arrived with her newly finished gown, shortly before the party. She was so upset that she pouted and said she would not go downstairs at all. "I won't be dressed. I will stay in my room. Mr. Lincoln can go down with the other ladies," she fretted. But the sight of the new dress—a flattering rose-colored moiré—spread on the bed seemed to soothe her fears and she was finally tempted to try it on. Then Lincoln, pulling on his white kid gloves, came in to sit on the sofa and watch his wife. His lavish compliments and a satisfactory reflection in the mirror gave her enough self-confidence to restore her humor, and she went downstairs on his arm, a picture of cheerful composure. Guests who were at the reception that night later remarked what a cheerful, delightful woman Mrs. Lincoln seemed to be.

Mary Lincoln, at forty-three, could swing erratically from dimpled good cheer to flushed irritation, and did so with distressing frequency. Her private secretary, William Stoddard, said: "It was not easy at first to understand why a lady who could be one day so kindly, so considerate, so generous, so thoughtful and so hopeful, could, upon another day, appear so unreasonable, so irritable, so despondent, so even niggardly, and so prone to see the dark, the wrong side of men and women and events." Another White House aide, less tolerant toward the unpredictable First Lady, complained: "The Hell-cat is getting more Hell-cattical day by day." Commissioner of Public Buildings Benjamin Brown French merely thought her eccentric, and wrote: "Mrs. Lincoln is—Mrs. Lincoln, and nobody else, and like no other human being I ever saw. She is not easy to get along with. . . ."

The President, however, had other worries besides his wife's behavior. On April 12, barely a month after he took office, the Confederates fired upon the Union-held Fort Sumter. Lincoln called for 75,000 troops, and soon soldiers were camping in the East Room and even in the corridors of the White House. Mrs. Lincoln passed them on her way to breakfast and on her way to bed each night; but they did not make her feel any safer. One night the whole family was taken ill, and poisoning was suspected —by the time it was determined that the culprit was tainted

Potomac shad, Mary Lincoln was hysterical. So many ugly letters of abuse and threats poured in to the White House, addressed to her, that she refused to look at her daily mail until her secretary, Stoddard, had screened it.

She did try, however, when she was not suffering from one of her headaches, to lighten the President's burden. She carefully brought him meals on trays when he worked late. She persuaded him to go for drives in the carriage with her, hoping he could relax briefly. She invited old, comfortable Illinois friends to breakfast to cheer him with casual chatter. She urged him to have afternoon tea with her, and read aloud from the Bible or recite a favorite poem. One such scene was observed by Mrs. Keckley, who later recalled that the President had come to his wife in a bleakly dejected mood. "Is there any news?" she asked softly. "Yes, plenty of news, but no good news. It is dark, dark everywhere," Lincoln sighed. Then he picked up the Bible and began slowly to read aloud, his wife knitting quietly by his side. After fifteen minutes, his face relaxed and the sorrow faded from his eyes—or so Mrs. Keckley thought.

In the South, a general named Nathan Bedford Forrest said: "War means fighting. And fighting means killing." Abraham Lincoln called it "this great trouble" and in despair watched the military telegraph click out the story day after day of Union retreats, mounting casualties. There was not a house in the nation, it seemed, that did not have relatives fighting against relatives. And the White House did not escape. The President and Mary Lincoln were very fond of Mary's half sister Emilie, and offered her husband, Ben Helm, a major's commission; but Helm chose to fight for the South. And before the war was over, Mary Lincoln had a brother, three half brothers and three brothers-in-law wearing Confederate gray. Some, including Helm, did not return. "It can almost be said that the Heavens are hung in black," the President mourned.

But life must go on, even in a Civil War. Robert, the Lincoln's oldest son, was sent to college, and the younger boys, Tad and Willie, romped virtually unattended through the White House. Mary Lincoln began to develop an obsession for penny-pinching, except where her clothes were concerned. She even went so far as to propose one day that her husband sell the manure from the White House stables to get a little extra money. But despite her petty economies, she made frequent trips to New York and Boston to shop. She continued to hold the usual receptions and dinners, although she was roundly criticized for her "callous and extravagant" entertainments. She opened the White House grounds to all visitors on Wednesday and Saturday evenings, when the Marine Band played on the lawn. The presidential family usually appeared on the south balcony, where they could watch the band.

Undoubtedly, the war did not make Mrs. Lincoln less difficult to get along with. She was uncontrollably jealous of her husband and could scarcely contain her fury in public when beautiful women flocked around the President. She could not abide the custom of the President's escorting the ranking female guest into dinner while she herself followed on the arm of the ranking male guest, so the custom was ignored and Mrs. Lincoln walked in to dinner with her husband. She objected so violently to each lady to whom the President spoke that once he replied in exasperation, "Mother, I insist that I must talk with somebody. I can't stand around like a simpleton and say nothing." She tried to strike the names of Secretary of Treasury Salmon Chase and his daughter from her dinner list, because she did not like them; but the President found out about it and had the names restored, braving a storm of wifely abuse to do so. She had so many loud arguments with Lincoln that soon their domestic turbulence was the gossip of the city. And Lincoln, for whom there seemed to be no rest, could lose his own temper—"Sometimes . . . being worn down, he spoke crabbedly," his wife wrote.

Lincoln searched for a general who could meet the military genius of Robert E. Lee of Virginia, who was leading the South to victory after victory. He could not find the right man; General George McClellan, who was in charge of the Union troops, mobilized and trained an impressive army, but he dallied and delayed and could not bring himself to fight. Lincoln despaired of the inactive troops, and called it "McClellan's bodyguard." Mary Lincoln, too, had her suspicions of McClellan. She called him a "humbug," and urged her husband to replace him. Finally, a week after she wrote Lincoln from New York that "many say they would almost worship you if you would put a fighting gen-

eral in the place of McClellan," Lincoln removed McClellan
from command. He was not acting upon her suggestion, but did
so because McClellan failed to follow up the advantage of his
first victory, at Antietam. It was well he didn't listen to her in
the matter of generals, for she promptly developed an intense
dislike for McClellan's ultimate replacement, Ulysses S. Grant.
At last Lincoln had found, in Grant, the man to lead the Union
to victory; but to his wife he was a "butcher" and had "no regard
for life." Lincoln, tired of hearing her complaints about his generals, finally proposed: "Suppose that we give you command of
the army. No doubt you would do much better than any general
that has been tried."

Mary Lincoln's dislikes were not confined to generals. She
resented Secretary of State William Seward's arrogance with her
husband, and once spit at him in a rage: "It is said that you are
the power behind the throne—I'll show you that Mr. Lincoln is
President yet!" She complained about this Secretary and that
Secretary so much that Lincoln sputtered, "Mother, if I listened
to you, I should soon be without a Cabinet." Secretary Stoddard
explained: "Her personal antipathies are quick and strong, and
at times they find hasty and resentful forms of expression." Mary
Lincoln was in the habit of telling her absent-minded husband
what to do about clothes, food, and etiquette, and she could not
stop when it came to other fields. She tried to tell him what to do
about appointments and other political matters, too. "My husband placed great confidence in my knowledge of human nature,
he had not much knowledge of men," she said proudly. She
dunned the President endlessly about his acceptance of what she
considered hypocrisy around him: "You are too suspicious. I give
you credit for sagacity, but you are disposed to magnify trifles,"
he told her.

Mary Lincoln revealed her attitude—that she had the right
to give unsolicited advice—in a letter to James Gordon Bennett,
editor of the New York *Herald*. She was replying to a letter Bennett had sent her suggesting a certain change in Cabinet membership, a repeat of a plea contained in another letter she had
just received. "Doubtless if my good, patient husband were here,
instead of being with the Army of the Potomac, both of these
missives would be placed before him, accompanied by my

womanly suggestions, proceeding from a heart so deeply interested for our distracted country. I have a great terror of strong-minded ladies, yet if a word fitly spoken and in due season can be urged, in a time like this, we should not withhold it," she wrote.

There is evidence of Mrs. Lincoln's frequent attempts to influence the President on appointments; there is no evidence of much success. She often wrote to Cabinet members on behalf of this person or that one, however, without her husband's knowledge, and with considerably more success. She accepted many expensive gifts—once even a carriage—from strangers, on the assumption such things were due her as the wife of the President, and then found it difficult to refuse when the gift-givers came around later seeking her help in getting a job. When the President discovered how she was being used by unscrupulous gift-givers, he "shut down on it," as he said.

In the Victorian 1860's, a woman's place was in the home, not in politics. A concerned gentleman came to the President to express his fear that Mrs. Lincoln had too large a voice in political affairs and too much influence over Lincoln's conduct. But Lincoln reassured him: "I myself manage all important matters. In little things I have got along through life by letting my wife run her end of the machine pretty much in her own way." Lincoln did not, however, explain what happened when his wife got confused about which "end of the machine" was hers.

Early in the war, Willie and Tad became suddenly very ill with typhoid fever, and Willie died. Lincoln grieved deeply, but he could not, even for a few hours, set aside his heavy responsibilities. Mary Lincoln collapsed in convulsions and lay prostrate on her bed for days. She did not rouse herself to attend the funeral, or to comfort little Tad, who was in miserable condition, sick himself and sobbing for his dead brother. She kept the White House swathed in mourning for days. She refused ever again to enter the room in which he died, or the Green Room, where he was embalmed. She banned flowers from the White House because Willie had loved them. She canceled the Marine Band concerts the next summer, because the sound of the gay, lively music drove her to distraction.

Ordinarily, Mary Lincoln's reaction to her bereavement

would have found sympathetic understanding among the sentimental mothers of that Victorian age. But in 1862 there was hardly a woman in the country who had not sent a husband or son to battle, and scarcely a home that had not felt the pain of a battlefield death. The newspapers printed one bitter mother's remark that at least Mrs. Lincoln had the privilege of seeing her son die, instead of having to send him out to be shot.

Lincoln, who had felt that Willie, of all his sons, was most like himself, could turn to no one for comfort. Instead he tried sympathetically, slowly, to calm his ailing, immature child-wife. He wrote to friends beseeching them to visit her. He did not journey outside the White House to visit an army camp without keeping her carefully posted on his movements. He gave himself a cavalry escort, because Mrs. Lincoln feared for his safety, although he considered it a nuisance. Later Mary Lincoln was to tell Emilie, her half sister, that "If I had not felt the spur of necessity urging me to cheer Mr. Lincoln, whose grief was as great as my own, I could never have smiled again."

Throughout it all, the newspapers continued to criticize Mary Lincoln unmercifully. Lincoln worried about the unkind "stabs given Mary." Everything she did, it seemed, found public disfavor. But the worst rumor of all was that she was a spy. With so many Southern relatives, it was easy to suspect her of being a Southern sympathizer. Stoddard, who opened all her mail, recorded: "The President's wife is venomously accused of being at heart a traitor, and of being in communication with the Confederate authorities." Mary Lincoln is clearly on record, through statements of friends and her personal letters, as being totally loyal to the Union. Like her husband, she believed before the war that slavery in the South must be tolerated by necessity, but that it must not be allowed to spread to the new Western frontier states. And, like her husband, she came to believe that emancipation of the slaves was the only just and proper answer. She even helped Mrs. Keckley raise funds for the Contraband Relief Association, an organization formed to help feed and clothe the Negroes who were being turned free without a cent. She headed the list of donors with a $200 contribution, and contributed frequently thereafter.

The accusations against Mary Lincoln's loyalty were so persistent, however, that a joint Senate and House committee, called the Committee on the Conduct of the War, was persuaded to hold a hearing to investigate. A senator later recalled that on the morning the hearing opened, Abraham Lincoln appeared at the foot of the witness table. Slowly, deliberately, he looked around the room at each congressman and intoned: "I, Abraham Lincoln, President of the United States, appear of my own volition before this committee of the Senate to say that I, of my own knowledge, know that it is untrue that any of my family hold treasonable communication with the enemy." The committee adjourned, and the subject was not brought up officially again. But the rumor continued in the streets.

Small wonder, with such hatred playing on her sensitive nerves, that Mary Lincoln's health did not improve. And on the day of the battle at Gettysburg, she was thrown from her carriage to the ground, where she struck the back of her head on a sharp rock. It was later discovered that the screws on the carriage seat had been deliberately removed so that the seat would come loose, in an attempt on the President's life. She was ill with an ugly head wound for three weeks. Two years later Robert was to say to his Aunt Emilie, "I think Mother has never quite recovered from the effects of her fall."

Few people in those days realized that Mary Lincoln's strangely overemotional behavior was the result of mental illness; indeed, much of the time, especially at social gatherings where she was on display, she was vivacious, quick-witted, and quite amiable. But Lincoln recognized that what he called her "nervous spells" were not normal. He hoped sadly that in time his love and steadying strength would cure her; in the 1860's psychiatry was unknown, and mental illness was regarded as an unspeakably horrible stigma. One day, long after the death of Willie, Lincoln stood by the window with his arm about his wife's shoulders as she sobbed uncontrollably. He pointed toward a building that housed mental cases, visible through the trees. "Mother, do you see that large white building on the hill yonder? Try and control your grief, or it will drive you mad, and we will have to send you there," he told her gently. Sometime later, a friend came to Lincoln with the story of how a scoundrel was deceiving his wife into using her influence for him. The visitor later recalled Lincoln was deeply troubled by the account. Finally Lincoln said, "The caprices of Mrs. Lincoln, I am satisfied, are the result of partial insanity." After a pause, Lincoln asked, "Is the malady beyond medical remedy to check before it becomes fully developed?" The visitor replied that he thought firmness and kindness seemed to be the only measures to use in such a case.

Emilie Helm stayed briefly in the White House after her husband's death, although she was a Rebel. She recorded in her diary that Lincoln and his wife were beset with concern for each other's health. Lincoln's face was lined and weary; he was showing the strain of caring for a sick wife and guiding the nation in war. He told Emilie, "I feel worried about Mary, her nerves have gone to pieces; she cannot hide from me that the strain she has been under has been too much for her mental as well as her physical health." He asked what Emilie thought about Mary's condition, and Emilie replied frankly: "She seems very nervous and excitable and once or twice when I have come into the room suddenly the frightened look in her eyes has appalled me." Emilie did not tell Lincoln, however, that his wife came to her in the night and said she had visions of Willie, and that sometimes he came to her bringing other dead relatives. "It is unnatural and abnormal, it frightens me," Emilie wrote in her diary. "It does not seem like sister Mary to be so nervous and wrought up. She is on a terrible strain and her smiles seem forced. She is frightened about Robert going into the Army."

Mrs. Lincoln's one pleasure was shopping; it intoxicated her. The war raged on, the casualties continued to mount; but she insisted on buying her finery. She was totally irresponsible about money. She spent so much on credit and had accumulated such huge bills, that by 1863 she was terrified lest Lincoln not win re-election. "If he should be defeated," she told Mrs. Keckley, "I do not know what would become of us all. To me, to him, there is more at stake in this election than he dreams of. I have contracted large debts of which he knows nothing, and which he will be unable to pay if he is defeated." Lincoln had no concept of the cost of female clothing; he only knew that his wife was happiest when she was shopping, so he was glad to let her shop whenever she wanted.

The President, too, for a vastly more important reason, was

worried about re-election. He had ordered an end to slavery, "the great event of the nineteenth century," but he had not yet ended the war. "The struggle of today is not altogether for today. It is for a vast future also," he said. But the South was still undefeated. The North, weary of the three-year struggle, was torn by dissension and disloyalty—and the long war was being blamed on the President. But Lincoln won renomination in 1864, and a few weeks before election day the North achieved the victories it had so long awaited. "I am a slow walker, but I never walk back," Lincoln said. The Confederacy, blockaded, exhausted of supplies and men, began to crumble. And the people, with renewed faith, re-elected Abraham Lincoln.

Kind-hearted, loving, confused Mrs. Lincoln said, "Now that we have won the position, I almost wish it were otherwise. Poor Mr. Lincoln is looking so broken-hearted, so completely worn out, I fear he will not get through the next four years."

For the second inaugural ball, Mrs. Lincoln wore one of her newly purchased gowns, a $2,000 white silk and lace with elaborate fan and headdress. But the Lincolns were not light-hearted; the President said to Harriet Beecher Stowe, "I shall never live to see peace; this war is killing me." Mrs. Lincoln, in her twisted way, betrayed her own innermost dread in that March of 1865 by purchasing along with her inaugural extravagances a thousand dollars' worth of mourning goods.

On March 23, President and Mrs. Lincoln sailed on the *River Queen* to City Point, Virginia, to visit General Grant's headquarters. Their son Robert was stationed there, as an aide to the general. (At Mary's tearful pleadings, the President had kept Robert out of the army until the last few months of the war, when he asked Grant to assign Robert to special duty in his headquarters, out of the line of fire. The President knew the nation would be angry at this show of favoritism, but he also knew what Robert's death would do to Mary's precarious sanity.) While the *River Queen* lay off City Point, Petersburg was evacuated and Richmond fell. Lincoln, in fact, entered the still blazing city of Richmond with Grant on April 4. With half a million dead, the war was over.

But in the triumphant moment of victory, Mary Lincoln had her first violent outburst in public. The President and First Lady were to participate in a field inspection of Grant's troops. Mrs. Lincoln arrived in a carriage with General and Mrs. Grant, and flew into a screaming rage when she saw her husband on horseback riding beside the beautiful young wife of General Edward Ord, commander of the post. Her jealousy always flared at the thought of her husband even speaking to a woman alone, and she wildly thought the troops would mistake Mrs. Ord for herself. In a frenzy, she yelled at Mrs. Grant, who was sitting beside her, "What does this woman mean by riding by the side of the President? Does she suppose that he wants her by the side of him?" When Mrs. Grant tried to soothe her, Mrs. Lincoln turned her full wrath upon her with the scornful (and prophetic) remark, "I suppose you think you'll get to the White House yourself, don't you?" With Mrs. Grant stunned into silence, Mary Lincoln shifted her fury back to Mrs. Ord, who had ridden up to pay her respects. She let loose such a flood of abuse that Mrs. Ord retreated in tears. For the rest of the day Mary Lincoln was in a temper, screaming at all who came near, temporarily out of her mind in full view of the officers and wives at City Point. With this one painful spectacle she destroyed the careful impression of four years in the White House during which she had managed to control herself in public. The next day she did not appear, but remained in her compartment on the boat; the President excused her, saying only that "she is not well."

The Lincolns returned to Washington the weekend of April 9, as Lee was surrendering to Grant at Appomattox, Virginia. They were both exhausted from emotional strain. Lincoln, in fact, had been bothered lately by strange dreams, which he attributed to his weariness. In one dream he had visualized a funeral in the East Room, and a soldier on guard explaining, "The President was killed by an assassin."

But the North was celebrating, and the gay spirits of Washington infected even the weary Lincolns. On Good Friday, April 14, the President told a visitor, "We are going to have good times now, and a united country." He and his wife planned to go to Ford's Theater that night to watch *Our American Cousin*, as part of the peace celebration. They had invited General and Mrs. Grant to accompany them, but the Grants begged off, no doubt because Mrs. Grant was still smarting from Mary's unwarranted fury. In the afternoon the Lincolns went for a drive together. He told her he wanted to be alone with her, for they had much to discuss now that they dared think of the future. As they drove companionably along, Mrs. Lincoln smiled, and said, "Dear husband, you almost startle me by your great cheerfulness."

"I consider this day the war has come to a close—we must both be more cheerful in the future—between the war and the loss of our darling Willie—we have both been very miserable," he told her gently. They talked of a possible trip to Europe, after Lincoln's second term. "I especially want to see Jerusalem," he said.

It was a happy drive; the Lincolns, in private, were an affectionate couple. But they returned early so as not to be late for the play that night. At 8:30 P.M., the Lincolns and their last-minute guests, Major Henry Rathbone and Miss Clara Harris, entered the flag-draped box at the theater. The quartet was in a good mood. The Lincolns chatted comfortably between acts, and during the third act Mrs. Lincoln pressed closer to her husband, clasping his big bony hand tightly. "What will Miss Harris think of my hanging on to you so?" she whispered coquettishly. "She won't think anything about it," he replied fondly.

When the assassin, John Wilkes Booth, struck, Mary Lincoln felt her husband's hand go limp in hers. She screamed and fainted, a tragic process she was to repeat through the long night as her husband lay dying, unconscious with a bullet in his brain. (The plotters also attacked Secretary of State William Seward in his home, and impaired him permanently, although he lived.) Lincoln was carried across the street to the nearest bed, in the home of a stranger, where he gasped his last at twenty-two minutes past seven in the morning. His wife frantically kissed his face, sobbed out her love, begged him to take her with him, beseeched him to speak to her. At dawn she looked on his face for the last time: "Oh my God, and have I given my husband to die," she sobbed. As the bells of mourning began to toll throughout the capital, the doctors took the distraught Mary Lincoln back to the White House. She could not bear to lie down in their bedroom, but insisted upon being taken to a guest room that Lincoln had never used.

Mrs. Lincoln remained in bed for five weeks, shrieking into

her darkened room, shuddering in private torment, weeping until her bedclothes were sodden. Tad, Robert, and Mrs. Keckley hovered nearby, but they could not comfort her. She did not rise for her husband's funeral, as she had not for Willie's. She told a minister years later that she had no recollection of those weeks after Lincoln's death. And he recorded that it was his opinion that "When her husband was shot down by her side her nervous system was completely shattered and her mind was unhinged by the shock."

While Mary Lincoln lay ill upstairs, souvenir hunters roamed the unguarded downstairs section of the White House, tearing off bits of expensive upholstery, carting away heavy tables and lamps, ripping down exquisite lace curtains, even cutting holes in the carpets. Finally Mrs. Lincoln regained enough composure to board a train with Tad and Robert for Chicago, where she decided to live because there she didn't know anybody who could remind her of Lincoln. When the damage to the White House was discovered, she was unjustly accused of stealing taxpayers' property, the nation's house goods—even then the press and her critics would not stop their abuse.

In Chicago, Mary Lincoln huddled in isolated misery. She refused to see any visitors or go out in public, yet she complained continually in letters to relatives and friends of her loneliness. Her fantasies about poverty increased; she had never thought rationally on the subject of money and now her exaggerated fears became a constant nightmare. Lincoln had left an estate of more than $83,000 (although it grew to about $110,000 before it was liquidated), to be divided equally among his wife and each of the boys. In the 1860's that was adequate for a prudent widow to live on for the rest of her days. But there were all those debts which she had accumulated for her fancy dresses. Now that she was no longer First Lady, her creditors pressed her for payment. When she was still in the White House, Mrs. Lincoln had hit upon the fantastic idea that Republican politicians should pay her debts, as fair return for her husband's favors to them. "Hundreds of them are getting immensely rich off the patronage of my husband and it is but fair that they should help me out of my embarrassment," she had explained to Mrs. Keckley. Obviously, her plan could not work; but it did make a number of Re-

publican politicians furious. Isaac Newton, then head of the
Agricultural Bureau, recorded—among others—his shock at the
strange scheme of the First Lady, who had come to him weeping
with the tale of her plight. So the debts remained unpaid—and
Mary Lincoln's unbalanced mind determined upon still another
incredible plot. She would sell her expensive gowns. It was a bad
blunder—the gowns did not sell, and the nation was aghast to
find a former President's wife so crude as to exhibit her clothing
for sale on New York's Broadway. Once again Mary Lincoln was
harshly criticized in the press, until she finally wrote in anguish
to a relative: "If I had committed murder in every state in this
blessed Union, I could not be more traduced. An ungrateful
country this." But the country could not know how Mary Lincoln
was; and, not understanding, it did not sympathize.

To escape public scorn, she fled to Europe with Tad. For six
years she wandered from city to city, lodging in cheap, cold ho-
tels, spending most of her time in bed, suffering from violent
headaches, rheumatic pain, and other infections, persecuted by
worries about her imagined poverty. She petitioned Congress for
a pension, and received one after five years, although even that
was not a large enough sum to assure her that she was financially
secure.

In 1871, after Robert and his wife had a baby, his mother
and Tad returned home to see the new grandchild. Tad was now
eighteen, a tall boy who resembled his father. He seemed older
than his years, for he had been his mother's only support in
Europe, her nurse through every illness, her companion during
her temper tantrums, and her servant on marketing days. But
shortly after they arrived in Chicago, Tad died. Mrs. Lincoln had
felt sorry for herself before; but now, without Tad, she was in-
consolable. She began to have delusions that someone wanted to
murder her. Her persecution complex was so extreme that she
could not enter a public room without trembling in fear. She was
afraid to eat, because the food might be poisoned. She was afraid
to sleep, because she would be attacked in the darkness of night.
She wandered nude into the hall of a hotel, and when Robert
forced her back into her room, she screamed, "You are going to
murder me." Her mania for spending now got the upper hand

over her mania about poverty. She shopped and shopped and shopped.

Robert could not seem to comfort his mother; he watched in horror as she dissipated her estate, and he began to fear that soon she would spend it all. The only way Robert could gain control over her finances, for her own sake, was to have her declared legally incompetent. So on May 19, 1875, in Cook County Court, a hearing opened concerning the sanity of Mary Lincoln, widow of a President. A parade of reputable physicians and witnesses testified that she acted hysterically and was, in their opinion, insane. Robert, weeping, said that he too believed her insane. "Oh, Robert," murmured his meek, black-draped mother, "to think that my son would ever have done this."

Mary Lincoln was committed under judgment of insanity to a nearby private sanitarium, where for the first time she was cared for by professional nurses and doctors who specialized in nervous and mental illnesses. She immediately began a campaign for release, enlisted the efforts of acquaintances who believed in her sanity, and after four months was permitted to live with her sister, Mrs. Ninian Edwards of Springfield. After nine months a second sanity hearing was held and she was judged "restored to reason," although there is no evidence that she had changed much in those few months since the first hearing.

Eventually Mary Lincoln forgave her son for what he had done to her, but she refused to live with his family. She lived quietly, ill much of the time, until her death on July 16, 1882. She was buried in Springfield next to her husband, and all the old acquaintances and former friends who had gossiped about her so meanly in life came to pay tribute to her. One of the guests was a former beau, James Conkling. Forty-three years before he had described her as "the very creature of excitement." And a far different girl she had been in those days than the tormented woman who lived in the White House.

Mary Todd at twenty was Springfield's most sought-after young lady of the season. She lived with her sister, Mrs. Edwards, who presided regally at the pinnacle of the city's social life. Mary brought to Springfield's society not only aristocratic breeding and a fine education but a merry heart, a quick tongue, a round, dimpled face, and a love of parties and gaiety. She was affectionate and high-spirited, and she was even interested in politics. "This fall I became quite a politician, rather an unlady-like profession," she said after the election of her favorite, General William Henry Harrison. Since marriage was the only honorable career open to well-bred women in that Victorian age, and Springfield abounded with unattached young males, Mary had been sent in 1839 by her family in Kentucky for an indefinite stay with her married sister—until she found a husband.

Abraham Lincoln, the junior law partner of Mary's cousin, John Todd Stuart, was admitted to Mary's exclusive, giddy social circle sometime during 1839 or 1840. He had come to Springfield in 1837, with all his possessions in two saddlebags, riding a borrowed horse. He was introspective, gangly, careless in his dress, poor, shy in the presence of cultured ladies. But he had a keen mind, a flair for politics, a wry sense of humor, a deep concern for mankind, a love of books—and he was in his third term in the state legislature, increasingly recognized for his legal abilities. In short, Lincoln had reached the point where despite his rough edges he was now acceptable in snobbish society.

From the beginning, Lincoln singled out Mary Todd. Mrs. Edwards recalled that Lincoln "was charmed with Mary's wit and fascinated with her quick sagacity—her will—her nature—and culture. I have happened in the room where they were sitting often, and often Mary led the conversation. Lincoln would listen as if drawn by some superior power, irresistibly so; he listened—never scarcely said a word." Mary's family thought Lincoln "the plainest man in Springfield." But one of their close friends said later, "She loved him as women of her nervous sanguine temperament only can love." And Lincoln told her repeatedly that she was "the only woman I ever loved." After a petty quarrel that resulted in a broken engagement, the young couple married on November 4, 1842.

A popular legend has it that Mary Todd tricked or forced the unsuspecting Lincoln into marriage. There is no conclusive evidence to support this; in fact, the bulk of evidence would seem to prove that they were both very much in love. Mary Todd's family objected strenuously to a marriage with Lincoln, whose social background they considered inferior to a Todd's. But Mary, spoiled, pampered, and headstrong, "wanted what she wanted

when she wanted it and no substitute," as a White House aide
was to describe her later. She defied her family to marry Lincoln,
but he certainly had made up his own mind in the matter by the
time he ordered her golden wedding band engraved "Love Is
Eternal." Part of the reluctant bridegroom myth is based on a
story which has a little boy watching Lincoln dress for the wedding. "Where are you going, Mr. Lincoln?" he inquired. "To the
devil," Lincoln quipped, certainly more in nervous jest than in
gloomy foreboding.

Seven days after his marriage, Lincoln wrote a friend: "Nothing new here except my marrying, which to me is a matter of
profound wonder." The newlyweds lived upstairs at the Globe
Tavern, in cramped, crude quarters for which they paid four dollars a week. "There never existed a more loving and devoted
husband," Mary Lincoln wrote, but there were some difficulties.
Lincoln had long periods of abstraction when he was oblivious to
everything, and everyone, around him, and he frequently sank
into protracted spells of depression. His wife was unaccustomed
to the poor, drab life she was now forced to live. Her family refused to see her now that she was Mrs. Lincoln; the invitations
to fancy parties and dinners trickled away. She was timid whenever she had to be alone, and Lincoln was gone for nearly six
months each year, practicing law in the courts of the area. Housekeeping was not easy. Springfield was smelly and dirty; hogs
rooted along the planks which served for sidewalks; chamber pots
and oil lamps were a hated daily cleaning chore; fireplace ashes,
mud from the streets, and dust from unscreened windows made
living a dirty business at best. As Mary Todd she had always been
waited upon by servants, and now she was forced to do all these
chores herself.

After baby Robert was born, the Lincolns moved, in May,
1844, to a story-and-a-half frame house at the corner of Eighth
and Jackson streets, where they lived until the presidential election of 1860. Mary Lincoln struggled constantly to domesticate
her brilliant husband. She watched his clothing, lest he walk out
with a trouser leg rolled up; she corrected his manners, lest he embarrass her in company; she tried to establish a comfortable
household routine so he could relax at home. But Lincoln proved
oblivious to much of the details of daily living which occupy a

woman's entire concern. He would wander in two hours late for dinner, and find the guests starved and the food burned. But he did not worry about his wife's protests. "Bring on the cinders," he'd say cheerfully. He pulled the bundled-up baby in a little wagon up and down in front of his house on Sunday mornings while his wife was at church, absorbed in reading a book as he walked. But once the baby fell out and lay squalling on the ground while Lincoln, still immersed in his book, continued on up the path, pulling the empty wagon. Small wonder Mrs. Lincoln shrieked when she discovered her baby's plight.

From the earliest days of their marriage Mrs. Lincoln suffered from the headaches which were to grow worse as years passed. Lincoln wrote her fondly in 1848: "Are you entirely free from head ache? That is good—good considering it is the first spring you have been free from it since we were acquainted. . . . I am afraid you will get so well, and fat, and young, as to be wanting to marry again." When she had a headache, she was cross, but when she felt well, she was bubbly and companionable. Lincoln, who had grown up without a mother or even much affection, spoiled his wife with his indulgence. After one of her outbursts of temper, he would merely say, "It does her lots of good and it doesn't hurt me a bit."

Mary Lincoln was proud of her husband, especially since he soon began to prove her family wrong and her own judgment correct. In 1847 she was introduced to a young man from another part of Illinois, who complimented her husband's ability. "Yes," she replied, "he is a great favorite everywhere. He is to be President of the United States some day; if I had not thought so I never would have married him, for you can see he is not pretty. But look at him. Doesn't he look as if he would make a magnificent President?"

The young lawyer was elected to the United States House of Representatives, and he was deeply involved in politics. In 1854 he sought the Republican nomination for senator, but was defeated. In 1856 he campaigned through Illinois for John Fremont, the first presidential nominee of the newly formed Republican party, although Mary was outspokenly for President Millard Fillmore, who was seeking re-election in the American party. (She felt "he made so good a President and is so just a man. . . .")

The breakthrough came in 1858. Lincoln was nominated for the Senate and it was in his convention acceptance speech that he said, "A house divided against itself cannot stand." Mrs. Lincoln could not follow her husband in his campaign because of their three children, the difficulties of travel, and her poor health; but she was confident that he would win. Lincoln told a young journalist during the campaign, "My friends got me into this business. I did not consider myself qualified for the United States Senate, and it took me a long time to persuade myself that I was. . . . Mary insists, however, that I am going to be senator and President of the United States, too. . . . Just think of such a sucker as me as President!"

Lincoln debated up and down the state with his opponent, Stephen Douglas, an old beau of his wife's. He lost the race. But the country had listened to the clear, logical words of a man who could lead them in their time of trouble; and the debates (as four televised debates were to do a hundred years later for John F. Kennedy) had transformed an unknown politician into a nationally recognized and respected figure. The word began to get about that Abe Lincoln might make a good President; and Lincoln himself, having "the taste in my mouth a little," launched an energetic two-year campaign for the Republican nomination. He spoke back and forth across the country; his fame spread. Finally, in Springfield, in May, 1860, they came to him and told him he had been nominated on the third ballot. "There's a little woman down at our house would like to hear this. I'll go down and tell her," he said with a broad smile.

Six months later, when the Springfield telegraph office tapped out the message that Lincoln had carried New York, and with it the election, he turned again immediately toward home, where his wife waited. He described election night later to Henry Bowen: "I told my wife to go to bed, as probably I should not be back before midnight. . . . On my arrival I went to my bedroom and found my wife sound asleep. I gently touched her shoulder and said, 'Mary.' She made no answer. I spoke again, a little louder, saying 'Mary, Mary' . . .

'We are elected!' "

Helen Herron

TAFT

❊ ❊

One shivery, snowy night in the winter of 1905, Secretary of War
and Mrs. William Howard Taft bundled up in their warmest
coats and rode in their carriage to the White House.

They dined alone with President and Mrs. Theodore Roosevelt by candlelight. The table talk was gay and animated,
ranging from the new electric lights to Edward Arlington Robinson's newest poem, from the growing controversy over prohibition
to the latest political intrigue.

The amiable Taft was feeling especially amiable; he had
finally been persuaded by Mrs. Taft to go on a diet and was
secretly delighted that he had already lost fifteen pounds. Mrs.
Taft, who was inclined to be serious-minded and intense, was
unusually light-hearted because a front-page story in the morning's Washington *Post* had mentioned her husband as a leading
possibility for the Republican presidential nomination in 1908,

since Roosevelt had already announced that he would not try for a third term.

After dinner President Roosevelt led his old friends into the library while his wife went off to tuck in the children for the night. He closed the library door behind them, and draped himself comfortably in a big easy chair. He smiled at the Tafts. Then, suddenly, with an innate sense of drama, he made a wide sweep with his hands to form a circle. "This is my crystal ball," he said.

Gazing mystically into his "ball," Roosevelt intoned in a deep, faraway voice:

"I am the seventh son of a seventh daughter, and I have clairvoyant powers. I see a man weighing three hundred and fifty pounds. There is something hanging over his head . . . I cannot make out what it is . . .

"At one time it looks like the presidency. Then again it looks like the chief justiceship!"

"Make it the chief justiceship," said Taft promptly.

"Make it the presidency," said Mrs. Taft.

Roosevelt's crystal ball could not foresee, of course, that Taft would become the only man in our history to win both honors.

At that time, three years away from the end of his own second term, Roosevelt was of two minds. He wanted to pick his successor, so that the Roosevelt policies would be continued. He liked Taft: they were longtime friends, and Taft rarely disagreed with him. But there were other men in the Cabinet, especially Secretary of State Elihu Root, whom he liked as well. And Roosevelt sorely needed a calm, pro-Roosevelt man like Taft on his Supreme Court.

Taft himself displayed little interest in seeking the rigors and responsibilities of the presidency. Ever since he was old enough to read, Taft's one ambition in life had been to attain the Supreme Court. His happiest days were spent as a federal circuit-court judge, and he longed only to go back to the comforts of judicial life. He refused to believe that the presidential nomination might be possible, and studiously ignored growing speculation about his candidacy.

Mrs. Taft, however, had one ambition since childhood, too. And that was to some day be First Lady of the land. When she was seventeen she spent a week in the White House with her older sister, as guests of President and Mrs. Rutherford Hayes, who were close friends of her parents. When she returned home to Cincinnati, young Nellie, as she was called, promised herself that she would only marry a man who could become President and take her back to live in that glamorous white mansion.

Through the years, Mrs. Taft prodded the husband she had selected toward the goal she had set for him. The judicial life that spelled comfort and dignity to Taft spelled boredom to her . . . "an awful groove" that she thought "quite too settled." So she became his chief political adviser, his severest critic, and always the dominant influence in his life.

Perhaps even more than to his own efforts, William Howard Taft owed the fact that he became the twenty-seventh President of the United States to two people. Without Roosevelt's public support and private political maneuverings at the 1908 Republican convention, Taft would never have been nominated. And without Mrs. Taft's continual, fierce struggle to keep him from the Supreme Court, Taft would not have been available for the nomination.

On March 4, 1909, when Taft was inaugurated, the Washington *Post* commented: "There is every reason why she [Mrs. Taft] should feel satisfaction in her husband's success, for had it not been for her determination to keep him from becoming a Supreme Court Justice he would not have been able to accept the nomination. . . . 'I want you to be in line for the presidential nomination,' she told him, and he followed what turned out to be excellent and timely advice."

The new First Lady herself was quoted that day as saying, "It always has been my ambition to see Mr. Taft President of the United States, and naturally when the ceremonies of the inauguration were in progress I was inexpressibly happy."

The White House was a long journey from snow-covered Mount Auburn, where they first met. The young set of Cincinnati's leading families was having a coasting party. Chubby Will Taft, a fledgling lawyer just out of Yale, asked Miss Helen Herron to ride with him on his bobsled. Later it became Taft's favorite joke to reminisce with the remark, "And Nellie and I have been sliding downhill ever since."

When she met Will Taft, Helen Herron was eighteen, and quite an exceptional young woman for her times. Her father was a prominent judge; she was the fourth in a family of eleven children. Miss Herron was not beautiful; but she was petite, candid, and intelligent. She always said just what she thought—and she had an opinion on everything. She was not intimidated by the popular theory that girls who displayed brains never caught a man. On the contrary, she even organized her own "literary salon" which met weekly to discuss books, music, and politics. Once in a while, salon discussions degenerated into juicy local gossip, but on the whole, they were conducted on a high moral and intellectual plane.

The forceful Miss Herron overwhelmed Will Taft. His mother had advised him that "a tall wife would be so becoming to you, showing off your broad proportions to full advantage." But young Taft was more interested in personality and wit than in physical stature.

"Do say that you will try to love me. Oh, how I will work and strive to be better and do better, how I will labor for our joint advancement if you will only let me," a smitten Will wrote Nellie in May, 1855. Even then Taft was listening to Nellie's advice and weighing her opinions seriously.

Their courtship was a long one, and its course was not always smooth. More than once Taft was moved to apologize for what Nellie considered an ungentlemanly slur on her intelligence.

"Far from holding your opinions lightly, I know no one who attaches more weight to them or who more admires your powers of reasoning than the now humbled subscriber. . . ." Taft wrote in one impassioned love note.

William Taft and Helen Herron were married in 1886—the same year President Grover Cleveland, so long a bachelor, married in a lavish White House ceremony and a young widower named Theodore Roosevelt took his second bride.

William Taft soon discovered that the clever tongue which expressed so many opinions could also grow sharp on occasion. "I know that I am very cross to you but I love you just the same," his wife wrote him in 1890. She frequently rebuked him in public.

The future President had some bad habits, however, which perhaps needed rebuking. For instance, he frequently got so involved in conversation at the dinner table that he forgot his duties as host. Carving a steak, he would get so busy talking he would pile two-thirds of the meat on one plate and leave very little for all the other guests. Finally, in exasperation, Mrs. Taft took over the carving chores herself.

And there was Taft's disturbing habit of dropping asleep anywhere at any time—at the dinner table, during conversations that didn't interest him, even during a funeral. Mrs. Taft called him her "Sleeping Beauty." She tried to keep him awake in public, and to cover up for him when she couldn't. A friend observed: "Sometimes she would carry on the conversation for him, for she was a brilliant woman, and she did know his views."

Once Taft managed to fall asleep while a typhoon raged outside their home in the Philippines, breaking windows and rocking the foundations. Mrs. Taft grumbled later, "The chair was shaking—how could you sleep?"

"Now, Nellie," answered Taft blandly. "You know it is just my way. I knew you could handle it."

Mrs. Taft didn't like it very much, but handle it she did— just as she briskly and capably handled everything else that came her way in life.

The newlywed Tafts were both deeply interested in politics, and active in Republican party activities in Ohio. Taft was rapidly building an excellent reputation as a lawyer, and was appointed a judge of Cincinnati's superior court when he was only twenty-nine. He discussed everything with his young wife—his legal cases, political developments, people he met every day in court. "You are my dearest and best critic and are worth much to me in stirring me up to best endeavor," Taft told her.

In 1890 Taft was offered the post of Solicitor General. He was reluctant to leave his home town and beloved judicial bench. But his wife persuaded him to take the job in Washington, because she had already begun to fret under the narrowing effects of the legal robe. "I was very glad because it gave Mr. Taft an opportunity for exactly the kind of work I wished him to do. . . ." she wrote later.

The Tafts lived in Washington for two years. It was during this period that Taft became friendly with another young political "comer"—the chairman of the Civil Service Commission, Theodore Roosevelt.

President Harrison appointed Taft to a circuit-court judge-
ship in 1892, and they moved back to Cincinnati. Taft was away
from home a great deal, covering his circuit, so his wife resumed
a neglected childhood interest: the piano. She organized Cincinnati's first orchestra association. But she worried that Taft, associ-
ating every day with judges at least twice his age, was becoming
stuffy. Her complacent husband, who tended to take things too
easily, needed a new challenge, she thought.

Meanwhile, Judge Taft was becoming influential in the Ohio
Republican party. At one point he led a delegation to President
McKinley, seeking a federal appointment for Roosevelt. He was
successful, and later wrote his brother: "We got Theodore into
the Navy Department [as Assistant Secretary]."

At least once during those years, however, Mrs. Taft proved
herself more politically attuned than her husband. He was so
scrupulously honest that he returned some government money he
had not spent that had been alloted him for travel expenses. A
judge's salary in those days was not extravagant, and Mrs. Taft
became "dreadfully upset" when she heard what he had done.
She pointed out that all the other judges, including the Supreme
Court justices, would not appreciate an associate who appeared
more economical than they. So for the sake of preserving his
own popularity, the honest Judge Taft thereafter took a more
liberal view of the function of expense allowances.

Suddenly, in 1900, President McKinley sent for Judge Taft
and asked if he would head a new commission to the Philippines.
The islands were still under martial law after Spain's surrender
of them to the United States. The purpose of the commission was
to set up a civil government there.

Again Taft hesitated to leave the bench; again Mrs. Taft was
eager for the new adventure. Taft extracted a promise from
McKinley that acceptance of the task would eventually mean
judicial promotion for him. And then he asked for a week to
think it over so that he could go home to Ohio and consult his
wife.

Mrs. Taft was delighted. "I wasn't sure what it meant, but I
knew instantly I didn't want to miss a big and novel experience,"
she recalled later.

Spurred on by his "council of war," as he affectionately called
her, Taft accepted and they were off to the Philippines. By this

time they had three young children: Robert, Helen, and Charles. Popular belief then held that the Philippines, where few Americans had ever visited, was the world's jumping-off place, a pest-ridden hole where white children surely sickened and died. But Nellie Taft was never a woman to be intimidated by the dubious or unexpected. As it turned out, she enjoyed their strange life, and so did the rest of the family. "I learned to accept the gifts of the gods without comment, which is the only thing to do in the East," she said philosophically.

Eventually Taft became governor of the Philippines, and his old friend Roosevelt succeeded President McKinley. In October, 1902, what Nellie Taft had always dreaded came: Taft was offered a Supreme Court appointment. There was an opening on the bench, and Roosevelt had remembered his friend's main ambition.

Taft, however, was deeply involved in the transition of the Philippines into a self-governing state. He felt, regretfully, that he could not leave the Philippines with so much left to do; Mrs. Taft, of course, agreed fully. Taft wrote Roosevelt that "I look forward to the time when I can accept such an offer, but even if it is certain that it can never be repeated must decline . . . gravity of situation here."

At first Roosevelt would not accept "no" for an answer. He practically ordered Taft to come home. But when word began to get around the islands that the governor was about to leave, Filipinos rioted and petitioned the President not to let him go. Between them, Taft and the native demonstrators convinced Roosevelt that all the years of effort to bring the islands to independence would be lost if a successor were substituted for the popular Taft.

Then Roosevelt offered Taft the post of Secretary of War. The Philippines came under the charge of the Secretary. Taft felt he could be of more use to the Filipino people in Washington than in Manila. Mrs. Taft was all for it: "This was much more pleasing to me than the offer of the Supreme Court appointment, because it was in line with the kind of work I wanted my husband to do, the kind of career I wanted for him and expected him to have, so I was glad there were few excuses for refusing to accept it open to him."

However, it was a curious sort of promotion. As First Lady of the Philippines, Nellie Taft had lived like a queen. In Washington, the wife of a Cabinet member had nothing like those privileges, and certainly had much less prestige. Nevertheless, she was delighted to be back in the capital city. The War Department was next door to the White House.

The final crisis was now upon her. Both the Supreme Court and the presidency were within reach. She determined that her husband should not sacrifice the possibility of the presidency for the certainty of the Supreme Court. For his part, Taft still only aspired to become Chief Justice.

By the winter of 1905 Nellie was complaining about the "rather annoying frequency" with which the subject of her husband's appointment to the Supreme Court cropped up. Their youngest son, Charles, heard the Supreme Court discussed at home so often he assumed it was the only honorable ambition for a man to have, and told everyone that it was his ambition, too.

A phone call the summer before had set it all off. The Tafts were staying with friends, Mr. and Mrs. John Hays Hammond, at Lakewood, New Jersey. Their vacation was interrupted one hot, quiet afternoon by a call from President Roosevelt. The butler called Secretary Taft to the telephone, and when he returned the carefully casual expression on his face made clear that something exciting had just happened.

His wife and hosts waited expectantly for Taft to explain. He settled his huge bulk slowly into a chair, perfectly aware that the suspense was becoming unbearable for the other three. Then he looked at his wife. Roosevelt had just told him that another Supreme Court appointment would be open next year, and had offered it to him. Taft said he had told Roosevelt he thought he might accept.

Mrs. Taft flushed. "You didn't!" she burst out. The Hammonds were just as dismayed. Mrs. Taft and John Hammond argued that Taft's chances for the presidential nomination in 1908 were very good. The newspapers already had mentioned Taft—along with several other prominent men—as a possible contender. Together, the Hammonds and Mrs. Taft were able to get Taft to postpone any decision at least until the seat should become vacant.

Taft remained undecided, pulled one way by his wife and another by his own preference, all that winter. In January, 1906, Roosevelt renewed the offer; still Taft hesitated. The subject was discussed several times, and in March, Roosevelt began to get impatient. On March 9 Taft went back to his office after a meeting with Roosevelt and recorded in his diary: "I also explained . . . that Nellie is bitterly opposed to my accepting the position and that she telephoned me this morning to say that if I did, I would make the great mistake of my life. The President has promised to see her and talk the matter over with her and explain the situation. . . ."

The very next week, Nellie Taft had a half-hour's confidential talk with Roosevelt about her husband's future.

She was not entirely successful, for the following day Roosevelt wrote Taft a formal letter officially offering a Supreme Court appointment. But Mrs. Taft had made some telling points with Roosevelt on the advantages of Taft for the presidency.

Roosevelt urged Taft to accept the appointment, outlining in detail the reasons he believed Taft might serve his nation more effectively there than by seeking the nomination. He warned that campaigning for the presidency carried with it the danger of defeat and an enforced return to private life.

But Roosevelt also added that "after a half-hour's talk with your dear wife . . . my belief is that of all the men that have appeared so far you are . . . most likely to receive the . . . nomination . . . and . . . I think the best man to receive it."

Roosevelt gently complained that perhaps he had been mistaken about Taft's own wishes. "I gathered that what you really wanted to do was to go on the bench, and that my urging was in the line of your inclination."

With the picture of a very resolute little woman still sharp in his memory, Roosevelt concluded his letter with a bit of pointed advice for the equivocal Taft. "No one can with wisdom advise you . . . you must decide," Roosevelt warned.

The Supreme Court offer was now public, but Taft continued to find excuses for delaying a decision. Roosevelt and the two Tafts discussed the problem frequently. Roosevelt began to press Taft to accept; he was beginning to lean toward Elihu Root as his heir-apparent. While Taft was away on a War Department inspection trip, Mrs. Taft had another conversation with Roosevelt. She got the impression that Roosevelt was discouraged over Taft as a possible candidate because he had not co-operated satisfactorily with some important political groups in the West.

In vexation, Mrs. Taft wrote her husband that Roosevelt had told her he might have to support Charles Evans Hughes, because he felt Taft was such a poor politician. She pleaded with Taft to show a little more enthusiasm for his own candidacy.

Taft merely sent her back a good-natured reply telling her not to be upset because there was "plenty of time." He added that, in any case, he had analyzed the public feeling and it was not running in his favor at all.

Taft also sent a letter to Roosevelt, however, with the notation that "Mrs. Taft writes me you are disposed to lecture me. . . ." This sequence of letters ended with an irritated message from Roosevelt to Taft, protesting that Mrs. Taft had misunderstood him. Roosevelt insisted that he hadn't told her he was going to support Hughes, or anybody. What he'd actually said was that unless Taft stopped being so aloof, there might be no choice but to support someone else.

One of the private meetings of the Tafts and Roosevelt was recalled by a White House usher, Ike Hoover, in his autobiography. Hoover overheard Roosevelt bring up the question of the Supreme Court appointment, and heard Taft say he wanted to take it. But, he recalled, "it was only through the pleadings of Mrs. Taft that he was not appointed. I can remember the exact hour of the famous visit when Mrs. Taft, in the face of opposition of both the President and her husband, the Secretary of War, carried her point. From that time on, the President seemed to feel that Mr. Taft should be his successor."

By May, Roosevelt was inclined to think that Taft might be best as a presidential candidate after all. But it was Taft himself who was still reluctant to make a decision. He wrote to his wife one day after a long talk with Roosevelt that "he was full of the presidency . . . he wants to talk to you and me together. He thinks I am the one to take his mantle."

With Roosevelt increasingly indicating that Taft would be his choice as successor, and his wife more persistently than ever encouraging him to run, Taft finally declined his heart's desire. On July 30 he wrote an official letter to Roosevelt turning down the Supreme Court offer, on grounds that he would like to continue as Secretary of War until the development of the Philippines was further along. He could not resist adding: "I would much prefer to go on the Supreme Bench for life than to run for the presidency, and that in twenty years of judicial service I could make myself more useful to the country than as President, even if my election should come about."

Even now, after rejecting the bench, Taft made little effort to add momentum to a presidential boom for himself. But there were others who would do that for him. His brothers began immediately to gather funds for the pre-convention campaign.

The winter of 1906-1907 was so full of activity that Mrs. Taft could recall almost nothing about it in her memoirs. It was "a hazy nightmare lightened in spots by contemplation of the delightful possibilities contained in a rapidly growing presidential boom. . . ."

Taft applied himself to his tasks at the War Department. There was no official word from the White House concerning the 1908 presidential race until April, 1907. Then Representative Nicholas Longworth, President Roosevelt's son-in-law, announced his preference for Taft. The President, however, said nothing.

The Republican party was in turmoil. There were many candidates, but none seemed to muster overwhelming enthusiasm. In December, six months away from the Republican convention, Roosevelt's supporters threatened to start a boom for him, despite his insistence that he would not break the third-term tradition. Roosevelt's secretary, William Loeb, warned him the party would soon tear itself apart unless he let his supporters know his choice for successor.

Roosevelt told Loeb, "Call Elihu and tell him that he is my first choice." Roosevelt knew that Elihu Root, who was convinced he could never be elected, would decline to run. And when Loeb called him, Root replied that he was honored but did not choose to become a candidate.

Then Roosevelt told Loeb to go to Taft and tell him that Roosevelt was placing the mantle around his shoulders. Roosevelt phoned his favorite correspondents and "leaked" the news that Taft was his choice. The next day's newspapers left no doubt about the authenticity of their stories about Taft's selection, although the President made no formal announcement.

Roosevelt was able to control the convention in June even to the point of squelching an effort to nominate him. When the chairman, Henry Cabot Lodge, paid tribute to the Roosevelt years during the opening session, the delegates began a cheering, foot-stomping demonstration. It lasted for forty-five minutes, breaking all previous records for both parties.

Taft's name was placed in nomination the next day. In the Taft headquarters near Convention Hall, Nellie Taft squirmed restlessly, her face taut with tension as she listened to the noisy proceedings. Taft's supporters began a wild ovation at the mention of his name. As the cheers rose, his wife's face relaxed into a smile. "I . . . want it to last more than forty-five minutes. I want to get even for the scare that Roosevelt cheer of forty-five minutes gave me yesterday," she said.

Nellie Taft made some appearances with her husband during his campaign, but for the most part she remained at home, peppering him with letters of advice and encouragement. She wrote to him every day and received a daily letter back from him. "I got completely worn out as a mere onlooker," she sighed, ruefully adding that she felt the strain more than her husband seemed to.

After her first experience watching Taft speak and propel his huge ungainly body through a crowd, shaking hands until his muscles ached, Mrs. Taft had a new appreciation of the rigors of politics. She told Taft, "My political enthusiasm waned slightly—though temporarily."

Taft didn't enjoy campaigning very much, either. He complained wearily to Roosevelt that he was sick of it all. Roosevelt replied, "Poor old boy! Of course you are not enjoying the campaign. I wish you had some of my bad temper!"

Taft, portly and perspiring, was campaigning against the golden-tongued orator of the Midwest, William Jennings Bryan, who was making his third try for the presidency. Against the eloquence of the Great Commoner, Taft often became discouraged with his own efforts. His wife's letters were a great source of comfort to him, for she never failed to cheer him on and assure him he was doing just fine. Once she wrote him: "Never mind if you cannot get off fireworks. It must be known by this time that that is not your style . . . if people don't want you as you are, they can leave you, and we shall both be able to survive it."

On November 3, 1908, William Howard Taft and James S. Sherman defeated William Jennings Bryan and John W. Kern by an electoral vote of 321 to 162. The nation that had elected the easygoing Ohioan as its new leader was in transition from a prosperous country to a world power. America did not yet quite realize what was happening, but it was growing up. Thomas Edison, interviewed by a reporter, reflected on his awareness of the country's provincialism: "We've got to start to make this world over."

During the uneventful administration, Taft was to watch the nation learn to cope with its new status as a world giant, seeking "the good life." He signed the bill providing for a personal income tax, which would change the nation's economic structure and develop the great middle class. He supported the growing campaign for woman's suffrage. He bought the first stamp advocating votes for women, and was asked what he intended to do with it. "I'll put it on a letter to Mrs. Taft," he said and grinned.

Taft gave the first woman in American history a presidential appointment. He named Julia Lothrop as chief of the Children's Bureau. And he was the first President to acquire an automobile, which was parked in the stable with the horses.

Nellie Taft became immediately absorbed in the problems of White House housekeeping and the duties of a First Lady. "My own problems became to me paramount and I began to give them my almost undivided attention, and to neglect the political affairs which had for many years interested me so intensely. Perhaps with my husband safely elected, I considered all important affairs satisfactorily settled. . . ." she said.

"My very active participation in my husband's career came to an end when he became President. I had always had the satisfaction of knowing almost as much as he about the politics and intricacies of any situation in which he found himself, and my life was filled with interests of a most unusual kind. But in the White House I found my own duties too engrossing to permit me to follow him long or very far into the governmental maze which soon enveloped him."

Taft was inaugurated March 4, 1909, after an all-night blizzard that ruined parade decorations and clogged transportation into the city. The Roosevelts invited the Tafts to spend the inauguration eve with them in the White House. In the morning, when they arose and saw the deep snow outside, Taft said to Roosevelt, "I always said it would be a cold day when I got to be President of the United States."

The inauguration ceremony was impressive, despite the cold and snow. Mrs. Taft noted with satisfaction that although Charlie, then eleven, had brought along *Treasure Island* to ward off boredom, he was so fascinated that he never opened the book.

Mrs. Taft's first act as the new First Lady was to break tradition and seat herself beside her husband in the carriage for the ride back to the White House. The inaugural committee protested that no woman had ever ridden down Pennsylvania Avenue beside a newly inaugurated President. But Mrs. Taft paid no attention.

The new President was entirely willing to share his proudest moment with his wife, just as they had shared his career for more than twenty years. Mrs. Taft recalled later: "That drive was the proudest and happiest event of inauguration day. Perhaps I had a little secret elation in thinking that I was doing something which no woman had ever done before."

When she became First Lady, Mrs. Taft was an energetic, gray-haired and still trim-figured forty-eight years old. William Taft was fifty-one. In its inauguration story, the Washington *Post* noted: "In the matter of mental attainments she is probably the best-fitted woman who ever graced the position she now holds and enjoys."

Mrs. Taft, however, was not to enjoy that position for long. After only two and a half months in the White House, she fell suddenly ill. Her doctors announced only that she suffered from nervousness and excitability; White House employees said later that she had a stroke which impaired her speech for a time and left her in delicate health for the rest of her life. Mrs. Taft herself only referred to it as her "serious attack of illness."

On his inauguration day, Taft had waggled a finger at his

wife and warned, "Well, now I'm in the White House, I'm not going to be pushed any more." But however exasperated he might have been sometimes at his wife's propulsive ways, Taft proved himself a devoted husband during her long illness.

He sat by her bedside several hours every day, reading to her and helping her practice forming words to regain her speech. He strained to be jolly and cheerful in her room, and thought up jokes to tell her. Most days he brought her flowers from the White House gardens. The first time he tried to pick a bunch the gardener came upon him, thought he was a thief, and yelled at him to stop. Thereafter Taft presented his daily bouquet with a flourish and the greeting, "I stole these for you!"

President Taft never fell asleep during these vigils by his wife's bedside, a measure of his devotion in itself. He was still in the habit of dozing off at the most embarrassing times.

With such good care, Mrs. Taft recovered steadily and by September was able to assume her full White House duties. During her illness her sisters had acted as hostesses in her place for social occasions. After the first two months she was sitting up in bed and "from my apartments on the second floor I directed arrangements for social activities almost as if I had been well."

President Taft wrote his brother in August that "she is quite disposed to sit as a pope and direct me as of yore, which is an indication of the restoration of normal conditions."

The strong-minded Mrs. Taft resumed her tasks as First Lady that fall with her usual thoroughness and determination. She made only two concessions to her weakened health. For long reception lines and tiring official entertainments, she wore low heels, although they offended her sense of fashion.

And she persuaded Taft, who slept best in a well-heated room under a mound of blankets, to sleep in a cold bedroom. Doctors had advised her that cool, fresh air was good for her health and she should stop sleeping in a stuffy room with closed windows.

Mrs. Taft was not a universally popular First Lady, although the Tafts gave lavish parties and held twice as many social affairs as any previous administration. She sometimes seemed aristocratic and distant to her guests, because of a natural reticence and because she overtired easily. Cruel gossips criticized her for her unusually large role in her husband's career, and called her "pushy."

Mrs. Taft tried to run the White House with the same concept of gracious living she had enjoyed as First Lady of the Philippines. Some of her changes were unpopular with the public, who thought she was putting on airs. She insisted the White House doormen wear livery, because she did not think it dignified for them to stand at their posts in ordinary suits. She decided to have the houseboys wear full dress uniforms to add a further touch of elegance. But she changed her mind one day when she overheard one houseboy grumble to another, "Won't we look fine cleaning windows in tails?"

Gracious living did not mean extravagance. Mrs. Taft had always controlled the family finances, and President Taft gave her $2,000 a month to invest against the day when they would leave the White House. She pinched pennies wherever she could. She stopped having refreshments for parties catered, because it was cheaper to have the food prepared in the White House kitchens. She even bought a cow, which grazed on the White House grounds. Twice a day the milk was delivered to the kitchen. Mrs. Taft nicknamed her cow "Mooly-Wooly," and took considerable ribbing because of its presence.

Taft was the first President to be paid $75,000 a year. This included the cost of all his state and official receptions. When Taft was elected, all White House domestic help was also paid from this personal payroll. Mrs. Taft, however, suggested to the President that the government should pay all White House salaries. And before the end of their term Congress made that change.

After the rollicking, carefree Roosevelt family, Mrs. Taft's insistent demands for economy and orderliness created such tension among the White House staff that Ike Hoover, the chief usher, complained of "unrest." This he attributed in fine male sarcasm to "the more than ordinary influence exerted by the female members of the household."

Mrs. Taft, however, just felt that she was doing her duty as it should be done. "I could not feel that I was mistress of any house if I did not take an active interest in all of the details of running it," she said.

In fact, it was Mrs. Taft who introduced democracy among the servants. She discovered that servants with the highest positions ate at a different table than those of lesser rank, and were served better food. She decreed that all the help should dine together and eat the same food.

Nellie Taft is best known for two achievements during her four years as First Lady. She introduced the custom of holding musicales after official White House dinners. Now this custom is highly popular, but Nellie was publicly criticized when she began it. Former First Lady Frances Cleveland was the honor guest at Mrs. Taft's first musicale. She was so horrified at this innovation that she rudely stalked out before the concert was over.

Mrs. Taft's other contribution to the nation's pleasure was the cherry trees which circle Washington's Tidal Basin. The trees provide such a lovely pink cloud of blossoms every spring that the city now celebrates an annual Cherry Blossom Festival. Mrs. Taft remembered the lush gardens of Manila, and envisioned a similar bower around the basin. When she had difficulty finding enough cherry trees for her purpose, the mayor of Tokyo shipped three thousand trees to her as a gift for the city.

Mrs. Taft was, however, far more influential in the conduct of the nation's business during her term as First Lady than these two projects would indicate. Despite her own disavowal that she did not follow the President far into the governmental maze, there is evidence that the President continued to rely on her good sense and advice as he had since their marriage.

She kept track of official appointments for him. Taft had a deficient memory when it came to such details. He seated different people in different rooms and then forgot which room to go to next. Taft frequently expressed his amazement at his wife's memory. She could repeat things accurately after a lapse of many days.

Mrs. Taft also attended nearly every important White House conference. She would come in, unasked and unannounced, and seat herself quietly near the President. She never openly expressed an opinion, but she listened carefully. And after the meeting was over, she usually had an opinion, or two or three, which she expressed to her husband in private.

Mrs. Taft's presence at White House meetings served a

double purpose. By gentle prodding behind her fan, she kept the President awake whenever he seemed about to doze off.

When she decided something, she generally had her way. Taft told her that he was appointing Nicholas Longworth as minister to China. Longworth wanted the post, he said. But she objected. She had never gotten along well with Alice Roosevelt, and now she argued that neither Longworth nor his wife was fitted for the post.

Longworth did not get the post. Taft put it on different grounds, but the real reason for his refusal was the opposition of his wife.

Toward the close of Taft's administration, a fad called the "New Thought" treatment swept the country. Mrs. Taft had not felt well for a few days, so a guest at a White House party suggested to the President that she try "New Thought." Taft asked what it was. The guest described the treatment as "teaching people to rely on themselves."

The President's huge bulk shook with laughter. "Mrs. Taft has been using 'New Thought' for years," he said. "She's about the most self-reliant person I have ever known."

Both Tafts very much wanted a second term in the White House. When former President Roosevelt announced that he was so unhappy with Taft's conduct in office he would oppose him for the Republican nomination in 1912, Taft was surprised. His wife wasn't, however. She had feared Roosevelt long before her husband thought that his old friend could have any ground for political grievance.

Mrs. Taft had never completely trusted Roosevelt's support of her husband, dating from their struggle over the Supreme Court appointment. When she heard Roosevelt's announcement, she turned to Taft disgustedly. "I told you so four years ago, and you would not believe me," she said.

"I know you did, my dear," Taft sighed. "I think you are perfectly happy now. You would have preferred the Colonel to come out against me than to have been wrong yourself!"

But Mrs. Taft was not perfectly happy to be right in this case, because Roosevelt's split with the Republican party caused her husband's defeat. While Taft and Roosevelt, running on his

own Bull Moose party, divided the Republican votes, Democrat
Woodrow Wilson was elected President.

Mrs. Taft was so miserable on the day of Wilson's inauguration that she did not even say good-bye to her staff. A reporter
asked her daughter Helen if her mother was relieved to be free
of the responsibilities of the White House. Helen replied, "Mother
was never much for relief. She always wanted something to be
happening."

Taft accepted a professorship at Yale, and they settled into
a quiet existence. Eight years later, however, Taft's fondest dream
came true after all. President Warren Harding appointed him
Chief Justice of the Supreme Court. This time Mrs. Taft did not
object.

Edith Bolling Galt

WILSON

❀ ❀

On October 2, 1919, at 10:00 P.M., White House physician Admiral Cary Grayson issued to the public a terse, uninformative bulletin. "The President," it said, "is a very sick man."

President Woodrow Wilson lay helpless in his bed, his entire left side paralyzed by a sudden stroke. His mind did not seem impaired, but he had great difficulty speaking and moving; the doctors warned he might not have long to live.

The President's handsome second wife, Edith, and Dr. Grayson decided that the truth should be kept from the people. They also determined to hide the President's condition even from his Cabinet members and closest advisers. And so began one of the strangest periods in American history—for six weeks nobody but Edith Wilson and Dr. Grayson went into the sickroom, and for a long time after that, Joe Tumulty, the President's secretary, was the only other person allowed to see the President about government matters. Even then Edith Wilson stood at the head of the bed to shake her head at Tumulty when she thought the President had had enough.

A bewildered, worried nation watched with alarm the drawn shades at the White House windows, the new guards posted at the locked gates, the total ban on visitors, the abrupt silence of the fluent presidential tongue. The White House was like a tomb. Rumors spread through the countryside: the President was totally paralyzed, the President was unconscious, the President was a raving madman. People noticed for the first time the barred White House windows, which had been fixed that way in President Theodore Roosevelt's term to keep his children from batting balls through the panes.

Inside the cloistered mansion, a team of medical specialists had solemnly warned Mrs. Wilson that the President might live five days, or five months, or five years. It all depended, they said, upon his being protected from "every disturbing problem." Dr. F. X. Dercum suggested that in order to take some of the President's burdens off his mind, Mrs. Wilson screen every government problem. She should weigh each one for its importance and effect upon the President's mental state, and discuss with him only the most vital of matters. "Every time you take him a new anxiety or problem to excite him you are turning a knife in an open wound," he warned her.

In her memoirs Edith Wilson claimed that she suggested her husband resign. But the doctors told her that as long as his mind remained clear, his responsibilities as President were the greatest incentive to recovery; that jobless, he would lose his will to live. It was Mrs. Wilson's final responsibility to decide upon a course of action: she chose to hide her husband's disability and take upon herself those Constitutional burdens of the presidency which could not be set aside.

Edith Wilson insisted upon referring to this period as her "stewardship"—which implies management within delegated authority, but no assumption of independent policy-making authority. Charles Thompson, a White House reporter, called it her "regency." Some held bluntly that she ran the country. Others said Mrs. Wilson was "acting President." One observer wrote in *Liberty* magazine that "Edith Bolling Wilson was not only acting

President, but secretary to the President and Secretary of State."
Reporter David Lawrence commented: "Between the President
and the outside world stands Mrs. Wilson, as devoted and faithful a companion as ever nursed a sick man ... it is doubtful if ever
a woman in American history had such a burden." The London
Daily Mail observed: "Though Washington tongues are wagging
vigorously no suggestion is heard that Mrs. Wilson is not proving
a capable 'President.' " But only President and Mrs. Wilson really
knew whether she served as a "steward" or a "President" in those
dark weeks—and President Wilson made no comment.

Historians cannot even agree as to how long Edith Wilson's
stewardship, or substitute presidency, lasted. For a total of seventeen months, until the end of Wilson's second term, Mrs. Wilson
and Dr. Grayson were protectively "taking care of Woodrow,"
and only his closest top-level advisers saw him. On October 30
Mrs. Wilson did permit King Albert and Queen Elizabeth of
Belgium to peep in at the President in his bed—the first "outsiders" to visit him since the stroke. Later the Prince of Wales
was also allowed to pay a brief bedside call, because Mrs. Wilson
felt visiting royalty would amuse the President. The curtain remained down to all of Washington, however. After six weeks
Tumulty was occasionally allowed to see the President. On November 18 President Wilson made his first appearance out of
bed, sunning himself in a wheel chair on the south portico. On
December 3 the President sent a message to Congress, the first
unmistakable evidence that he still commanded the same precise,
eloquent style. By February the President was well enough to
fire his Secretary of State, Robert Lansing, who had had the
temerity to suggest to Tumulty after Wilson's stroke that the
presidential powers be transferred to the Vice-President. It was
not until April, however, that the President, crippled, speaking
with difficulty and looking tired, felt strong enough to hold a
Cabinet meeting.

All that winter reports circulated that Wilson was insane,
that the presidency was, in effect, vacant. Senators publicly expressed their concern for the nation's welfare. Finally, the Senate
Democratic minority leader, Gilbert Hitchcock of Nebraska, and
a Republican senator, Albert Fall of New Mexico, were sent to
the President on the pretext of consulting about United States–

Mexico relations, but actually to check on the President's sanity. They found the President propped up in bed, freshly shaved. "Well, Mr. President, we have been praying for you," Fall said. "Which way, Senator?" wryly quipped the sick man. Mrs. Wilson sat on the opposite side of the President's bed and painstakingly wrote down every word of the three-way conversation. Annoyed, Senator Fall observed, "You seem very much engaged, madam." Mrs. Wilson snapped, "I thought it was wise to record this interview so there may be no misunderstanding or misstatements made." Her precaution turned out to be unnecessary. The "smelling committee," as Wilson called it, reported to eager reporters at the front door that the President was indubitably in his right mind. Afterward Dr. Grayson even remarked that he thought the little encounter had done the President good.

Edith Wilson repeatedly and solemnly insisted that "I myself never made a single decision regarding the disposition of public affairs. The only decision that was mine was what was important and what was not; and the very important decision of when to present matters to my husband." She also declared that her "stewardship" lasted only six weeks, not six to seventeen months. "At first," she admitted, "I was only able to discuss affairs of state with him for about ten minutes a day." But she added that he made rapid progress—"Within two weeks of his stroke the President was able to sign public documents," and by December 3 she was going over every communication with him, whether it was important or not.

But a number of questions which concern the true extent of her role seem destined to remain forever unanswered. How fully did the President comprehend those papers she gave him to sign? And what about all those matters which Mrs. Wilson, who had no political, philosophical, or administrative training except that provided by her four years as First Lady, took it upon herself to keep from the President? Not only was she exercising censorship by selection, but she was also coloring the major problems she discussed with the President by her own abbreviated interpretations. Who can accurately estimate the effect of Mrs. Wilson's interpretation of a subject upon the ultimate decision, particularly when that decision was made by a man totally isolated from other opinions or information? Furthermore, the

Wilsons left no record of which problems she discussed with the President and which she did not—possibly because of the Constitutional questions such a record would raise.

In a recent biography of Edith Wilson, *First Lady Extraordinary*, written with Mrs. Wilson's approval and assistance, the author, Alden Hatch, suggests: "The truth is that even to this day Mrs. Wilson does not realize the power that she wielded. She simply acted as she thought she must." When Hatch asked Mrs. Wilson, then in her late eighties, how she had decided which things were important enough for her ailing husband's attention, she snapped curtly, "I just decided."

It is difficult to determine how close she came to being "acting President," but it is true that Edith Wilson knew completely and intimately just how President Wilson thought about every key aspect of government conduct and policy. For four years Wilson told only her his innermost ideas and opinions. He discussed each day's government problems with her. Before her marriage she had never been troubled by a single political thought; and so Wilson molded her naturally quick, but inexperienced, mind in his own image. Edith Wilson concentrated her whole being on serving as her husband's companion, and between them there existed a deep affection and intimacy. Tumulty, who had reason to dislike Mrs. Wilson, nevertheless recorded generously: "No public man ever had a more devoted helpmeet, and no wife a husband more dependent upon her sympathetic understanding of his problems."

Wilson could not seem to come to a decision until he had talked out the situation with his wife and received her assurance that the course he chose was the correct one. He did not meet people easily, and he trusted few. The two men on whom he once relied heavily, Tumulty and Colonel Edward House, became "outsiders" like the rest of his associates after his marriage, largely because his wife did not like either man. So Wilson proceeded in his abstract, intellectual manner, substituting the unquestioning devotion of his wife for, in today's terms, the support of an advisory staff.

During the months of the President's illness, Edith Wilson displayed a calm and efficient command of White House operations. But there was one vital, disturbing difference between her interpretation of the presidency and her husband's: whereas Wilson put concern for the nation's welfare above all else, his wife put concern for the President's welfare above all else. "Woodrow Wilson was first my beloved husband whose life I was trying to save ... after that he was the President of the United States," she said.

Immediately after Wilson's stroke Mrs. Wilson quietly set up what she described as "a workable system of handling matters of state." Every document, letter, or paper from the Senate, the Cabinet, or the public addressed to the President went to her. She arose early and stayed up far into the night, studying each document carefully. If she felt that a presidential decision was required, she wrote out a brief digest of the problem, which she read to him. Then she carefully wrote down his answer and transmitted the decision to the parties involved. If a subject seemed important but likely to irritate the President, Mrs. Wilson sent for the official involved and discussed it with him, urging him to solve the matter without the President. If it still remained insoluble, she reluctantly brought up the subject with her husband and recalled the official later to her sitting room to repeat the President's words. She gave all such instructions orally, for she did not want to leave a written record of her role as presidential spokesman.

In her memoirs Mrs. Wilson recalled: "He asked thousands of questions, and insisted upon knowing everything, particularly about the Treaty [the Peace Treaty of World War I, which contained a provision setting up the League of Nations, then up for Senate ratification]. He would dictate notes to me to send to Senator Hitchcock, who was leading the fight for the treaty in the Senate. Or he would tell me what senators to send for, and what suggestions he had to make to them. These directions I made notes of, so in transmitting his views I should make no mistake. . . ."

Mrs. Wilson did not even permit Hitchcock, who was trying valiantly to squeeze Wilson's treaty through the Senate, to see the President. The doctors had advised her that personal encounters, especially about official matters, would sap the President's limited strength and she protected him zealously from visitors, no matter how influential. She served this go-between function for six months, and to a modified degree until the end of his term.

In desperation, Hitchcock came to see the First Lady on November 18, to warn that unless the Democrats accepted compromise limitations upon League participation, the whole proposal would be defeated. Mrs. Wilson wrote later that she had gone immediately to her husband's bed and pleaded, "For my sake, won't you accept these reservations and get this awful thing settled?" Wilson looked at her with sorrowful, bitter eyes. "Little girl, don't you desert me," he whispered. "Better a thousand times to go down fighting than to dip your colors to dishonorable compromise." Mrs. Wilson did not try to persuade him further: she went back to Senator Hitchcock, feeling "like one of his betrayers," with the message that the President did not wish the Democrats to compromise. As Hitchcock had warned, the Senate thereupon rejected membership of any kind in the League. Isolated, unaware that public opinion, lulled by peace, was no longer ardently idealistic, stubbornly clinging to the hope that the League would be saved by some miracle, President Wilson had killed with his own sickly hand his dream of a democratic world government led by the United States. The League of Nations opened in Geneva in 1920, without United States participation.

Whenever she addressed administration officials, the First Lady was careful to attribute her remarks entirely to the absent President. Secretary of Agriculture David Houston recorded a good example of her technique. On January 25, 1920, he received a summons from the First Lady to come to the White House. Although Houston was one of Wilson's original appointments seven years before, Houston had not been in direct contact with the President since early September. He arrived promptly at the appointed time, 4:30 P.M., and was served tea. "You are wondering why I wanted to see you . . ." the First Lady began. "The President asked me to tell you that he is very anxious for you to accept the Secretaryship of the Treasury. He is reluctant to have you give up Agriculture, but he still thinks he now needs you more in the Treasury. . . ." Houston promptly accepted. Then Edith asked him for recommendations for a new Agriculture Secretary, and wrote down the names which Houston proffered.

Houston was surprised to be also asked whether he had anybody in mind to suggest for Secretary of Interior. He had no inkling there was to be a vacancy. But Mrs. Wilson explained: "The President is somewhat embarrassed. Secretary [Franklin] Lane has resigned in the press. The President has not yet been officially informed of his going. He would like your judgment." Houston shortly departed; he was not asked to visit the President.

Lane did resign on March 1. And Mrs. Wilson conveyed the offer of the secretaryship to Judge John Barton Payne in much the same way she had notified Houston. Before the interview, Mrs. Wilson "went to get my instructions from the President as to what to say." Payne accepted the offer; like Houston, he did not see the President.

By January the President was replying to Cabinet member requests by notes in his own handwriting. "He was now able to do more each day, but I eased things in every way possible and never left him if I could avoid it," Mrs. Wilson said. Secretary of State Lansing was virtually ignored. "I did not see much of Lansing," Mrs. Wilson recalled, "for I never liked him."

The President held his first Cabinet meeting on April 13. The meeting had been suggested by Dr. Grayson, who hinted in his own memoirs that he suspected Edith was being a bit overprotective. Grayson felt a Cabinet session might stimulate the President and bring him out of the bleak mood of depression which had settled upon him after the defeat of the League. Wilson was so gloomy he even discussed resigning with his wife and Dr. Grayson, both of whom argued ardently against it. After the Cabinet session, Grayson said the President "plainly showed that it had done him a lot of good."

The Cabinet members, however, were shocked at the President's appearance. David Houston recorded: "The President looked old, worn and haggard. It was enough to make one weep to look at him. One of his arms was useless . . . when he tried to speak there were marked evidences of his trouble. His voice was very weak and strained . . . he put up a brave front." After an hour's discussion, to which the President contributed little, "Mrs. Wilson came in looking rather disturbed and suggested that we had better go." Secretary of Navy Josephus Daniels recalled that thereafter at each Cabinet meeting "Mrs. Wilson was never far away."

What Edith Wilson felt during this demanding, trying

period can only be imagined. In her memoirs she allotted only eighteen pages to those days, and avoided entirely any illuminating reference to her own burdens. But the tension to which she was subjected must have at times seemed unbearable. Because no one knew the true nature of the President's illness, she had no one in whom she could confide her worries. Dr. Grayson, by her own admission, advised only on the President's illness and never had anything to do with the handling of political matters. The newspapers were full of insulting comments about her husband's mental condition, as well as angry criticism of her own role. She hid all these papers from Wilson, so that he would not know how the public had turned against him. Her maid recalled years later that she had come upon Mrs. Wilson huddled miserably over the newspapers one day, whispering, "I just don't know how much more criticism I can take." But out of concern for her husband's memory, her distaste for the unkind sentiments of the press, and alarm for the probable unconstitutionality of what she was doing, Mrs. Wilson took it all in silence.

This remarkable, intelligent woman who could rise to such incredible demands was Woodrow Wilson's second wife. His first, Ellen Axon Wilson, died in the White House on August 6, 1914. She had been a sensitive, gentle woman who treated the austere intellectual whom she married almost as much like a god as a husband. They were both deeply religious; he the son of a Virginia preacher, she the daughter of a Georgia minister. Ellen Wilson gave up a promising art career to marry Wilson and rear three daughters, Eleanor, Jessie, and Margaret. By the time Wilson was elected to the presidency, her health was already weakened by Bright's disease and tuberculosis. She exhausted herself in her new role of First Lady by preparing fabulous White House weddings for Jessie and Eleanor. She embarked upon a personal crusade to clear up Washington's festering slums, dragging congressmen through the slum areas to inspect the drab shacks of the poor. As she lay dying, Congress passed her slum clearance bill.

Wilson had thrived in this household of all women, who doted on him, cared for him, and, in all truth, spoiled him terribly. For months after her death the President wandered listlessly through the empty White House corridors, abstracted, lonely, and forlorn. Two daughters now lived elsewhere; Margaret was too absorbed in her own singing career to be much company for her melancholy father. Four days before his wife's death France was invaded by Germany; the World War had begun and Wilson was faced with the struggle of trying to keep America out of it. When he most needed soft, comforting words, he was alone. "God has stricken me almost beyond what I can bear," the anguished President wrote a friend.

The President was not the only lonely person in the White House, however. Helen Bones, a young cousin who had been practically reared by the Wilsons, lived in the big mansion with no female companionship and little to do to keep herself busy. Dr. Grayson felt sorry for Miss Bones; so one day he introduced her to the guardian of his fiancée Alice Gertrude (Altrude) Gordon—a weathy, beautiful widow named Edith Galt. At forty-two, Mrs. Galt had an ample, well-shaped figure, a cameo complexion, thick dark hair, and delicate features; she was generally considered one of the best-looking women in the city. Her late husband, Norman Galt, had been a successful Washington jeweler. They had no children, and so she, too, was lonely.

Helen Bones, and later the President's three daughters, took a great liking to Mrs. Galt. The women began to spend long hours together.

Edith Galt was genteely reserved, dignified, and poised. She did not care much for the parties and dances of Washington society; she preferred traveling, or a quiet evening at the theater, or simple dinners with a few old friends. She was not, in any sense, gregarious. She was given to black-and-white opinions; if she did not like a new acquaintance, she could not tolerate to pretend otherwise. Her life had been secluded, her only contacts with a small, rather stratified circle—she knew little of the world and its variegated humanity. In her way she was a great romantic, with an idealized view of love and marriage which was to be reflected in her maternal, possessive, awe-stricken, and dispassionate but all-absorbing adoration of President Wilson.

Edith, born October 15, 1872, was one of nine children of Judge and Mrs. William Bolling; she grew up in an impoverished rural Virginia town named Wytheville. Her parents had owned vast plantation lands, but had lost all their possessions in the ravages of the Civil War. Edith's father and grandmother taught her to read and write and figure, and even to speak a smattering of French. In the evenings Judge Bolling gathered his large brood around him and read aloud from the classics—Dickens, Shakespeare, and Milton. Judge Bolling's meager purse, however, could not stretch to educate both his boys and his girls. So Edith had only two years of formal schooling—one year at Martha Washington College in Abington, Virginia, and one year at Powell's School in Richmond.

The winter she was eighteen, Edith went to visit her sister, Mrs. Alexander Galt, in Washington. The Galts lived five blocks west of the White House, on a shady cobblestoned street. The wide-eyed girl from rural Virginia was thrilled by the excitement of the city. It was here, too, that she met Norman Galt, the younger brother of Alexander. With maidenly prudishness Edith said that Norman was a "lovely person" who wooed her faithfully for four years before he "finally wore me down." Galt was a stolid, rather dull young man, but he was a hard worker, and the family jewelry store prospered. The Galts lived very comfortably. They traveled frequently to Europe, in an age when only the rich could afford to do so. Mrs. Galt wore only gowns by M. Worth, then the leading couturier of Paris. She became the first woman in Washington to have an electric automobile.

When Galt died in 1908 he left his wife the sole owner of the store, which she supervised for two years and then sold, for a tidy sum, to its employees. Childless, Edith Galt took under her wing Altrude Gordon, the teen-age daughter of a close friend who had died. She and Altrude filled up their empty lives with travel, even making a canoe trip together in the rugged wilderness lakes of Maine. Then, in the winter of 1914, Dr. Grayson brought Helen Bones to Edith Galt to be mothered.

Edith and Helen took long walks together, went for rides in Edith's little electric, and chatted cozily over tea in the afternoons. They always, however, had tea at Edith's house, not the White House. Finally, one day in March, after their friendship had ripened for several months, Helen invited Edith to tea in the mansion, with the promise that "Cousin Woodrow will be out playing golf." The pair trudged, laughing, to the White House, tramping in with muddy shoes, rumpled clothes, and wind-blown, untidy hairdos. But as Edith emerged from the elevator, her first time in the upstairs living quarters of the mansion, she collided with a slender man as disheveled as herself. He had just come down the long corridor with Dr. Grayson, having walked up the front stairs after a game of golf. "Cousin Woodrow," sputtered Helen, "I should like to present Mrs. Norman Galt." The quartet laughed self-consciously; and Edith remembered thinking, "At least I'm disheveled in a suit by Worth."

She could have been wearing burlap for all the President seemed to notice. He could not take his eyes from the rosy cheeks, round smiling face, and large violet eyes. He invited the ladies to join him for tea in the Oval Room.

Tea that day was a great success. After a friendly, frivolous hour of light-hearted nonsense, the President invited Mrs. Galt to stay to dinner. For the first time in months, the President had assumed a cheerful attitude. She refused, out of timidity or propriety; but their friendship had begun. Dr. Grayson and Helen Bones were elated over the meeting—one might almost suspect they had planned it that way, although neither ever admitted it. A few days later the President joined Helen in a drive through the countryside with Mrs. Galt. This time when he asked her to dinner she did not refuse.

The President pressed his courtship eagerly. They went for frequent drives, accompanied by Helen; he sent her books and flowers; he invited her to quiet family dinners at the White House. From their first meeting the President talked openly of state affairs with Mrs. Galt, displaying an impetuous, even reckless, confidence in the discretion of this woman he barely knew. On May 3, two months after they met, the President proposed. Overwhelmed, Mrs. Galt could not think what to say. She could scarcely believe that this great man loved her on such short acquaintance; she was both attracted and awed by the inevitable glamour of the presidency; she was sympathetic with the President's loneliness but she felt guilty that it was less than a year since his first wife died; and she was terrified at the vast social responsibilities and attendant publicity which she would bear as First Lady. Not sure of her own feelings, Edith asked for time to think it over.

All summer the President continued his courtship, while the

family tried to preserve the fiction that Edith Galt visited the White House so frequently merely to see the female occupants. There is no place, however, so difficult to keep a secret as in the White House. The gossips were soon linking their names romantically. Edith Galt joined the Wilson family group for a vacation in New Hampshire; she sailed in the small private party aboard the presidential yacht *Mayflower* to review the Atlantic Fleet in New York harbor. Each time she was seen with the President, speculation increased.

The President was already seeking Mrs. Galt's uninformed opinions and comments on crucial state matters, although more as a sounding board for his own thoughts than as any kind of serious advice. She was the only person, for instance, with whom he discussed the critical problem of determining whom to entrust with the conduct of foreign policy under the shadow of war. As they sailed to view the Atlantic Fleet, President Wilson confided to her that Secretary of State William Jennings Bryan, a pacifist, had requested permission to resign. Bryan felt he could no longer carry out Wilson's foreign policy, which he considered as leading the nation into war. The conflict in Europe was inexorably sucking in the United States: the *Lusitania* had been torpedoed without warning by a German submarine, and sank with 1,198 aboard, 114 of whom were Americans. Wilson, although hopeful of staying out of the war, had sent Germany a warning note demanding "strict accountability," reparation, and steps to prevent a recurrence. The President asked Mrs. Galt if he should accept the resignation of the Great Commoner, a man of formidable reputation, and a three-time presidential nominee. Her reply was deplorably flip and naïve: "Take it, sir, and thank God for the chance," she said. They discussed the war for a long time, and in the end Wilson did as she had recommended (although in all likelihood he would have done the same regardless what she said). Wilson appointed Robert Lansing as the new Secretary; and as things turned out, Mrs. Galt did not like Lansing any better than Bryan.

Despite all the hours they spent together, Edith Galt still could not quite face up to the responsibilities of being First Lady. She left to spend two months with friends in New York, promising only that if Wilson were defeated the next year she might marry him. When she returned to Washington on September 3, 1915, she was promptly invited to the White House for dinner. Helen Bones and Margaret Wilson upbraided her before she could even remove her hat: the President, they reported, was tense and fretful and grumpy, and it was all her fault. He had missed her.

In her memoirs Mrs. Wilson described their reunion in flowery phrases that stressed her own maidenly primness and her sweetheart's noble motivations. However, no reliable record of their personal emotions during the courtship exists but hers, so we must accept her word for the events that transpired. Mrs. Wilson said that the President, Helen Bones, herself, and a Secret Service man took a drive along the river her first night back in Washington. The President confided that the war situation was worsening. "I doubt if anything I can in honor do will keep us out of war," he said. In view of this, he added sadly, he had no right to ask his "little girl" to share such a burden with him, out of pity. Mrs. Galt, faced with losing him, flung aside her prudery and clasped her arms about the President's neck. She vowed that she would marry him as soon as he wanted.

President Wilson's daughters and his cousin Helen heartily approved of their engagement, even though Ellen Wilson had been dead barely a year. They knew how lonely President Wilson had been, and they liked Edith Galt. The Cabinet and the Democratic leaders, however, took no such charitable view. A second marriage, they feared, would be so distasteful to the public that the President would not be re-elected. Democratic officials talked of little else but the pending engagement but no one had the courage to brave the President on the subject. Colonel House, Wilson's closest personal adviser, was especially distressed at the President's infatuation. He complained peevishly in his diary that Wilson was spending too much time on affairs of the heart and too little on affairs of state. Besides, Wilson no longer spent confidential, intimate hours revealing his every thought to House; he now talked to Mrs. Galt instead. House could sense the change. He determined to get rid of the meddlesome widow.

House, Tumulty, and Secretary of the Treasury William McAdoo, the President's son-in-law, concocted a plot to halt "this terrible business." During the campaign of 1912 it had been rumored that Wilson was conducting a torrid love affair with a Mrs. Thomas Peck; although evidence indicates this was false, it caused painful embarrassment to the President and his family. Now the three plotters determined to revive the rumor. McAdoo and House warned the President solemnly that newspaper friends had told them Mrs. Peck threatened to publish love letters from the President if he announced he would marry someone else. Wilson had, in truth, written Mrs. Peck several affectionate letters, but they were the letters of a warm friend, not of a lover. Mrs. Peck actually had no intention of publishing them; in fact, she did not even care that Wilson was engaged. (Years later, however, when the President introduced his wife to Mrs. Peck, Mrs. Wilson displayed some thinly veiled female jealousy, noting pettishly that Mrs. Peck was a "faded, rather sweet-looking woman" who talked too much and over-stayed her welcome.)

President Wilson was so upset at the thought of putting his fiancée through the possible recurrence of the rumors of the 1912 campaign that he developed a splitting headache and retreated feebly to bed. Unwilling even to see Edith he sent Dr. Grayson to release her from the engagement. When Dr. Grayson explained the problem to her, she was stunned. As before, when the President had proposed, she could not think what to do. She told Dr. Grayson only that she would write, and fled to the comfort of her library, where she sat in a chair, staring straight ahead at the walls, thinking, until dawn. Edith Galt was outraged at the possibility of having her proud name publicly besmirched. In the cloistered Victorian atmosphere of her Southern heritage, such things only happened to women of loose and questionable morals. Finally she rose to the occasion, as she had the previous time it seemed she was about to lose Wilson. She penned a thoughtful, loving note, pledging: "[I] am ready to follow the road 'where love leads' . . . I am not afraid of gossip or threat with your love as my shield . . . my dearest one, I will stand by you."

She sent off her reply, and eagerly expected a prompt response from the White House. But one, two, three days passed, agonizingly, without answer. She grew frightened, then angry, suspecting a giant insidious conspiracy within the administration to keep her from marrying the President. Several times she considered phoning the White House, but each time pride kept her from doing so. Suddenly, on the third day, Grayson appeared at her door. The President, he said, was ill; would she come? She went with him immediately, her other fears paling beside this new one. At the White House, she found the President in bed, his face drawn with pain. They were alone together for some time; and when she emerged from the bedroom it was announced that their engagement would be revealed without delay. Whatever the President's malady, he quickly recovered. Later, during their honeymoon, the new Mrs. Wilson asked whatever had become of her letter. Sheepishly, Woodrow Wilson, the visionary prophet who was to lead America to world power, admitted in boyish embarrassment that "I was afraid to open it." From a pocket he pulled her crumpled letter, still sealed.

When their engagement was announced, it created such a public stir that even the war was crowded out of the headlines for a day. The papers made a big fuss about the fact that Mrs. Galt was a ninth-generation descendant of Pocahontas, and general public reaction to the forthcoming marriage was favorable. Democrats breathed a sigh of relief and decided to be cordial to the future bride, after all.

During the two months of their engagement the President talked out every one of his government problems with his fiancée. He had a telephone line installed directly from his study to her house. He sent her inside information on international and domestic issues via special messenger, and then called her later to ask her opinion of the material. "In this way," Mrs. Wilson said, "I followed day by day every phase of the mosaic which he was shaping into a pattern of statecraft, and we continued this partnership of thought and comradeship unbroken to the last day of his life. . . . I always sat in when one or two people we knew came to discuss politics. In that way I was never a stranger to any subject, and often able in small ways to be of help."

Particularly disgruntled at Mrs. Wilson's "sit-ins" was Colonel House, who was accustomed to having the President to himself. It affronted him deeply to be forced to listen politely to the opinions of a Southern gentlewoman who had no experience in or knowledge of politics. Worse, he had to pretend the same deference toward her that the President clearly demonstrated.

House, a student of politics and history, had personally shep-
herded Wilson's rise from college professor to governor to President; there were times when his ego deluded him into believing
that he, not Wilson, really ran the government. After House's
abortive attempt to stop the marriage, Edith Wilson could hardly
be expected to like him. And she did not like the weakness in
Wilson which, she thought, his reliance on House's advice indicated. Their struggle for the President's attention was conducted
politely, behind a mask of cordiality. But within a couple years
Mrs. Wilson had so alienated the President from House that he
was no longer invited to the White House. And during the President's illness Edith refused to show him House's affectionate letters offering his help—although obviously the President could
have used the help of such a devoted, astute adviser just then.

President Woodrow Wilson and Edith Bolling Galt were
married in her home on December 10, 1915, in a simple Episcopalian ceremony. Edith wore a plain black velvet gown with
orchids at the waist. The President was eighteen days short of his
fifty-ninth birthday; his bride was forty-three years old. They
had known each other just nine months. As they set off on their
honeymoon President Wilson was observed dancing a jig the
length of their private railroad car, loudly whistling, "Oh, you
beautiful doll . . ."

On January 1, the day before she moved into the White
House as its First Lady, the new Mrs. Woodrow Wilson began a
diary. She brought with her a few pieces of her own furniture, to
make the rooms more homelike—a roll-top desk, her piano,
stacks of books, and a sewing machine. Margaret teased her
mightily about that sewing machine, but it unexpectedly came in
handy after all—during the war Mrs. Wilson and the other White
House women used it to sew pajamas and hospital shirts for the
Red Cross.

The Wilsons soon established a routine of daily activities.
They breakfasted about 8:00 A.M., then played a game of golf.
Mrs. Wilson was actually a better golfer than her husband, who
played more for exercise than enjoyment. The couple returned to
the White House by 10:00 A.M., and Mrs. Wilson walked with
her husband through the rose garden to his office. Then she returned to their living quarters to answer her own mail, stacked

on the social secretary's desk. At noon the President joined his wife for lunch and afterward she again escorted him back to his office. Afternoons as he worked she received callers. If they were not having official guests, the Wilsons took a short drive before dinner. After dinner they worked on affairs of state, played pool in the basement, read, or simply talked.

The President was increasingly disturbed about the war. He worried that the people did not realize the imminence of the danger, and he decided to embark upon a cross-country speaking tour to warn the nation of the need for preparedness. As much as he hoped for peace, he knew that public opinion had to be aroused to support a military build-up—just in case. This trip was Mrs. Wilson's first experience with the physical effort involved in politics. The President would not consider leaving her behind—in all their married years he refused to travel anywhere without her, and their longest separation was one week.

There were mixed results from that trip. It was so successful that Congress felt the public pressure for preparedness, passed a naval construction bill and ordered the training of a strengthened national army. But the trip also gave Wilson the impression that he did not need Congressional co-operation—whenever he wanted something, he could go over the head of Congress to the people. It was partly this conviction that led him to treat the Congress so high-handedly over the issue of the League of Nations. He took none of the Congressional leaders into his confidence during the formation of the peace treaty, but simply presented the Senate a complete treaty to accept or reject. The Senate, which jealously guards its prerogatives, resented the fact that it had not been consulted, and promptly demonstrated that the President is not the only instrument of "the people's will."

In March the Wilsons were distracted from their war worries by a raid in New Mexico boldly conducted by Pancho Villa, the Mexican bandit. Seventeen Americans were killed. The United States teetered on the brink of war with Mexico as Wilson dispatched the National Guard to the border. While Wilson labored to work out a peace formula with Mexico, Mrs. Wilson discovered how much he relied upon the comfort of wifely adoration in times of serious mental stress. She devoted herself to his welfare. Dr. Grayson warned her that physical exercise was necessary to relieve the President's agonizing tenseness under strain. So Mrs. Wilson, who suffered herself from frequent neuralgic headaches, insisted gaily that they keep up their golf, rides, and yachting weekends. Edith Benham, her social secretary, said, "She used all sorts of persuasions and ruses to make him exercise and get away from his problems."

Edith Wilson was completely upset by the rigors of campaigning during the President's fight for re-election in 1916, but she sat on the platform for every speech and traveled with the President to each rally. When she heard his first political speech, her romantic sensibilities cringed. "I like the other kind so much better," she told him. Campaign headquarters was a rented summer home at Spring Lake, New Jersey, which was a huge gingerbread Victorian monstrosity full of dusty potted palms, ornate statuettes, and strange beaded objects. It is typical of Mrs. Wilson that she ordered a marble statue of a nude woman, which stood unblushingly in the front hall, draped "as much as possible." Wilson campaigned on the record of his New Freedom programs. He had established the Federal Reserve System, which set up the first uniform banking code in the United States; he set up tariff reforms; he created the Federal Trade Commission to curb unfair competition; he achieved an eight-hour day for railroad workers. But the nation was concerned only about war—and the potent argument of the campaign was the slogan "he kept us out of war."

Mrs. Wilson's favorite moments during the campaign came when she sat quietly in a corner of the room while Wilson answered mail with his secretary, Charley Sweem. "As Mr. Wilson spoke and Sweem wrote, a panorama of world affairs passed before me," she recalled. As each letter was finished, she placed it in front of Wilson for his signature, blotting it as she slipped the next letter in place. Once the President looked up, smiled, and sighed, "When you are here work seems like play."

One issue which Wilson tried heartily to avoid was woman's suffrage. But the suffragettes gave him no peace; for years they picketed the White House; they formed clubs; they demanded the right to vote in such loud voices that the wise politician dared not ignore them. Wilson capitulated to their pressure, although he had little sympathy for their cause. For her part, Mrs. Wilson found the conduct of the suffragettes disgraceful. She called them "disgusting creatures" and "detestable suffragettes." She wrote in her diary that "the only speech of my Precious One that I ever failed to enjoy" was delivered at a suffragette meeting. "I hated the subject so it was acute agony. I had orchids from the suffragettes." Female independence, and traditional male rights such as voting, did not fit into her concept of a Southern lady's proper behavior.

Orchids were rapidly becoming the First Lady's trademark. It was her favorite corsage, for orchids brought out the violet color of her eyes. All her life she preferred wearing one large orchid rather than jewelry, and rarely used necklaces or pins.

As the campaign ended, both Wilsons felt that they had surely lost. On election night, November 7, 1916, the Wilsons ate a quiet dinner in the family home at Princeton, and played a dispirited game of "twenty questions" with relatives. About midnight, convinced that Charles Evans Hughes was the new President, Wilson took a glass of milk and climbed the stairs sadly to bed. His wife followed him; she sat on his bed, holding his hand, talking pseudo-cheerfully about all the things they could do now they were free, until he finally fell asleep. The election was so close that it was three days before Wilson's re-election was assured. When they returned, triumphant, to the White House, Mrs. Wilson felt that the historic mansion "looked so big and aristocratic."

Now Wilson was free to turn his thoughts to one more last great effort to end the war in Europe. He called Ambassador Thomas Page from London and Ambassador James Gerard from Berlin for consultations. Gerard was struck by the fact that "Mrs. Wilson was present . . . and at times asked pertinent questions showing her deep knowledge of foreign affairs." Wilson began to work on a note to all the belligerents, offering to meditate a just peace and proposing an association of nations in which the United States would join. As he labored, he called upon his wife for comments and reassurance. She noted in her dairy: "I helped Woodrow in the study until nearly twelve. He was writing what he says may prove the greatest piece of work of his life."

President Wilson labored over his note for two weeks, and it was indeed a daring proposal. For the first time an American President was thrusting his country into international leadership; since the collapse of the Greek Empire, world leadership had rested squarely in Europe. And since the time of George Washington, America's firm policy had been to avoid entanglements with other countries. The world, however, was not ready for such revolutionary concepts; everywhere Wilson's note was misunderstood and reviled. His last great effort failed.

On December 18, his first wedding anniversary, Wilson sent off his finished note. Then, at dawn, he tiptoed into his wife's room to present her with his anniversary gift, a black opal and diamond pendant. They then went off gaily for a round of winter golf; that evening they went to the theater. Wilson the President always found time to be Wilson the husband.

Wilson had kept the United States out of the war as long as he honorably could—too long, some historians have charged in retrospect. "I'd do anything else in the world rather than head a great military machine," he said wearily. But, in the end, the choice was not Wilson's; it was Germany's. A nation-wide plot of espionage and sabotage conducted secretly from the German Embassy was discovered and diplomatic relations with Germany were broken off; the German government announced unrestricted submarine warfare and four American unarmed ships were torpedoed. Wilson could wait no longer.

On the night of March 31, not quite a month after his second inauguration, Wilson took his typewriter out on the south portico, where he could feel the soft spring breezes, and began to compose a message to a special session of Congress called for Monday, April 2. Mrs. Wilson sat upstairs, reading, in the Oval Room, listening to the lonely sound of the typewriter keys tapping. Once she went to the kitchen, fixed him milk and crackers, carried the tray to him, and left without a word. She waited up for him, knowing that the presence of the lighted window above him provided some small measure of comfort. On Sunday, Wilson finished his dismal task. Monday morning, before the speech, his wife insisted upon a round of golf to ease the tension. She rode with him to Congress and sat in the gallery, full of pride and patriotism as he called for a war "to make the world safe for democracy." Congress met his call to war with a thundering ovation. On the way back to the White House, the Wilsons sat in silence, tightly holding hands. Tumulty met them in the study, and noticed immediately the President's extreme depression and weariness. Tumulty watched in amazement as the President "let his head fall down on his big, old desk and sobbed like a child." A few days later, April 6, the President signed the formal declaration of war with a small gold pen he had once given his wife.

Wilson kept the conduct of the war, and the whole United States foreign policy, tightly in his own hands. Secretary of State Robert Lansing was little more than an errand boy; Mrs. Wilson called him "that clerk." Lansing did not even know the secret code with which the President communicated with his emissaries abroad. In Washington, only the President, Mrs. Wilson, and Colonel House knew the code. Wilson dispatched House on a special fact-finding tour of the war front. Mrs. Wilson decoded every one of House's gloomy, despairing messages from Europe, and coded the President's longhand replies. The decoding task became one of her special wartime duties, and it gave her a complete, detailed picture of the conduct of the war.

Now the Wilsons found the days too short to accomplish everything. They arose at 5:00 A.M. instead of 8:00 A.M. They closed the White House grounds to the public and stopped all entertaining. When the President worked on problems she could not share, Mrs. Wilson sat near him, knitting for the soldiers. She joined a Red Cross canteen, and sometimes brought the President with her to the train station to greet the doughboys embarking for French battlefields. She passed out gum and cigarettes to the soldiers, most of whom were unaware of her identity. She was present at all the President's war councils. She adamantly dragged the President out for relaxing excursions in the car or for horseback riding (they no longer could afford the time for golf). The First Lady carefully observed at the White House all the meatless, wheatless, gasless, and heatless days called for by the government to relieve national shortages. She bought a flock of sheep to crop the White House lawn, and had their wool auctioned off for the benefit of the Red Cross. It netted approximately $100,000. A war garden was added to the White House grounds.

Mrs. Wilson also took upon herself the task of naming American ships—88 taken from Germany and all the new ones being built. This proved to be more difficult than she had anticipated, for every time she thought up a good name, she'd check in Lloyd's

Register and find it already in use. Disgusted, she finally sent to the Library of Congress for an Indian dictionary and gave all the ships Indian names.

In December of 1917 Colonel House returned from Europe, full of discouraging information about the progress of the war. Mrs. Wilson sat in the study with her husband, House, and Chief of Staff Tasker Bliss while the trio revised American strategy in light of the new information. "Fascinating talk," she reported.

In January, President Wilson outlined his Fourteen Points and pledged these would be the basis of any peace treaty to which the United States was a party. He specified that Germany should not be annexed, that Poland be liberated, that true freedom of the seas be assured, and that "a general association of nations" be formed to provide "mutual guarantees of political independence and territorial integrity to great and small states alike." All winter the war dragged on; but by late summer the tide had turned. More than two million United States soldiers were in France; the German attacks had been stopped; the Allies were now on the attack. Tentative peace feelers were sent out by Germany, but there seemed to be an interminable series of delays. On Sunday, November 10, Mrs. Wilson spent the evening after dinner translating a long coded note from French leader Clemenceau. At 1:00 A.M. she finished and joined the President in the study. At 3:00 A.M., as they were still talking, the news came of the armistice. "We just stood there dumbly, knowing the news was true, but unable to feel it," Mrs. Wilson recalled.

The war was won, but there was no rest for the President. He had already begun to lose the peace. Just a few days before, the Democrats had lost both House and Senate in the midterm Congressional elections. The President himself was partially responsible for his party's defeat. During the war he had said "politics is adjourned," and Republicans had given him their full cooperation. But in October, on the brink of the war victory, Wilson appealed to voters to keep the Democrats in control of Congress. Republicans were indignant, and apparently the American people were too. Wilson had been warned by several advisers, including his wife, about the hazards of injecting partisanship into the war effort and the subsequent problems of peace. Wilson refused to listen to them. "That message was the greatest mistake Woodrow ever made," Mrs. Wilson said later. The turnover of majority control in the Congress spelled defeat for Wilson's League, partially because it promoted Wilson's bitter enemy, Senator Henry Cabot Lodge, to the chairmanship of the Foreign Relations Committee—the select group which would first consider any negotiated peace treaty. The hatred between Lodge and Wilson was blinding and deep-rooted; Mrs. Wilson called the senator "that stinking Lodge," very strong language for her ladylike tongue.

Wilson felt that he should attend the peace conference in Paris, although it shattered all precedents for an American President to leave the country for such a prolonged period. But Wilson knew that the European statesmen who had watched German troops ravage their villages and towns were concerned more with revenge than with the justice Wilson sought in his Fourteen Points: if the Points were to be the basis of the treaty, Wilson would have to fight for them himself. Wilson's concept of "peace without vengeance" and "self-determination for the little peoples" was not exactly what the European politicians, with their eyes on the conquered spoils, had in mind. One newspaperman said that Wilson at the peace conference was "like a virgin trapped in a brothel, calling sturdily for a glass of lemonade."

Mrs. Wilson, of course, sailed for Europe with the President. They spent most of the cruise in their suite, being briefed by experts and discussing the problems ahead. The other commissioners, including Secretary Lansing, complained that Wilson never spoke to them, and did not even bother to tell them what he intended to ask at the conference. The President was so absorbed in his wife's company, in fact, that Edith Benham, her social secretary, wrote in her diary during the cruise: "The more I am with the Wilsons, the more I am struck by their unrivaled home life. I never dreamed such sweetness and love could be. . . . It is very beautiful to see his face light up and brighten at the very sight of her, and to see her turn to him for everything, though she is a woman of a lot of spirit."

That woman of spirit discovered she had long, dreary hours with nothing to occupy herself seriously during the conference, which opened on January 18. The President was very busy: mornings he received callers and reports from his staff; afternoons he met with delegates, eventually in special sessions with just the Big Four; and evenings he chaired the commission set up to propose a covenant for a League of Nations. Mrs. Wilson did not have any particular interests of her own, outside of being her husband's companion. So she filled up her days by shopping at the Paris couturiers, visiting hospitals and factories. She always made a careful point of being home by the time Wilson returned, weary and frustrated, from the long tiresome sessions. The President was overworking; he grew thin and his hair went from gray to white. His wife's concern over his health grew, but she could do little else but try to get him to relax when with her and take a brief drive once in a while. The President was battling with all his strength to keep the League covenant an integral part of the treaty; if it were not included, he feared it would never be adopted at all.

Finally the President was ready to read his draft of the covenant to the conference. Mrs. Wilson begged to be allowed to attend, although the strict rule was "no women allowed." The President always gained strength from her presence in the audience, and so he arranged that she be smuggled into a small antechamber hidden by red brocade curtains. There she listened, sneaking a careful look from time to time through the curtains, "hot but happy." The delegates were swept away by the force of Wilson's eloquent, audacious vision of a world body to improve life for all nations—and unanimously approved the covenant. Mrs. Wilson wrote in her diary: "As he stood there, slender, calm and powerful in argument, I seemed to see the people of all depressed countries—men, women and little children—crowding round and waiting for his words."

Wilson, after this triumph, returned briefly to the United States. He stayed just long enough to receive a statement from Senator Lodge, co-signed by thirty-seven senators—more than the one-third of the membership needed to defeat ratification—warning they would not vote to approve the covenant in its present form. Wilson, blinded by his personal fury at Lodge and the shining inspiration of his belief in the rightness of his cause, flung his challenge back at the Senate: he would not change a line of the covenant and the people would force the Senate to accept it anyway.

Not only the United States Senate had reservations about the loss of sovereignty implicit in a League of Nations. Back in Paris, Wilson found that without his leadership the Allies had maneuvered to get the covenant out of the treaty and had inserted harsh reparation clauses. Edith blamed Colonel House, who had been left in charge, for compromising away all that Wilson had sought to achieve, but this was hardly fair, for poor Colonel House had been left with no authority to do much of anything except keep conversations going in the President's absence. Wilson had to do everything all over again, for the conference had all but written off the League. He grew weak from overwork, and fell ill with influenza. Over his wife's protests, he continued the Big Four discussions at his bedside. After four months the treaty was finally finished; Wilson had compromised on harsh reparation provisions in order to retain his beloved League.

Miss Benham, who watched the Wilsons during all this, wrote in her diary: "Probably no one will realize fully . . . how much Mrs. Wilson has done to make it [the President's work] possible. She is the most wonderful wife in the world to a man who needs love and care more than any I have ever seen. Without it, I don't believe he could live."

The peace treaty was signed at Versailles on June 28, 1919. That morning the President gave his wife a corsage of orchids and a beaded bag of gray and blue, which he had ordered made to match her gown. He also gave her a red rosebud, with the comment, "This is the nearest I can get to making it our American red, white and blue." Mrs. Wilson went with him to Versailles, where she sat on the sidelines as he and the other powers signed the treaty. That very night they left Paris for home; and as the train pulled out of the station, the Wilsons stood wearily at the window, watching the blurry countryside go by. "Well, little girl, it is finished. And as no one seems satisfied, it makes me hope that we have made a just peace. . . ." the President sighed.

The Wilsons were glad to be back at the White House, the only home they had known together. She wrote: "How good to be surrounded once more by the simple dignity of the White House, spick and span with cool linen on the chairs and flowers everywhere."

Still there was no rest for the weary Wilson. The Senate, with its Republican majority, was almost evenly divided on the issue of the treaty and its provision for the League. A great number of senators, reflecting the suspicions of the countryside, did not like the clause of the covenant which committed member nations to come to the defense of each other in case of outside aggression. The people did not want to be forced into another European war. The President, however, considered this offending clause to be the most important single part of the covenant. And so once again he decided he must take his case to the people; he must persuade them of its importance. Mrs. Wilson and Dr. Grayson, who worried about his frail and fatigued condition, tried desparately to dissuade him. But the President insisted the cause was greater than his health; he would make a nation-wide whistlestop campaign. "It may kill you," Grayson warned.

Long before he became the White House occupant, Woodrow Wilson had once written: "Men of ordinary physique and discretion cannot be Presidents and live, if the strain cannot be somehow relieved." There seemed to be no way to relieve the strain on Wilson himself; the task he had set was too far-reaching and too difficult. On September 3, 1919, the presidential train left Washington. Mrs. Wilson, aboard, wrote: "Dr. Grayson's disregarded warnings against attempting the tour haunted my sleep. . . ." The President delivered forty speeches, most of them an hour long; traveled eight thousand miles, took part in a dozen parades, shook thousands of hands, attended luncheons, dinners, and receptions for twenty-two days through the hot midlands of a sleepy America already bored with the whole idea of the League. A reporter in Oregon, who did not know that by now the President had splitting headaches, insomnia, and persistent asthma, recorded: "The President can truly say that Mrs. Wilson sustains him. As Mr. Wilson, standing in his auto, bowed right and left, waving his brown fedora in answer to the cheering thousands, she constantly held her hand against his back, supporting him against the possibility of a fall."

Mrs. Wilson tried daily to persuade the President to stop and rest, but he drove himself onward in a blur of heat and exhaustion. On the night of September 25, the train rattled through the silent prairies toward Wichita, Kansas. The President knocked on his wife's adjoining door about midnight. "Can you come to me,

Edith? I'm terribly sick," he pleaded in a weak voice. All night she sat by his bed, while he tossed feverishly and could not sleep. In the morning light she could see that the left side of his face was drawn up unnaturally and was unusually deep-lined. Still the President wanted to continue the tour; so she bluntly, sadly, told him that the public must not see him as he was. Weeping, he gave in. The tour was abruptly canceled, the tracks cleared, and the train sped back to Washington as mournful, mysterious, and silent as a funeral cortege. All the way, Mrs. Wilson sat beside him, trying miserably to keep him company with cheerful small talk. The public was not told what had happened, only that the President had a "digestive upset."

The President was barely back in the White House when he suffered the stroke which took away the use of his left side. The silence which settled upon the White House then remained, to more or less degree, even through the 1920 Democratic convention. One of the presidential candidates was William McAdoo, and everybody thought that surely the President would speak out in support of his son-in-law. But Wilson remained silent, and neutral; some said it was because Mrs. Wilson had not forgiven McAdoo for his part in the plot to prevent their marriage. After forty-five ballots, James Cox and Franklin D. Roosevelt were nominated to carry the Democratic banner in the 1920 campaign.

Wilson bequeathed his battle for the League to Cox, and hoped that a sweeping Democratic victory would put his party in control of Congress and assure approval of his League at last. Now that the reign was ending, life was relaxed in the White House. The President worked in the mornings, lunched, napped, and took drives with his wife. In the evenings they watched movies on a screen in the East Room, played solitaire, or Mrs. Wilson read to the President. He depended upon her for everything, and they were seldom apart more than a few minutes. Her only interest was to keep him happy. "I read innumerable books to Woodrow—everything from Bagehot to detective stories. I hate detective stories," she recalled. They spent hours planning the house to which they would retire, selecting one not far from the White House.

The Wilsons decided to live out their retirement in the capital so that the President could be near the Library of Congress to do research on a book he planned. All that was ever written of it, however, is the dedication, which Mrs. Wilson included in her memoirs. It reads: "To EBW—who has shown me the full meaning of life. Her heart is not only true but wise; her thoughts are not only free but touched with vision . . . her unconscious interpretation of faith and duty makes all the way clear; her power to comprehend makes work and thought alike easier and more near to what it seeks."

When Cox was defeated, Wilson felt the final blow to his spirits; the people had not been behind him after all. They had chosen Warren Harding, and isolationism.

The Wilsons moved into their new home on S Street, after Harding's inauguration. They lived quietly, in near-seclusion. Mrs. Wilson arranged their furniture as nearly as it had been in the White House as she could manage; she even ordered a replica made of the giant Lincoln bed in which Wilson had slept during the White House years. But the President, despite his wife's unfailing care, never regained full health. On February 3, 1924, after three years of retirement and three days of semi-consciousness, Wilson died. Mrs. Wilson had held his hand almost constantly those final days—"he would lift his hand and take mine," she murmured sadly.

The widow did not make a public appearance for over a year after the funeral. But gradually her energetic spirits began to revive. She traveled: in the twenties and thirties she went to Europe seven times, once around the world, and twice to Japan. Each trip she attended a session of the League of Nations. She made scattered public appearances, but only at events in connection with Wilson's memory or the causes in which he believed. She answered volumes of mail: every query about the President, no matter how trivial, received a polite reply. She took an active part, as a director, in the Woodrow Wilson Foundation to promote international co-operation. She was active in making the Manse at Staunton, Virginia, Wilson's birthplace, a national shrine. At the age of eighty-five, she served as a member of the Woodrow Wilson Centennial Commission.

Edith Wilson went out socially very little. She was seen in Washington social circles so rarely in her later years that residents forgot she was still alive. She appeared at the Democratic conventions of 1928 and 1932 with friends and even campaigned a bit for Roosevelt in 1932. Her last public appearance was at President Kennedy's inauguration in 1961, although a blizzard the night before and bitter cold weather kept many a less hardy soul away.

On December 28, 1961, Edith Wilson died, at the age of 89. Her home, where Wilson had spent his last years, was left to the National Trust for Historic Preservation to become a museum.

Florence Kling
HARDING

❀ ❀

Thirty-four men occupied the White House between the terms of President George Washington and President John F. Kennedy. Of them all, only one totally and miserably failed the trust of the American people.

The presidency is the master force for shaping public policy; and as Franklin D. Roosevelt put it, "pre-eminently a place of moral leadership." Woodrow Wilson noted that "the President is at liberty, both in law and conscience, to be as big a man as he can."

Warren Gamaliel Harding, truly the tragic manikin of fate, was a little man all his life, and he did not know how to grow up to the demands of the presidency. His inability to cope with the power and responsibilities of the White House resulted in incredible shame and corruption. Harding was, by historians' agreement, our worst President.

Harding himself had grave doubts that he was suited for the presidency. Possessed of a kind heart, little courage, and less intelligence, he desired only to be popular. He did not want the presidency; but unhappily there were others who wanted it for him. On the day of his election Florence Kling Harding turned to her husband and boasted, "Well, Warren Harding, I have got you the presidency; what are you going to do with it?"

The new President-elect, who hadn't the vaguest notion what to do with it, murmured prophetically, "May God help me, for I need it."

Harding had displayed rare personal conviction against running for the Republican nomination in 1920. He was then the Senator from Ohio, and popular enough to stay in the Senate the rest of his life without much effort. Ohio's political boss, Harry Daugherty, however, had greater ambitions. He tried to persuade Harding to jump into "the big circus," but Harding, in a profane burst of temper, threw him out of his Senate office. Then Daugherty went to Florence Harding, for, he recorded, "I knew I would have to cultivate her to carry out my plans for the advancement of her husband." Mrs. Harding wasn't difficult to cultivate, for she liked the idea of being First Lady. She set to work on her amiable husband, who was long accustomed to her sharp-tongued domination. As always before, Harding gave in; he had such a reluctance to face unpleasantness that he was not used to exerting his own will. "The two of us," Daugherty later recalled, "backed him against the wall and made him stick."

To the American public in 1921, it seemed as though the handsome Hardings, fresh from Main Street in Marion, Ohio, were just what the country needed. Harding promised the nation a return to "normalcy" after the turbulence of a world war, and his smiling wife assured everyone they were just "plain folks." The people, after twenty years of exhortation from leaders with burning convictions for reforming life in the name of great causes, were tired. They wanted a rest.

Harding at fifty-five "looked" the part of a President. His sensitive mouth, dark olive skin, black hair, well-chiseled, expressive features fairly reeked of sincerity. He had a clear, silvery voice that could inspire the multitude even when it uttered the most banal of platitudes. (And in the days before loudspeakers that was doubly important.)

And Mrs. Harding, who was always at his side, had such a charming manner. She seemed inexhaustible, although she was five years older than Harding. She was friendly, vivacious, handsomely dressed, and she had kept her figure. There were those who felt she was a little too mechanically marceled, too heavily lipsticked and rouged, and too meticulously tailored. But kinder souls found in her sturdy features the reflection of a typically devoted Midwestern housewife, and they felt akin to her.

On inauguration night Mrs. Harding threw everything wide open. During the war years and the illness of President Wilson, the White House gates had been closed and guards posted at the entrances. But Mrs. Harding welcomed the crowd of sightseers who came to peer at the President's house once again, snapping pictures of each other posing on the steps of the north portico, leaning against the pillars, and strolling along the walks and driveways. She even pulled up the window shades and smiled at the curious faces which pressed against the panes. "It's their White House," she said. "Let them look in if they want to."

With the Hardings installed, the White House throbbed again with a gay social life. The new President and his wife appeared frequently at public events, waving and smiling. The First Lady, particularly, was generous with her time, lending her name and august presence to a variety of good works and charitable causes. She regularly visited welfare institutions, and became a favorite of the injured and ill soldiers at Walter Reed Hospital. Once she held a garden party for veterans on the White House lawn, and insisted upon wearing a dilapidated old hat with her new party dress: "The boys are accustomed to it, and as soon as they see it, they know where I am," she explained.

Florence Harding felt deeply the symbolic importance of her position as First Lady, and she was tireless in her contacts with "the people," which she considered one of her most vital duties. Frequently she slipped downstairs while visitors were touring the public first-floor rooms of the mansion, introduced herself, and walked the delighted crowd through the rooms to point out objects of interest. She always insisted on purchasing and using

American-made articles, and always wore American-tailored dresses. She never sagged in public, although she had a recurrent kidney ailment and was not always feeling well. Once, at a White House New Year's reception, a friend observed that the First Lady had stood perfectly still, shaking hands, for over two hours, and offered sympathy. "Oh, now," the First Lady said and laughed, "my hand is good for two hours yet." That afternoon she shook 6,756 hands, and her own was swollen for days afterward.

It soon became common gossip, however, that the presidency meant far more to Mrs. Harding than it did to Mr. Harding. He continued to behave in the White House the way he had always behaved; that is to say, he did nothing of great importance. He tried piteously to pretend that he was not the President. He frequently surprised Washington hostesses and guests by showing up at private parties unannounced, pleading, "Forget I am President. Just relax." He played poker regularly with his cronies, generally at stag affairs that lasted until dawn. His friends included a number of men who frequented a mysterious "little green house" on K Street, the hangout of a jolly collection of assorted blackmailers, money-grabbers, and crooks called "the Ohio gang." Strange things were reported as going on there, and no decent lady dared pass the house alone at night. Sometimes Mrs. Harding went to the poker games, where she was permitted to mix the drinks. The Hardings kept a full supply of liquor in their private quarters, blithely ignoring the prohibition law. Because of the law, however, they never served liquor or wine at official White House dinners.

Harding tried to avoid the fuss and feathers of the presidency just as he tried to avoid its duties. He insisted, for instance, on continuing his good Ohio practice of picking his teeth after every meal. The first time he called for toothpicks on the White House table, the status-conscious servants nearly went into shock. "That's being too much a man of the people," the butler grumbled. But the toothpicks stayed.

"I am a man of limited talents, from a small town . . . oftentimes, as I sit here, I don't seem to grasp that I am President," he confessed.

But on the other hand—"Mrs. Harding wants to be the drum major in every band that passes," the President sighed. In truth, she was not a bit modest. She often boasted that she had always known "what was best for Warren" and that without her, he would not be President. The President encouraged her arrogance by showing her a great deal of deference in public. He called her "the Duchess," as did most of his old Ohio cronies. At public functions, when asked to do something, he invariably replied, "I'll have to check with the Duchess." The Duchess watched over him like a fiercely possessive mother, and it was said that in public her eyes seldom left his handsome face. She dominated him, drove him, and in her own way loved him. She would condone anything that would promote her husband's career. She once told an interviewer, "I have only one real hobby —it's my husband." She daily wore around her neck a diamond sunburst on a ribbon, which was Harding's inauguration present to her.

Mrs. Harding meddled constantly in official White House business. She did not like to let the President out of her sight, it seemed. She rewrote part of his inaugural address. She was consulted on the major federal appointments: it was she, not the President, who insisted that Charles Forbes, a member of the Ohio gang, be appointed Chief of the Veterans Administration. Forbes was eventually charged with stealing and wasting millions appropriated for crippled or sick veterans, and was sent to prison for bribery and conspiracy. As a Christmas present their first year in the White House, Harding let her choose which of the convicts in penitentiaries should be given holiday pardons. An acquaintance later observed, "He allowed her great latitude in this, as in other official matters."

Mrs. Harding was soon well informed on current governmental affairs. She sat in on most White House conferences, regardless of their level. An intuitive, shrewd woman, she must have been disturbed at Harding's continued inability to grasp his job; she told friends that the President always did well when he followed her advice and poorly when he did not. There is no evidence that Harding ever possessed much understanding of big political issues and principles; he simply did what other people told him. His wife, however, was opinionated and positive, and seemed to understand politics better than her husband. For instance, one of Harding's basic philosophies was a belief in isolationism and a hatred for the League of Nations and the visionary "one world" concept it represented. In the Senate, Harding had been part of what President Wilson called "a small group of willful men" who killed Wilson's hope that the United States would join the League. Yet his comprehension of what he had done was so slight that during the campaign, while stumping on an isolationist platform, he declared that "an association of nations" was necessary. Mrs. Harding was at least consistent in her political philosophy and alert to the significance of each presidential utterance.

Harry Daugherty, who had been appointed Attorney General by the grateful Hardings, recalled in his autobiography that one night he was hastily summoned to the White House. Daugherty wrote: "The President and Mrs. Harding were waiting for me in the library. There was an air of restraint between them. I caught it instantly. I thought at first it might have been a little domestic spat over something trivial, but changed my mind the moment Harding spoke: 'I want to read to you the message I'm going to deliver tomorrow.' Mrs. Harding's face was still flushed and the President's was set in unusually stern lines. She took a seat on a long stool before us, and I sat in my usual chair beside his desk. The President read in even tones and when he reached a paragraph relating to the League of Nations, I stiffened in my chair and saw Mrs. Harding smile as I said:

"Wait a minute, Mr. President, are you saying there exactly what you intended?"

" 'Certainly,' he said.

" 'Why,' I interrupted, 'my interpretation of that would head us straight into the League of Nations, destroy the policy of your party, and ignore the pledge of the last election.'

"Mrs. Harding sat bolt upright, her eyes flashing. 'Exactly what I've been telling him.' "

Daugherty reported that the argument went on until midnight, with the President still stubbornly unwilling to agree to a substitute paragraph. At midnight Secretary John Weeks came by, was read the speech, and agreed with Daugherty and Florence. But at 2:00 A.M. the conference broke up with the President's message unchanged. The next day Daugherty and Weeks rode to the Capitol together to hear what they believed would be a fatal address. As the President began to speak, Weeks sighed, "Good-bye, Washington. I'll go back to Boston beans and good old codfish cakes."

Then Harding reached the key paragraph, and as he read, Weeks whispered, "Glory to God. We're saved. He's reading the substitute word for word."

Daugherty was grinning. "A wise little woman!" he murmured.

Mrs. Harding based part of her aggressiveness on a smug, childlike belief that she was a special woman of destiny. She was very superstitious, with a particular weakness for fortune tellers. And, to hear her tell it, she had had some very remarkable experiences with them. While still a senator's wife, she visited a "Madam Marcia" with her close friend Evalyn Walsh McLean, the fabulously wealthy owner of the Hope diamond. Mrs. Harding did not identify herself to the fortune teller, but called herself a "President-maker" and a "President-ruler." She asked the fortune teller to cast the future for a man born on November 2, 1865, at 2:00 P.M. The "madam" pretended not to recognize her visitor, but she was later quoted in an article in a way that indicated she easily figured out who "President-maker" was. "Madam Marcia" told Mrs. Harding that the man was a statesman and would become President of the United States. She added, however, that he would not live to complete his term. Then, mercilessly, "Madam Marcia" threw in an analysis of the man: "sympathetic, kindly, intuitive, free of promises and trustful of friends, enthusiastic, impulsive, perplexed over financial affairs. Many clandestine love affairs; inclined to recurrent moods of melancholia."

There is some indication that the "clandestine love affairs" part, at least, was reasonably accurate. Harding's name was linked in scandalous gossip with a variety of women throughout his life. He was generally known as a "ladies man," with all the title implies. This, apparently, was the one aspect of Harding's life which his wife could not control. The servants gossiped that she tried to keep her husband at home evenings, but was not very successful. One of the servants reported seeing her leaning over the balcony, purple with rage, shouting, "You are not leaving this house tonight!" Harding, the story goes, didn't even look up at her as he stalked out.

And there was the case of Miss Nan Britton. Miss Britton had the audacity to write a book entitled *The President's Daughter*, contending that President Harding sired her illegitimate child. She claimed that she worked for Harding's newspaper while a teen-ager, and after he was elected senator she wrote to ask help in finding a job. They agreed to meet in a hotel lobby in New York —and finished their conversation in his room, where they were more comfortable, and where they met frequently thereafter. According to Miss Britton, after the first meeting "he tucked thirty dollars in my brand-new silk stocking and was sorry he had no more that time to give me."

Miss Britton chronicled secret meetings that lasted from 1916 until Harding's death. She made no complaint about this arrangement; Harding, she said, kept her comfortably enough. Their daughter, she charged, was born on October 22, 1919.

The story caused a sensation, of course, and has become such a part of the tragic Harding story that it cannot fairly be ignored. There is some indication that Harding did, indeed, know Miss Britton rather well—but there is considerable doubt about her allegation. In the first place, Miss Britton produced not one document to substantiate her story of the love affair: not even a faded love letter. Second, she claimed in the book that the President never saw his child, although he continued to meet her after the child's birth. Given Harding's gentle, harmless nature and his apparent love for children and dogs, it seems incredible that he would not once in four years want to take a look at his only child. Third, the President and Mrs. Harding had no children of their own, although she had a son by a previous marriage. Mrs. Harding reportedly put the blame for their childless state on Harding. Fourth, Miss Britton sued Harding's estate for support of her child, but a jury returned a verdict against her. And fifth, Richard Wrightman, the ghost writer of her book, was subsequently sued for divorce by his wife for his association with Miss Britton.

Whatever his weaknesses, Harding was at least a more likeable personality than his strong-willed wife, who was subject to temper tantrums and could be downright vindictive. If the First

Lady took a dislike to someone, that hapless individual soon knew it. For example, Mrs. Harding never warmed to the taciturn Vice-President Calvin Coolidge and his pretty wife. The Vice-President's reserved manner annoyed her. When a bill was proposed in Congress to buy a fine residence for a permanent Vice-President's house, Mrs. Harding whipped into action. She personally put pressure on every politician who had cause to be wary of, or grateful for, her influence over her husband, and she got the bill killed. Exultant, she said, "I just couldn't have people like those Coolidges living in that beautiful house."

Mrs. Harding carried her grudges forever. She wrote down in a little red book the names of people she felt had "snubbed" her. Alice Longworth, former President Theodore Roosevelt's daughter, said in her memoirs that Mrs. Harding confided to her that she kept this record because "these people were to realize that she was aware of their behavior."

Mrs. Longworth, whose husband Nicholas, Speaker of the House, was also from Ohio, saw the Hardings frequently while he was still a senator, mostly to play poker. "Harding was not a bad man. He was just a slob," she said. As for his wife: "She was a nervous, rather excitable woman whose voice easily became a little high-pitched, strident." She added that in retrospect it seemed odd to have seen so much of people whom she had never liked.

Mrs. Harding's predecessor, First Lady Edith Galt Wilson, was not an admirer either. She invited Mrs. Harding, according to custom, to tea the day before Harding's inauguration. She reported she was greatly annoyed, first because Mrs. Harding was so gauche as to ask if she could bring along a friend (which Mrs. Wilson politely refused); second, because Mrs. Harding talked too much; and third, because Mrs. Harding took one look at the housekeeper and bluntly announced she would no longer be needed. (Mrs. Harding, incidentally, later changed her mind, and the housekeeper stayed.) Mrs. Wilson also thought that Mrs. Harding sat too stiffly in her chair and that her husband slouched too much.

In fairness to Mrs. Harding, however, it must be pointed out that both Mrs. Longworth and Mrs. Wilson were inclined to be very aristocratic. And Florence Harding remained always as she had presented herself during the campaign: just "plain folks." She never acquired much sophistication, and felt more at home with "the Ohio gang" than with the social elite who came to her parties.

The Hardings seemed to love a good time, and gave many parties. Publicly they were gregarious. They surrounded themselves with other people and rarely dined alone. But the tensions began to build up after their first year in the White House. Florence Harding strove for perfection in everything she did, to make up for her husband's laxity. She worried about aging, since she was older than her husband, and had a specialist visit the White House every day to give her a facial. She drove herself to appear gay even when she did not feel well. She nagged Harding relentlessly, trying to get him to apply himself to business. They quarreled so much that it became a matter of common gossip throughout Washington. Mrs. Harding complained piteously to a White House maid that her husband was "ungrateful" for all she had done for him, and acted as if he thought he didn't need her any more. An observer recorded that she was "at all times jealous and most times suspicious" of Harding.

One day the President accidentally met a friend taking a short cut across the rear White House lawn. Harding, in a melancholy mood, confided that his life had been unhappy and empty. "And he cried," the dismayed friend recalled. Charles Forbes was invited to share the Hardings' first Christmas in the White House, but when he arrived he was greeted with a scowl. "This is a hell of a Christmas," Harding growled at him. "What is the matter?" asked the startled Forbes. "Everything's the matter," the President complained, stalking away. The White House doctor, Charles Sawyer, who had also been invited for Christmas dinner, signaled to Forbes behind the President's back. "They had a hell of a row this morning," Sawyer muttered under his breath, warning Forbes to be extra charming at dinner.

The storm clouds were gathering. The nation was still content with its good-looking First Family; but within the administration growing rumors about corruption and misdeeds were too persistent to be dismissed as fantasy. Mrs. Harding, who was too alert not to have heard the rumors, grew increasingly jittery. She was so upset she asked for a Secret Service agent to be assigned to her, although no agent had ever before guarded a First Lady. She kept him sitting in the hall outside her bedroom door at night to protect her, although it was never clear from what. The President suffered frequent spells of depression, and he seemed unable to relax. He could not fall asleep except in a half-sitting position.

The combined strain of her deteriorating relationship with her husband, her fears that his weakness in the presidency might be discovered, and her uneasiness over the persistent suspicion that their Ohio gang friends were betraying them, brought on Florence's old kidney trouble. When they moved to the White House, she had brought her family doctor, Brigadier General Charles Sawyer, and his wife from Marion to live with them. Sawyer prescribed a strict diet which had hitherto kept her in reasonably good shape. But in September, 1922, Mrs. Harding became very sick. One kidney had blocked and she was expected to die. The specialists who were called in wanted to operate, but Sawyer refused them permission because he feared she was too weak to survive such an operation. Under his care, she gradually rallied.

Once recovered, after many weeks, she saw nothing around her conducive to good cheer. There is no record of the Hardings' thoughts and actions in that winter of 1922-23, for Mrs. Harding carefully burned all the President's private and official papers after his death. As far as can be determined, they simply watched helplessly as the disaster grew. Harding, who had sought only the modest goal of being history's "best-loved" President, behaved as though he could smile and make it all go away, like a bad dream, and his wife, his tower of strength, could not bring herself to do anything that might destroy the illusion she had helped create of Warren Harding, great leader. Harding's hair turned white; his olive complexion faded to a sallow yellow; lines appeared around his mouth. Mrs. Harding gave up her battle against age; she was tired and ill, and she looked it.

Warren Harding had come to the White House already the captive of unscrupulous men, although he did not know it—he had plenty of obligations and so-called "friends," but no personal convictions. The Ohio gang, which was Harding's chief source of political strength back home, was a faction of the state's Re-

publican party led by Daugherty and composed of certain greedy
big business interests, notably the Standard Oil Company. Oil,
by 1920, had become a powerful financial giant elbowing the rail-
roads and investment bankers for dominant political influence.
The oil barons were concerned with only one thing—protecting
and expanding private oil interests without interference by government regulation. Testimony in numerous oil suits brought later
by the government clearly indicated that these big oil barons
controlled the Republican convention of 1920. They worked
chiefly through a band of senators, including Harding, who were
already indebted to them for political support. The Republicans
were badly split in 1920, and when the weary convention dead-
locked over General Leonard Wood and Governor Frank Low-
den, the oil barons decided quietly in a smoke-filled room to settle
upon an inoffensive compromise, Warren Harding.

It is doubtful that Harding realized the significance of what
the oil interests planned to demand of him, or that he would have
had the intelligence and moral courage to oppose them if he had.

In the presidency, Harding recognized that he must have
help. He turned to a kind of makeshift brain syndicate, which he
assembled out of men that he trusted. He made a few good appointments, including Charles Evans Hughes as Secretary of
State, Henry Wallace as Secretary of Agriculture, and Herbert
Hoover as Secretary of Commerce. But for the most part, Harding's trust was incredibly misplaced. He filled his administration
with politicians who were neither career men, administrators, nor
intellectuals. They made their decisions in terms of party good,
not the national good, and it never occurred to Harding to question what they were doing in the jobs he had given them.

And some of Harding's cronies, it developed, were just plain
corrupt. The Veterans Bureau chief, Charles Forbes, was quietly
lining his pockets; when it began to be suspected, his legal adviser committed suicide. The Alien Property Custodian, Colonel
Thomas Miller, was busily conspiring to make away with public
funds, and was eventually convicted. District attorneys across
the country were indicting many of the President's big business
friends for violations of the anti-trust laws. The Ohio gang was
collecting money in blackmail through Jess Smith, a grubby man
who roomed with Attorney General Daugherty. Mysteriously, as

the scandals began to break, Smith committed suicide—or was murdered. Gaston B. Means, a confidence man and professional scoundrel, was handling a variety of dirty chores for Daugherty through the Justice Department's Federal Bureau of Investigations, where Daugherty had conveniently assigned him. Means was later convicted for bribery, and wrote a salacious book entitled *The Strange Death of President Harding*, in which he accused Mrs. Harding of poisoning her husband. Means, however, like Nan Britton, never produced a shred of evidence to back up his sensational charge. Meanwhile, in the lower levels of the Harding administration, suicides and mysterious resignations broke out like a rash.

Harding was barely installed in the Executive Mansion before the oil barons had proceeded with their plans to separate the United States from her oil reserves. Their intrigue was to result in the Teapot Dome scandal, the biggest exposé of government corruption in United States history, in which Secretary of the Interior Albert Bacon Fall was to gain the dubious distinction of being the only Cabinet member ever to be convicted of conspiring to make away with public funds. The Teapot Dome oil fields in Wyoming and the Elk Hills field in California were federally-owned oil reserves set aside for the future use of the Navy. Fall persuaded Secretary of the Navy Edwin Denby that the Interior Department was better equipped to handle government oil fields than the Navy, and got Harding to issue an executive order making the transfer. Harding apparently endorsed Fall's manipulations without really understanding why the transfer was important. He remarked flippantly to a friend, "Well, I guess there will be hell to pay, but those fellows seem to know what they are doing." Once in control of the oil fields, Fall was in a position to dole out permits for leases to private companies. He received $100,000 from oil magnate Edward Doheny in a "little black bag" and similarly impressive sums from Harry Sinclair, in exchange for complete rights to pump the Teapot Dome oil reserve, which would net the magnates millions of dollars that rightfully belonged to the government. New Mexico attorneys, however, became suspicious when Fall suddenly displayed amazing affluence for a man with a salary of $12,000 a year: within a few months, his run-down New Mexico ranch had been transformed with new blooded stock, expensive repairs, and the addition of $124,500 worth of new land.

An investigation was threatening Fall in June, 1923, when President and Mrs. Harding set out on a vacation trip across the country to Alaska. There were indications that a suspicion of the burgeoning corruption had begun to reach the people, and Harding hoped to recapture his old popularity by making several speeches en route. The Hardings still desperately believed that his personal warmth could somehow smooth over the troubles, as it had always masked his inadequacies before. As they left, the President sighed, "Some day the people will understand what some of my erstwhile friends have done to me in these critical times when I depended so much upon them." Both Hardings left for their trip with a show of good spirits, as though by leaving Washington they left the scandals behind them.

The day before they began their trip the President called in Daugherty, whom he still relied upon, and made his will. Neither Harding was well, but Florence Harding was thought to be in worse condition than the President. Reporter William Allen White noticed that, after a heavy schedule of speeches across the nation, the President's "lips were swollen and blue, his eyes puffed, and his hands seemed stiff when I shook hands with him." As the train sped through the country, the personal torment of the two hapless individuals inside must have been dreadful. They could put physical miles between themselves and the shocking eruptions in the administration, but they could not put mental miles between them. At Kansas City, Mrs. Fall paid a furtive call on the President in his hotel room. Mrs. Harding was not present. The two talked for an hour; and if the President still had any illusions about his Secretary of Interior, he did not have them when Mrs. Fall left. Afterward he was fretful and could not conceal his agitation. He complained to an associate on the train the next day: "In this job I am not worried about my enemies. It is my friends that are keeping me awake nights." Mrs. Harding kept to her own room and was visited only by her doctor and the President. For a talkative woman, she was strangely silent throughout most of the train trip.

A few days later, in Alaska, the President received a long coded message from Washington. The message sent him into a state of collapse for a day. He asked reporters traveling with him bewilderedly what a President should do whose friends had betrayed him. Mrs. Harding, for once, had no advice. In Washington she had always, unknown to her husband, "kept in touch through private conversations with officials of the administration," according to Ike Hoover, the chief usher. But now she was thousands of miles away, in poor health, and unsure of whom to trust any more.

On July 28 President Harding fell ill, but after a few days he seemed to be slowly rallying. On Friday evening, August 3, his wife sat by his bed, reading a magazine article which defended the President against the mounting tide of criticism. Harding was pleased, and said "That's good." "Go on," he urged, as she paused. At that moment a blood clot formed on his brain, and a short time later he was dead.

The President's funeral train crept slowly back across the continent, the First Lady alone with her dead husband and her thoughts for five days. The train reached Washington late in the evening, but the First Lady immediately began receiving callers and did not retire until 1:00 A.M. Her friend Mrs. McLean stayed with her that night in the silent White House. She recorded that as soon as the visitors left, the First Lady descended the great staircase to the East Room, where her husband lay in state, as handsome as in life. With Mrs. McLean beside her, Mrs. Harding sat quietly talking calmly to his body. "No one can hurt you now, Warren," she whispered. She had never had much interest in the beauty of flowers, but that night she carefully selected a small bunch of wild field flowers from the masses of floral displays which banked the casket and laid it atop the casket. "The ones Warren would like," she murmured to herself. At 3:00 A.M. she went back up the stairway. She had not shed a tear. At the funeral, she was dignified, expressionless, and calm. "She has turned to ice," an observer said.

Mrs. Harding retreated to her home in Marion, Ohio. She cut off all ties with old acquaintances, and even refused the sympathetic advances of President Coolidge and his wife. She gave the servants Laddie Boy, the President's collie, and her own canary.

She had once said, when her husband was nominated for the

presidency, that despite her own ambitions "I have a presentiment against this thing." And once he was buried, the shame came out in a rush. In October a Senate subcommittee under the chairmanship of Thomas Walsh of Montana opened hearings in its investigation of the Teapot Dome oil leases. By the next June ex-Secretary Fall, Sinclair, Doheny and his son were indicted on charges of conspiracy and bribery. After a long series of trials, mistrials, and appeals, Fall was found guilty and sent to jail for one year in July, 1931. In death defenseless, President Harding's name became synonymous with the corruption and his reputation was forever blackened in the minds of a horrified public. History will never know whether Mrs. Harding was trying to hide his ignorance or his folly—or her own collaboration —when she methodically destroyed all of his personal and official papers.

One year and one hundred days after the death of President Harding, his "President-maker" died. She lived just long enough to see much of the sensational scandal her husband was spared— but it was his name, not hers, which she watched go down in infamy.

Florence Kling Harding had nobody but herself to blame for picking such a weak man as her husband. She had done it on purpose, in reaction against the two selfish, egotistical, and strong-willed men in her life.

Her father, Amos Kling, was the leading banker and wealthiest man in the small town of Marion. When Florence was born, on August 15, 1860, he was bitterly disappointed, for he had wanted a son. He never seemed to forgive her for daring to defy him on this vital matter. He was an obstinate, vigorous, quick-minded man whose forceful personality made him a virtual dictator over his family. He sent his daughter to the best school in Marion, and later to the Cincinnati Conservatory of Music to study piano. But while Florence was still in her teens her mother died, and she returned home to teach piano and live with her father.

Florence had inherited her father's toughness, and her years away had given her a heady taste of independence. Kling demanded blind obedience; Florence defied him; and the two locked in a lifelong battle of bitterness. Kling set down rigid rules of conduct. If Florence dated a boy of whom he did not approve, or stayed out beyond his 11:00 P.M. deadline, he would simply lock her out and let her fend for herself overnight. As the town's richest man, Kling felt that no man was good enough for his daughter. Florence suffered while her father rudely drove away beau after beau. She was rather ordinary-looking, and never very popular because of her overbearing ways; her father didn't seem to understand that she had a hard enough time attracting eligible young men without his interference.

When she was nineteen, Florence met Henry DeWolfe, a neighbor who came from an old and wealthy Ohio family. DeWolfe was the first man who was not intimidated by her spiteful father—he was probably hardened to disapproval, for his own family deplored his excessive drinking, his instability, his spendthrift ways, his predilection for lower-class ladies and shady men. Florence, however, was inexperienced enough to consider him dashing and bold, and her best chance to escape from her father's tyranny. They eloped. In the next year they had a son, Marshall Eugene DeWolfe, and moved to Galion, Ohio, where DeWolfe accepted a job managing a roller-skating palace. On Christmas Eve, however, two days before the "Ice Palace" was to open, DeWolfe vanished. He left behind him a bewildered young wife barely out of her teens, with an infant son, no money, no food, and no friends in a strange town.

Florence was learning, the hard way, how to fend for herself; the harsh, aggressive shell to protect her from further pain was forming. Carrying her baby, she went to the train station, where she persuaded the conductor to let her ride free to Marion on a promise that she would pay the fare later. Cold, hungry, and lonely, she arrived at Marion in the middle of the night. But then she lost her courage: she could not face her wrathful father. She was not even sure that he would forgive her enough to take her back, for he had not spoken to her since the marriage. So Florence crept into a vacant house near the train station, where she huddled, nearly frozen, with her son until dawn.

She made her way to the home of old friends, still afraid to approach her father. She had good reason to be worried, for when the friends told Kling he coldly refused to see his deserted daughter and grandchild. So other friends helped Florence find a place to live, and she persuaded Simon DeWolfe, her father-in-law, to provide her with food and other necessities. She boarded little Marshall temporarily with another couple. She borrowed a piano and began giving piano lessons again, and eventually earned enough to support herself and her son.

Once she had shown she could manage without him, Amos Kling relented. Florence got a divorce. Kling let her return to live in the biggest house in town and he adopted her little Marshall. (Marshall lived inconspicuously in Marion all his life, and died at the age of thirty-five.)

Within the Kling household the cold war raged for ten years, and Florence never knew the meaning of affection. Whatever warmth she had left in her own hardened heart was bestowed upon her son. Then she met handsome young Warren G. Harding, publisher of the Marion *Star*, which he had recently purchased with two other men for three hundred dollars. Harding was the son of a poor doctor and a domineering, doting, overpossessive mother, who had well conditioned him for a woman who would tell him he was wonderful at the same time she told him what to do. The accounts of their courtship vary, but there is little disagreement on the question of who was the aggressor. Florence was thirty, a lonely divorcée with a child, and she determined to marry Harding. With his kindly attitude toward life, his devil-may-care air, his easy popularity, his gift of gab and charm, Harding was everything that Florence would have liked to be, but was not.

Kling, of course, flew into a rage when he heard the gossip about Florence and Harding, whom he considered an irresponsible scalawag, and a penniless one at that. Kling trapped Harding one day on the courthouse steps and threatened to shoot him if he set a foot on his premises. He stomped around town charging that Harding came of "mixed blood." It was thought at the time that Kling was the instigator of a full-page article which appeared in the *Mirror*, Marion's other paper, alleging that Harding's family had always been regarded as Negroes, and treated as such, in their former home town of Blooming Grove.

Kling's outrageous opposition once again drove Florence into defiance. She married Harding secretly on July 8, 1891. She was thirty; he was twenty-five. It was seven years before her father would pass her on the street with any sign of recognition, and fifteen years before he visited their home, although it was only a few blocks from the Kling edifice. The Hardings never seemed very affectionate, but Florence had gotten away from her father, into a home of her own, and Harding—well, he was a nice chap who could never say "no" to anybody. Somebody who had known Harding nearly all his life once commented that "If Warren had been a woman, he would have been pregnant all the time."

Surprisingly, virile, healthy-looking Harding developed an ailment shortly after their marriage which affected his digestive and nervous systems. His father prescribed a long rest, and Florence Harding went down to the newspaper office to fill his place for a while. She stayed fourteen years, reorganized the bookkeeping system, trained and bossed the delivery boys, and generally ran the whole business operation. Norman Thomas, one of her former newsboys, recalled: "She was a woman of very narrow mentality and range of interest or understanding, but of strong will and, within a certain area, of genuine kindliness. . . . It was her energy and business sense which made the *Star*. . . . Her husband was the front. He was, as you know, very affable; very much of a joiner and personally popular. He was a fine small-town or city booster and wrote editorals telling how Marion, Ohio, had more miles of Berea sandstone sidewalks than any town of its size in the United States. Nay, he ventured to say, in the whole world. This was his best line. . . ."

Thomas continued that "in the days of my youth, Mrs. Harding and his tailor had not discovered how well Warren could be dressed up. . . . He was always more personally popular than his wife, but I am quite sure that most folks . . . would have told you that it was she who was the real driving power in the success that the Marion *Star* was unquestionably making in its community."

The *Star* grew from a weekly to a daily. Harding, freed by his wife of the *Star*'s time-consuming duties, grew from an occasional orator at community club luncheons to a faithful spokesman at local Republican party functions. His flowing oratorical style made him in great demand at public events. He seldom understood what he said, but he certainly said it well. Mrs.

Harding encouraged her husband's appearances, for it increased their standing in the community and gave her reflected prestige. She wanted to show her father, for one thing, that he had been wrong—and she right—about Harding. So Florence Harding worked all day at the newspaper, then pedaled home on a bike each night a half hour ahead of her husband to broil their dinner steak.

One day, Ohio national committeeman Harry Daugherty heard Harding expound at a Marion Republican committee function. "This man looks like a President," he thought. Daugherty introduced himself to Harding, and as they parted, saluted, "See you in Columbus." Thus began their fateful relationship. And after Harding ran and was elected to the state senate in 1900, he did see plenty of Daugherty. Harding easily became a spokesman for Daugherty's "Ohio gang," but he was never admitted to the inner political councils where policy was determined. In the senate, Harding was not the most able of representatives but he was one of the most popular. He was elected lieutenant governor, and his popularity grew. Back in Marion, Mrs. Harding continued to run the newspaper; its editorial and news columns were filled with the statesman-like deeds of the lieutenant governor. Harding had ordered his editor to keep his name out of the newspaper, but his wife promptly and decisively overrode him.

In 1910 Harding was nominated for governor. Alice Longworth recalled sitting near Mrs. Harding at the state convention, that she was "very much excited, cheering and waving." He lost, however, and returned home to Marion to pick up his role as local publisher-orator. Daugherty still had ambitions for his political protégé, however, and frequently visited the Hardings in Marion. Daugherty himself had run for Congress, the Senate, and the governorship, and been defeated every time; he had given up hopes of holding elective office. If he was ever to have high political power, he had to win with a "front man" he could control. Daugherty reported in his autobiography that Florence Harding was always co-operative and helpful. "She trusted my judgment, as a rule, against Harding's on political issues," he noted. "She knew that he was a man easily fooled by his enemies."

Harding would have been content to remain in Marion, a

relatively big fish in a little pond. But Daugherty and Mrs.
Harding persuaded him to run for the Senate in 1914, and he was
narrowly elected. Florence Harding, proud and pleased, went
off to Washington with him. It was correctly observed at the
time that "no man could be as much a senator as Harding
looked." He put up a magnificent appearance (by then Florence
and his tailor had learned how to dress him up), was well liked
by his colleagues, and did very little. His stirring voice led him,
inevitably, to a position as unofficial party spokesman on the
national scene. He appeared everywhere on behalf of the Republican cause, and was a tireless campaigner for Charles Evans
Hughes in 1916. Mrs. Harding went all over the country with
him; she told a friend she thought the way to hold Warren
Harding was to "always have reserve food in the icebox, and
never let my husband travel without me." They were both as
happy as they had ever been, or indeed would be. "I like the
Senate. It is a very pleasant place," was Harding's astute observation.

Daugherty had his puppet in the Senate, but he wasn't
satisfied. He maneuvered his forces toward the presidential nomination in 1920. The Republican party was badly split, and he
felt certain that a dark horse compromise would take the convention. When approached with the idea, however, Harding balked
violently. "If I don't run for the presidency I can stay in the
Senate all my life," he protested. Mrs. Harding, too, was at first
cautious. Harding was up for re-election, and if he was defeated
for the presidency he would be not only out of the White House
but out of the Senate. "I like being a senator's wife," she pointed
out. Daugherty, however, persuaded her to join forces with him
once again, in a "President-maker" role. He admitted that he
probably could not have manipulated Harding without her:
"Harding was very fond of her and held the profoundest respect
for her judgment, which had been sharpened by five years of
contact with public life in Washington as a senator's wife. . . . If
she backed our candidate he would make the fight. If she opposed
it, the issue would be doubtful."

Harding entered the primaries, but he did not have his heart
in the campaign. One day in Indiana he decided that the fight

was not worth the goal, and he told his wife that he intended to withdraw his candidacy. Mrs. Harding, disturbed, consulted a fortune teller. The crystal-gazer told her that her husband would be victorious, just as "Madam Marcia" had predicted earlier. So she browbeat Harding into staying in the race.

Harding's discouragement in Indiana had been based on realistic appraisal. When the results of the primary came in, he had won not one instructed vote. Harding, who received the returns with his wife at the home of Senator and Mrs. Harry New, was crushed. Without a word he stalked across the room and picked up the phone. Mrs. Harding, deep in conversation with the News, heard Harding ask for Daugherty in Ohio. She jumped out of her chair and snatched the phone from Harding's hand. As someone came on the other end of the line, she shouted, "Hello, this is Mrs. Harding. Yes, *Mrs.* Harding. You tell Harry Daugherty from me that we're in this fight till hell freezes over."

Mrs. Harding and Daugherty kept their faint-hearted candidate going until the convention. Whenever Harding faltered, she propped him up again.

At the Republican convention Mrs. Harding behaved superbly. She said just the right things to the reporters. And she insisted that Harding follow Daugherty's advice in everything. She sat in her box at the convention hall every day, smiling and receiving visitors. The morning after fifteen tired men settled upon Harding as their candidate, Daugherty joined Mrs. Harding in her box to share the moment they had both worked for so long. The sweltering heat of the crowded hall was almost suffocating, and Mrs. Harding had wilted considerably under the temperature and the tension. She had removed her hat from her iron-gray hair, and sat slumped forward in her chair. In her right hand she gripped the two enormous fashionable hatpins she had taken from her hat. "I've come up here to ask you to keep cool," Daugherty said as he sat down beside her. "That's some joke." She scowled in irritation. "It's a hundred and ten in this place and you advise me to keep cool!"

Daugherty leaned over and whispered that her husband would be nominated on the next ballot. Mrs. Harding fairly leaped out of her chair, her arms jerked outward, and she accidentally stabbed both hatpins into Daugherty's side. Daugherty, surprised, nearly fainted from the excitement of it all. But the wound turned out to be a scratch and the blood he thought he felt was nothing but nervous perspiration.

Mrs. Harding, of course, was overjoyed at her husband's nomination. Once in a while she grew uneasy as she remembered the warning of "Madam Marcia," but those moments of misgiving were quickly smothered. In a reflective mood she said, "I can see but one word written over his head if they make him President, and that is tragedy." Florence Harding didn't behave as though she was very disturbed, however, for she threw herself energetically into the presidential campaign. Since this was the first election in which women were allowed to vote, Mrs. Harding traveled with the candidate on his one speaking tour. Her job was to appear at women's groups, where she shook hands and smiled and insisted modestly, "You know you really shouldn't ask me to talk politics. My husband will do that."

Most of Harding's campaign, however, was conducted from his own front porch. Pictures of the house in Marion, with the Hardings standing like "plain folks" on the porch, were circulated throughout the country. Mrs. Harding later claimed this particular campaign tactic as her own idea. "I want the people to see these pictures so that they will know we are just folks like themselves," she said, unconsciously using the singular pronoun as though she, instead of Harding, was the candidate.

Florence Harding is credited with another major campaign policy decision. The Democrats dredged up the old rumor about Harding's supposed Negro heritage. Harding's advisers called a council of war to shape a denial of the charge, but his wife alone faced them down. She was imperious in her wrath. Warren Harding would not by a single word dignify such a ridiculous lie with an answer, she informed the advisers. Thus ignored, the rumor died a-borning.

Daugherty, who had ample reason to be favorably disposed toward Mrs. Harding, praised her tireless work during the campaign. He also observed charitably, "They were of more help to each other than any man and woman I have ever known. She was intensely interested in his work and watched carefully to see that he made no mistakes. If he did she was keen to 'pick him up,' though she did it in a way that never nagged."

There were those who would have disagreed with that last phrase of his. And as for the newly elected President—"I have lost my freedom," he said.

Anna Eleanor

ROOSEVELT

❀ ❀

Rhode Island University officials thought up the title. And three American Presidents, United Nations diplomats, foreign heads of state, short-order cooks, plumbers, secretaries, miners all called her "The First Lady of the World." There has never been, and perhaps never will be again, a First Lady like the incredible Anna Eleanor Roosevelt.

Some people hold to the idea that a woman's place is in the home—but to Eleanor Roosevelt, home was the land, the sea, and the air. She was First Lady for twelve years, longer than any other. And she is the only First Lady who increased her own prestige and her efforts on behalf of mankind after her husband's death. More than any other First Lady, she was a full partner in the tasks of the presidency, deeply involved in politics, in the operation of government agencies and in the conduct of public affairs. She was the eyes and ears—and the conscience—of a man who is considered by historians one of the nation's greatest Presidents, Franklin Delano Roosevelt. She shattered all precedents in her energetic efforts to represent the President where his own crippled limbs could not carry him. She voiced always the ideal of government for the many rather than for the few. Let any worthy cause rear its head, and she came running.

Neither the tributes after her death, on November 7, 1962, nor the honors heaped upon her in life were adequate measures of the deep impact Eleanor Roosevelt made upon the people of America and the world. United Nations Acting Secretary-General U Thant said, "Mrs. Roosevelt was truly the First Lady of the World and we, in the United Nations, salute her memory for her warm humanitarianism and her deep concern for the underprivileged." Upon her death, the United Nations General Assembly stood a minute in silent tribute—only the second time in its history that it offered such an honor to an individual.

Former President Harry Truman said, "She had interest not only in the United States but in the world." President John Kennedy said, "It is my judgment that there can be no adequate replacement for Mrs. Roosevelt." Secretary of State Dean Rusk said, "She had no capacity for hate, but much for indignation, which led to her passionate protests against disease, poverty, injustice, prejudice. . . ." Even the Soviet Ambassador to the United Nations, Valerin Zorin, a man not ordinarily given to kindly thoughts about Americans, was moved to say, "In her heart we could always find warm feelings for all people."

For thirteen consecutive years the Gallup Poll showed that Eleanor Roosevelt was "the most admired woman in the world." Her son James called her "a sort of roving one-woman task force for social reform and international good will," and "Father's invaluable and trusted right arm."

Eleanor Roosevelt herself was more self-effacing. She wrote: "When I went to Washington I felt sure that I would be able to use the opportunity which came to me to help Franklin gain the objectives he cared about. . . . He might have been happier with a wife who was completely uncritical. That I was never able to be . . . nevertheless, I think I sometimes acted as a spur even though the spurring was not always wanted or welcome. I was one of those who served his purposes."

The nation in the 1930's wasn't used to a First Lady with a mind of her own and the courage to express her views openly on controversial issues. Not everyone took kindly to her meddling at all levels of government activity and her persistent prodding on behalf of protégés or pet projects. Some people felt she should spend more time being a mother to her five children and less time gallivanting around the country. She earned the enmity of a large section of the South by her championing of Negro rights, and the anger of Catholic Church groups by adding her voice to the parochial versus public school controversy and by calling divorce "necessary and right, when two people found it impossible to live together." But Mrs. Roosevelt merely ignored her critics, and persisted in saying and doing what she felt was right. She was never inhibited by her austere position as First Lady; and President Roosevelt never seemed to mind having a controversial wife. "Lady, it's a free country," he used to tell her. "I have my own way of getting my views across to the American people. If you get me in hot water, I'll manage to save myself."

The trouble was that Mrs. Roosevelt never felt she was poking into other people's business. Her business *was* people. She was more New Deal than her husband. She never thought of people as "masses"—as politicians and blue-bloods (and she was both) generally tend to do—she thought of them as clerks and farmers and housewives, and she was deeply concerned about their welfare.

"She makes me feel as though I haven't done a thing with my life," an industrious, matronly civic worker said recently. Yet Eleanor Roosevelt, who did so much with her life, would have been a good candidate, until her thirties, for a "least likely to succeed" award. She was "an ugly duckling," to use her own words, the plain child of a beautiful mother and an alcoholic father. She was born October 11, 1884, to Anna Hall and Elliott Roosevelt, who were wealthy and socially prominent descendants of a long line of American aristocracy. But Eleanor's mother reminded her constantly that she was "a funny child" and bemoaned the fact that she was not pretty. Eleanor grew up shy, solemn, insecure, and lonely. "There was absolutely nothing about me to attract anybody's attention," she recalled.

Her mother died when she was eight, her father two years

later. She was reared by her grandmother and a collection of relatives who disciplined her severely and sent her to grim, strict schools. She had few friends and seldom smiled; she found the occasional debutante parties "utter agony." Her family despaired of ever marrying her off, despite her excellent social credentials.

But then, miraculously, her handsome fifth cousin, Franklin Roosevelt, began to dance with her at parties. He came from Harvard, where he was a student, to visit her. He met her sometimes at Rivington Street Settlement House in New York City, a community center in the slums set up by the Junior League, where she taught calisthenics and dancing. James contends that his father's visits to that settlement house "were the beginning of his education. Mother took him with her on a visit to one of her sick charges. He was absolutely shaken when he saw the cold-water tenement where the child lived, and kept saying he simply could not believe human beings lived that way."

In the fall of 1903, while still at Harvard, the popular, gay, ebullient Roosevelt asked to marry the innocent, homely, timid Eleanor. She promptly accepted. But Franklin's mother Sara, who completely dominated his life, thought the couple too young and hustled her son off for a nice long cruise in the West Indies. Eleanor waited, and Franklin persisted, and so a year and a half later they were married. Eleanor's uncle, President Theodore Roosevelt, gave her in marriage to Franklin on March 17, 1905, in New York City.

For the first ten years of her married life, Eleanor Roosevelt was absorbed in having children—she had six, of which five survived. She was awed by her active, virile husband and terrified of her mother-in-law. She was even afraid of the servants, so she left the running of her household entirely to the senior Mrs. Roosevelt, who lived near them. "I was not developing any individual taste or initiative, I was simply absorbing the personalities of those about me and letting their tastes and interests dominate me," she reflected later.

Franklin Roosevelt began to take an interest in politics, and in 1909 was elected to the state senate. In Albany, the capital, Mrs. Roosevelt now had to manage her own household, but she still depended heavily upon others for advice. "I do so want you to learn to love me a little," she wrote pleadingly to her mother-in-law, who had been left behind in Hyde Park. She meekly made public appearances with her husband, but she did not yet feel personally involved in politics. "I still lived under the compulsion of my early training; duty was perhaps the motivating force of my life, often excluding what might have been joy or pleasure. I looked at everything from the point of view of what I ought to do, rarely from the standpoint of what I wanted to do . . . so I took an interest in politics. It was a wife's duty to be interested in whatever interested her husband."

The First Lady looked back from the White House at that early colorless Eleanor Roosevelt with very little sympathy: "I had very high standards as to what a wife and mother should be, and not the faintest notion of what it meant to be either a wife or a mother, and none of my elders enlightened me. I marvel at my husband's patience."

Politics was beginning to interest her, but she resisted, refusing to be tugged out of her shell. Louis McHenry Howe, the political genius who was to become Roosevelt's closest adviser, managed his re-election campaign; but Mrs. Roosevelt didn't like him because she didn't approve of smoking, and he smoked. In 1912 Roosevelt insisted she accompany him to the Democratic national convention, but she understood little of what was going on: "The demonstrations all seemed senseless." Shortly afterward Roosevelt was appointed Assistant Secretary of the Navy, and his wife became a dutiful hostess, entertaining Washington officialdom. But every time she went to a party she wished "the ground would open and swallow me."

Roosevelt was nominated as the Democratic vice-presidential candidate in 1920, with James Cox as the presidential nominee. Cox had a strong personality and political sagacity, but very little else to recommend him. The First Lady, Mrs. Woodrow Wilson, remarked that young Roosevelt "could charm the birds from the trees" but she didn't think too highly of his ability. Cox and Roosevelt lost, but the campaign was a good training ground for the emerging high-powered team of Roosevelt, his wife, and Howe. Since 1912 Howe had been addressing his letters to Roosevelt as "beloved and revered future President." He managed the vice-presidential campaign—but more importantly he began the education of Mrs. Roosevelt. To break down her antagonism, Howe would knock at the door of her train compartment and ask for her opinion on a campaign speech he was drafting. "Before long, I found myself discussing a wide range of subjects," Mrs. Roosevelt recalled.

The following spring, while vacationing at Campobello, Roosevelt was stricken with infantile paralysis. He was unable to move. His mother insisted that he retire to Hyde Park, where he could live the life of a pampered invalid. But the doctors warned that his only chance for recovery lay in prodding him to take an active part in life. Mrs. Roosevelt and Howe, who moved into the Roosevelt household and stayed until his death in 1936, took the doctors' advice. They took turns massaging Roosevelt's useless legs—and they decided that since he couldn't go to politics, they would make politics come to him. "Do you really believe that Franklin still has a political future?" his wife asked. "I believe that some day Franklin will be President," was Howe's firm reply.

In a bitter struggle for dominant influence over her husband, Eleanor Roosevelt warded off Sara Roosevelt's attempts to smother her son. Encouraged by Howe, she joined the Women's Trade Union League, raised funds for the Democratic state committee, drove voters to the polls on election day, worked in local campaigns. She brought social workers, labor leaders, politicians, writers, and a wide variety of people home for dinner and to talk to her husband. She made speeches at civic and political meetings in his name, although in the beginning she "died" every time she got up on a platform. But the shrewd, patient Howe rehearsed her, wrote her speeches, taught her how to suppress her nervous giggles, and how to tone down her flat, high-pitched voice.

By 1924 Franklin Roosevelt had regained full use of his arms, although he was never able to walk or stand without ten-pound locked leg braces. He practiced law; he managed New York Governor Al Smith's pre-convention campaign for the 1924 presidential nomination (which Smith lost). The slow days of exercise had taught him patience and persistence and given him a tolerance and courage he did not have before. Mrs. Roosevelt, too, had developed new depths of personality. "More and more, I used the quickness of my mind to pick the minds of other people and use their knowledge as my own," she said. She was writing, doing regular radio broadcasts, and teaching current events, history, and literature at Todhunter School, a New York private school for girls.

Roosevelt nominated Al Smith for President at the 1928 convention, dramatically presenting the governor as "the happy warrior of the political battlefield." He headed Smith's business-men's division for the presidential campaign; his wife organized the women's committee. Smith wanted Roosevelt to run for governor, because he felt it would strengthen the national ticket in New York. He approached Mrs. Roosevelt at the state convention, beseeching her to ask her husband to run. She refused, because she felt it was too soon: he was not yet fully recovered. Smith finally persuaded Mrs. Roosevelt to call her husband at Warm Springs, Georgia, where he was vacationing, and present Smith's request. So she called her husband and handed the phone over to Smith without comment. She did not stay to hear the conversation, and later said, "I did not know until the following morning when I bought a newspaper that my husband had been persuaded to accept the nomination."

Eleanor Roosevelt worked in Smith's national campaign, rather than stump for her husband. A campaign co-worker was Frances Perkins, whom Mrs. Roosevelt was later influential in making Secretary of Labor, the first woman Cabinet member. Miss Perkins said that Mrs. Roosevelt was always concerned not just with the mechanics of politics but with the greater objectives in party policy and government philosophy as well. "She came to have a shrewd, independent judgment not only about policies but about politicians," Miss Perkins said.

Smith's protégé was elected while Smith himself was going down to defeat, and the Roosevelts took over the New York governor's mansion. The state became Franklin Roosevelt's experimental laboratory for legislation that was the forerunner of his New Deal. Prodded by his wife, Roosevelt's interest in "the underdog" was growing. He developed the hydro-electric power resources of the St. Lawrence River to supply cheap electricity, set up a farm relief program, sponsored old age pensions, wages and hours laws, pushed through a reform of the judiciary, established soil conservation and forestry programs. The Roosevelts rode around the state to visit prisons, insane asylums, state hospitals, and other institutions. Because walking was so difficult, he stayed outside in the car while his wife inspected the facilities. He instructed her to peer into the cooking pots on the stove, check the clothing hung in closets, and notice whether beds were folded up behind doors, which meant they filled overcrowded corridors at night. Sometimes, if she was treated to a delicious hot lunch with meat balls and vegetables, Mrs. Roosevelt would return to the institution unannounced several days later to see if the luncheon menu was the same, or if it was weak watery soup (it was frequently the soup). She became an expert observer on the condition of institutions, and she reported it all back to her husband, with appropriate exclamations of compassionate concern when she felt inmates were being mistreated.

Mrs. Roosevelt insisted that she never knew exactly when her husband decided to run for the presidency, although she was perfectly aware that everything Howe had undertaken for him for years had been with this goal in mind. She was not consulted on the decision. "From a personal standpoint, I did not want my husband to be President. I realized, however, that it was impossible to keep a man out of public service when that was what he wanted and was undoubtedly well equipped for. It was pure selfishness on my part, and I never mentioned my feelings on the subject to him," she said.

In 1932 Roosevelt was nominated for President, after a bitter convention fight. In his acceptance speech he promised "a new deal for the American people" and a helping hand for "the forgotten man." The Democratic theme song, stolen from a cigarette commercial, was "Happy Days Are Here Again." But President Herbert Hoover, seeking a second term, prophesied that if the radical Roosevelt was elected "grass would grow in the streets of one hundred cities" and "weeds overrun millions of farms."

The country desperately needed some happy days. One out of every four American workers was out of a job. Families, evicted from their homes because they could not pay rent, slept in tar-paper shacks or little tents put up beside the road. The lucky ones subsisted on pinto beans and black coffee. The unlucky ones scavenged like animals for food in city dumps, or stood in long, weary lines for a handout of soup and bread. Banks closed. Investors lost millions on the stock market. Factories which had filled the air with their ugly smoke and stench were now uglier in their abandoned silence. Veterans sold apples on street corners; college professors dug ditches. In New York State one-fifth of the public-school pupils suffered from malnutrition. Violence flared frequently as hungry men stole for their hungry families. Since the stock market crash of October, 1929, the national depression had deepened, and deepened, and deepened. Millions had no money, millions had no jobs.

Mrs. Roosevelt turned her observing eyes upon a discouraged countryside that fall as she campaigned with her husband. But Roosevelt believed there was "a vitality in the people that could be salvaged," and he believed he was just the man to do it. "I believe it was from his faith in the people that he drew the words of his first inaugural address: 'the only thing we have to fear is fear itself,'" his wife said.

The New Deal entered the White House with the Roosevelts, to make the government serve the people on a grand scale never before conceived. "We must act and act quickly," the new President said. In the first hundred days he launched a program of public works of such a scope as to put money in the pockets of the workingman, transform him into a consumer, and start the factories running again. He blithely closed down all the banks, and reopened them under a system guaranteeing personal savings deposits up to $5,000. The Public Works Administration put thousands to work building federal, state and municipal projects. The Civilian Conservation Corps set unemployed young men to a variety of tasks. The Tennessee Valley Authority was established, to demonstrate the blessings of cheap power; and the Rural Electrification Administration began to stretch power lines to farm homes. Legislation to provide loans for homeowners and farmers and other relief measures were pushed through the Congress. The new agencies from Roosevelt's "must" legislation eventually added up to more than thirty, functioning primarily on the principle of federal aid through matching funds with the states.

Mrs. Roosevelt, according to a New Deal official, was from the beginning "one of the best-informed and understanding citizens in this country on the plight of the unemployed." She had dreaded that she might be a "prisoner" in the White House, with nothing to do but receive visitors and preside over state dinners in handsome gowns. However, she settled her family in its new quarters within three days, had all her husband's naval prints hung within a week—and soon found something more interesting to do. Within a month the President sent her on her first inspection trip of a depressed area. She represented the President at social welfare organization meetings, and she urgently pressed on the President her ideas regarding several agency appointments and policies.

The country quickly became aware that Eleanor Roosevelt was no ordinary First Lady, content to sponsor good works from the comfort of the White House. She liked to see things and do things for herself, from running the White House elevator and personally hanging out her husband's bathing suits to dry, to making her own evaluation of her husband's bills rather than rely on his sketchy descriptions. When hordes of jobless veterans staged their second Bonus March on Washington, she herself went out to greet them at their camp. A year before, these veterans of World War I had marched on the city, demanding the compensation due them from the war, but President Hoover had ordered Army troops to drive them out with tear gas and burn their shacks. This time the Roosevelt administration provided them with tents in which to sleep and served them hot meals. The First Lady appeared on a rainy day and stalked unceremoniously through the camp, ankle-deep in mud, shaking hands and assuring the veterans of her help. She even joined them in singing "There's a Long, Long Trail A-Winding." One veteran cheered, "Hoover sent the Army. Roosevelt sent his wife." Within two weeks after her visit, most of the veterans had been assimilated into the Civilian Conservation Corps.

The President was soon sending his wife all over the country, to report on the depression and on how the New Deal was working. She drove her own car, rode buses, subways, and train coaches, cheerfully ignoring the special privileges that could have been hers as First Lady. She refused to have Secret Service men accompany her. "They can't keep up with her," the President said, chuckling. She logged up an annual average of 40,000 miles in her first eight years in the White House. She was in her fifties, but she was blessed with good health and she seemed indefati-

gable. "Such energy is depressing," moaned one reporter assigned
to cover her travels.

The President instructed his wife carefully on what to look
for. "Watch the people's faces," he told her. "Look at the condition of their clothes on the washline. Notice their cars." And he
accepted her accounts of conditions in the country as gospel. In
Cabinet meetings he often based some proposal or another on one
of her reports. "You know, my missus gets around a lot," he would
say; or, "My missus says they have typhoid fever in that district";
or, "My missus says the people are leaving the dust bowl in droves
because they haven't any chance there"; or, "My missus says that
people are working for wages way below the minimum set by
NRA in the town she visited last week." Secretary Perkins said
that the President was enormously proud of his wife's ability, although he rarely talked about it. Once he said to her, "You know,
Eleanor really puts it over. She's got great talent with people."

But Mrs. Roosevelt was more than a public-relations image
or a pair of legs for the President. She was, as her son James put
it, "a first-class thinking mechanism" too. She was continually
stirring the President to action in a variety of causes. For instance,
she was largely responsible for the National Youth Administration, which, among other functions, put college boys and girls
to work part time. Harry Hopkins, the head of the Works Progress Administration, and Aubrey Williams came to her with their
idea for a youth work program, because the President was too
busy to see them. Mrs. Roosevelt, who had worked with underprivileged youth in New York, added her own suggestions and
promised to try to enlist the President's support. After dinner,
just before he went to bed, she outlined the proposed project to
him. Roosevelt liked it. "If it is the right thing to do for the young
people, then it should be done. I guess we can stand the criticism,
and I doubt if your youth can be regimented in this way or any
other way," he said. The project turned out to be politically popular, and Mrs. Roosevelt said, "It was one of the occasions on
which I was proud that the right thing was done regardless of
political considerations."

Eleanor Roosevelt continued to be interested in the N.Y.A.
She visited its projects, recommended others, and showed its progress reports to the President. All aspects of the relief work

deeply concerned her. Harry Hopkins contended that she believed so passionately in the programs that she "tended to steady the President's nerve" whenever he considered cutting this or that budget when under fire for extravagance. "She continually impressed upon both of us," Hopkins recalled, "that we must not be satisfied with merely making campaign pledges, the President being under moral obligation to see his domestic reforms through, particularly the organizing of our economic life in such a way as to give everybody a job. She emphasized that this was an overwhelming task and she hoped neither the President nor I thought it was settled in any way by making speeches."

Rexford Tugwell, a part of the President's famous Brain Trust, called Mrs. Roosevelt "the keeper of and constant spokesman for her husband's conscience." And Mrs. Roosevelt herself conceded that without her prodding and the persistent efforts of others, her husband might have been just another "nice young society man."

The Morgantown Homestead project provides a good example of Mrs. Roosevelt's well-intentioned, but not always wise, efforts to help the nation's underprivileged. She had a great heart, but she did not always have good judgment.

Under the homestead project, the government bought land, built houses, acquired livestock and farm machinery, built roads, put in utilities, and then sold the developed plots to homesteaders, who paid for them over a thirty-year period. The President was asked to establish such a project near Morgantown, West Virginia, a poverty-stricken soft-coal region. He sent his wife to look things over, and the conditions she found were so miserable that she became convinced the country was on the brink of a revolution. One of her companions on the trip, a wealthy businessman, stepped into one of the filthy, smelly shacks where a large family huddled, but promptly retreated outside, into the fresh air, where he vomited. When Mrs. Roosevelt came out of the shack some minutes later, the man thrust some money into her hand, promising to donate more, "if only you won't make me go in there again." But Eleanor Roosevelt, all squeamishness forgotten in her sympathy, spent days talking with evicted families in similar smelly tents, patting children sick with typhoid, asking questions. A miner showed her his weekly pay slip, which left him less than a dollar in cash each week for his family after deductions for rent and bills at the company store. His six children lived on scraps Mrs. Roosevelt would not have considered suitable to feed Fala, the President's dog. One of the miner's children proudly showed her his pet white rabbit, which he clutched lovingly. Said his sister coldly, "He thinks we are not going to eat it, but we are."

Mrs. Roosevelt and Howe took the Morgantown project over as their own. Howe ordered fifty prefabricated houses, which turned out to be inadequate for West Virginia's harsh winters. They then called in an expensive team of New York architects to redesign and enlarge the houses. She insisted on providing all the houses with plumbing and other modern fixtures, although even in good times the mining families would not have been able to afford such conveniences. Secretary of the Interior Harold Ickes, under whose jurisdiction the homesteads fell, complained that "Mrs. R. took the Morgantown project under her protecting wing with the result that we have been spending money down there like drunken sailors—money that we can never hope to get out of the project." But when Ickes protested his budget problem to the President, the President brushed him off with "My missus, unlike most women, hasn't any sense about money at all." Unchecked, the costs mounted so rapidly that the Morgantown project became one of the most loudly criticized projects of the administration. A magazine complained that the taxpayers had put up a community for poor miners that had the look of a superior real estate development.

Mrs. Roosevelt got so interested in the functions of the Interior Department through her experience with homesteads that she began to try to tell Ickes how to run other aspects of his domain. Ickes grumbled to his diary that she was "the most outspoken critic" of the Interior operation. She suggested inefficient employees she thought Ickes should fire, and efficient employees he should hire. Sometimes he complied, but he refused to fire an administrative assistant she did not like. So Mrs. Roosevelt used indirect tactics: she took to criticizing the assistant at dinners, with other guests present. Ickes resigned himself to giving in, because "a constant repetition of these groundless charges on her part is bound to have an effect sooner or later on the President." Even so, Ickes confessed to his diary that "I am fond of her."

Mrs. Roosevelt frequently found the dinner table a good place to press her opinions upon her husband. Once she got into such a heated argument with him over some political issue that her daughter Anna interrupted: "Mother, can't you see you are giving Father indigestion?" And if the President steadfastly refused to give an appointment to somebody she felt he should see, she merely invited the person to dinner. One such evening she invited the N.Y.A. head, Aubrey Williams, who had an urgent problem to discuss. The President liked Williams, but was rather startled to see him at the table. During dinner Mrs. Roosevelt urged the President to see a young Chinese student she had just met who had a new insight into China. The President said he was too busy to take the time; when Eleanor continued to insist, he sputtered crossly, "Send your Chinaman to the State Department." She was not to be put off so easily. "Franklin, you know perfectly well that the State Department is on the other side politically so far as China is concerned and it will be useless in the matter," she said, daintily spearing a piece of fish with her fork. The President repeated flatly that he was not going to waste his time seeing her Chinese student. "Well, then I will have him to dinner as my guest," she murmured sweetly. Williams burst into laughter, and had to confess to the President that was why he was there, too.

To Mrs. Roosevelt, people were just people. Because she felt some groups weren't getting a fair representation in the national life, she championed Negro causes, spoke before labor pickets, and prodded her husband to appoint women to high posts. Up until 1933 Roosevelt had displayed no special concern for Negroes; Mrs. Roosevelt was a large influence in persuading him to advise the new federal agencies to take in colored workers. She insisted that the nation's capital desegregate its public facilities, and to this day angry white residents of the District of Columbia blame the city's predominantly colored population on "that Eleanor." She was an ardent advocate of the anti-lynching law, although the President soft-pedaled it because he did not want to alienate the large Southern Democratic voting bloc in Congress, whose support he needed for more urgent bills.

She looked over the President's new appointment lists carefully to see if he included women appointees. If not, she would tell him that she was weary of reminding him to remind his Cabinet and advisers that women were a factor in the life of the nation, and increasingly important politically. He would smile and say, "Of course, I thought a woman's name had been put on the list. Have someone call up and say I feel a woman should be recognized." Often she was asked to suggest a few names; she always did, and sometimes they were appointed and sometimes not.

If there was one aspect of a First Lady's role in which Eleanor Roosevelt failed to match the record of some of her predecessors, it was the social side. Not that her manners weren't excellent, or that she failed to give the customary staggering number of receptions. It was just that she was indifferent to the extensive preparations required for a White House dinner, and left the running of these things entirely to her staff. In an economy move, she served nineteen-cent luncheons to the President, who obediently ate them. To her, food was just something to be stoked like fuel into the body to keep it running, and guests continually complained about the terrible food they were served at the White House. She resented the protocol prescribed for official functions and circumvented much of it until she was persuaded that it was required for protection and orderly procedure. She raised a howl of public protest by serving the King and Queen of England hot dogs and mustard at a picnic, instead of plying them with an elaborate black-tie state dinner. She seldom wore lipstick and powder, could go off happily for a long trip with just one small suitcase, and never paid much attention to high fashion.

But for all her informality, Mrs. Roosevelt knew the White House and its occupants held a deep significance for the American people. So three times a week in winter months she shook hands with White House tourists for an hour or so. She also realized the meaning and value of certain social duties, and rarely failed to appear by her husband's side for important events.

Eleanor Roosevelt began writing a syndicated column, which proved so popular that even furiously anti-Roosevelt newspapers were forced to carry it. She called her column "My Day," and in it she commented upon favorite projects, controversial issues, the activities of her large family. She did regular radio broadcasts.

She held press conferences for women reporters, which no other First Lady has had the courage to do. Because she was speaking out so often on so many topics, the public gradually accepted her opinions as her own, and not necessarily her husband's. She did not seem to be overly concerned about possible flubs. "My press conferences did not bother me or my husband as much as they seemed to worry other people," she remarked.

She kept up her contacts with the people of the country through a voluminous correspondence that totaled over 300,000 pieces of mail her first year in the White House. They were not all flattering: she received at least twenty threatening letters a week. Every morning and sometimes in the evening after dinner she worked on her mail. She initiated a new system for handling the correspondence after she discovered that some of the stiff form letters available for the First Lady's use had been composed as far back as the Cleveland administration. And she collected samples from each day's batch of mail to put in the basket by her husband's bedside, on the theory that people who wrote to her were more uninhibited than those who wrote to him. He read them all, and sometimes used parts of them in his speeches.

In 1934 Hitler ranted: "Eleanor Roosevelt is America's real ruler." It was an exaggeration, of course, but she did seem to get involved in everything. She was a frequent caller at government offices, and kept her phone lines humming to officials at all levels. Usually she had some project she wanted to push or check up on, or some letter-writer who wanted a job. Most members of the Cabinet resented her interference; her naïve probing into the affairs of their agencies could sometimes be embarrassing. Secretary Ickes complained, "I wish Mrs. R. would stick to her knitting and keep out of the affairs connected with my department."

She peppered the President with suggestions for speech material. A Brain Trust speech writer, Sam Rosenman, said the President suggested that his writers seek her advice, especially on speeches dealing with youth, consumer interests, or the relief program. Rosenman talked the ideas over with her, then showed her the first drafts for approval. "Mrs. R. was very helpful on certain kinds of speeches," he said.

It was inevitable that all these activities, plus her habit of speaking her mind, would embroil Eleanor Roosevelt continually in controversy. Governor Paul Pearson of the Virgin Islands commented acidly that "The President's family handicaps him politically, especially Mrs. Roosevelt." In a radio broadcast she pleaded that Congress approve the President's request that the United States join the World Court. As a result, telegrams flooded congressmen, most of them bitterly criticizing Mrs. Roosevelt for getting mixed up in a Congressional battle; and Congress rejected membership in the World Court. She expounded on the evils of capital punishment after Bruno Hauptmann was sentenced to death for the kidnap-murder of Charles Lindbergh's baby. But public sentiment was on the side of the Lindberghs, and her statements were so unpopular she confessed to an aide, "Franklin will be furious." She resigned her membership in the Daughters of the American Revolution when they refused to permit Negro Marian Anderson to sing in the D.A.R.-owned Constitution Hall. Despite loud wails from the D.A.R., she defiantly rescheduled the concert for the public mall near the Lincoln Memorial, and later invited Miss Anderson to sing at the White House for the King and Queen of England. She felt that a Congressional investigation in 1939 of organizations suspected of Communist infiltration was unfair, so she offered to testify on behalf of those organizations in which she was interested. The committee never called her to testify, but she sat through the hearings as a spectator, and after the sessions invited the witnesses to the White House for lunch.

The most serious criticism leveled at Mrs. Roosevelt concerned her support of several groups in which Communists and fellow-travelers were active, particularly the American Youth Congress. She defended the A.Y.C. for some time, because she felt its leaders were idealistic and hard-working, and because she believed their assurances that they were not Communistic. She even persuaded the President to address the A.Y.C. on the White House lawn; but he gave them a strict lecture on democracy and they booed him. She said later that whether the A.Y.C. was Communist-inspired from the beginning she never knew, but she broke with the group when she found it was opposed to national defense, lend-lease, and the national draft. She pointed out later that her experience with this group had taught her that it was impossible to work with Communist-dominated groups.

"My work with the A.Y.C. was of infinite value to me in understanding some of the tactics I had to meet later in the United Nations," she said. She was always an ardent anti-Communist. "I think I should die if I had to live in Soviet Russia," she said. Yet, because of her connection with the A.Y.C. in the late thirties, she was attacked as a "pink" and "fellow-traveler" by enemies all her life. During the last speech she made before her death, two teen-age boys hooted at her from the crowd, shouting "dirty Communist." But she did not get angry. "They are either ignorant or they are being paid," she said mildly.

But even her critics had to admit that Mrs. Roosevelt's mistakes were made only because her zeal for helping individuals and good causes sometimes got in the way of her common sense. A Republican called her "an unscrupulous Girl Scout." She would ride miles into the suburbs to address a handful of people at a club meeting. Asked why she wasted her energies on such a small group, she replied, "Because no one else will." She would invite youth leaders to discussion dinners and argue philosophy of government with them. One night the young men argued back so vehemently that her son Franklin remarked they didn't seem to have very good manners. But his mother, always tolerant, silenced him by saying that they had not had his opportunities. One day as she rode through Tarrytown, New York, her motorcycle escort was thrown off his cycle and slightly injured. She went with him to the hospital, and stayed until she was assured he would be all right. Much later, driving through the city again, she spotted the burly policeman, with bandaged head. He recognized her, got off his cycle, and started toward her. "I will not have that poor man running to me," she exclaimed, and began running down the road toward him, her cape flying.

Mrs. Roosevelt's relationship with her husband by the time they reached the White House did not fit the traditional pattern of a devoted middle-aged couple. Demonstrations of affection were rare, although they were bound together by more than a quarter of a century of intimacy, dedication to a common political cause, and mutual respect for the other's intelligence and ability. Roosevelt relied upon his wife's help, but he did not share with her his innermost hopes and tribulations (nor with anyone, for that matter). Frequently they did not see each other for long stretches, and often he did not know whether she was in the White House or not. Once, when she was off visiting prisons with Representative Maury Maverick, in charge of prison industries, the President inquired of her secretary as to her whereabouts. "She's in prison, Mr. President," the secretary replied. "I'm not surprised"—the President grinned—"but what for?" The President's grown sons didn't see him as often as they would have liked, either, and complained that in order to talk to their father they had to make an appointment like everybody else. "I wish I knew what you really thought and really wanted," Mrs. Roosevelt protested wistfully in a letter to her husband.

Their son James said that between his parents existed "deep, unshakable affection and tenderness." The Roosevelts frequently disagreed, because both had firm convictions and active tongues. But the President became furious if anybody but himself rebuked his wife. One of Roosevelt's speech writers, Robert Sherwood, recalled sitting with the President one afternoon, listening to a radio broadcast. The commentator began a bitter attack on the First Lady for a trip she was then making; and the President, a twisted expression of pain on his face, abruptly reached out and snapped off the radio.

In her own writings Mrs. Roosevelt described her relationship with her husband as one of deep understanding, warm affection, and agreement on essential values. She did not mention the word "love." She indicated that she did not share her husband's total confidence: "Franklin did not talk a great deal about the work he was doing either at meals or in private family conversations." Rexford Tugwell suggested that this reticence in Roosevelt may be partially why Eleanor lavished her boundless love and energies outside her family upon the whole world: "Her life may have been a substitution."

Mrs. Roosevelt was aware that human misery on a large scale can only be alleviated by political means, and she was adept at cultivating and using these means. But she was forever disturbed by the compromises sometimes necessary in politics. Tugwell said Mrs. Roosevelt was "more matter-of-fact, more earnest and more unswervingly moral than Franklin. She understood the necessity of politics but she had many moments of doubt whether Franklin's compromises were worth the price." She frequently protested to her husband when she feared he was about to compromise on a principle of ethics, but he seldom took her advice in such matters. Rosenman pointed out: "If she had had her way there would have been fewer compromises by Roosevelt, but also . . . fewer concrete accomplishments."

Mrs. Roosevelt was modest about her own political talents. "The political influence that was attributed to me was nil, where my husband was concerned," she insisted. "However, one cannot live in a political atmosphere and study the actions of a good politician, which my husband was, without absorbing some rudimentary facts about politics . . . though Franklin always said I was far too impatient ever to be a good politician and though my sense of timing is nowhere near so trustworthy as his was, I have grown more patient with age and have learned from my husband that no leader can be too far ahead of his followers."

One political compromise that particularly irked Mrs. Roosevelt was the President's neutrality during the Spanish civil war. When she complained that the United States ought to back the Democratic government, the President explained patiently that the League of Nations had asked the United States to remain neutral. "By trying to convince me that our course was correct, he was simply trying to salve his own conscience because he himself was uncertain," she said. "It was one of the many times when I felt akin to a hairshirt." But this didn't stop her from nagging at him regularly for what she considered his "shilly-shallying." One evening she told Leon Henderson, an administration official, "You and I, Mr. Henderson, will some day learn a lesson from this tragic error over Spain. We were morally right, but too weak." She waggled a finger at the President as though he were deaf as a post, sarcastically saying, "We should have pushed *him* harder!" The President, Henderson recalled in amazement, said not a word.

Mrs. Roosevelt never gave up the good fight, even when the cause was long lost. Years later she had a "difference of opinion" with British Prime Minister Winston Churchill, during which she complained that the United States had not "done something" to help the Spanish Loyalists during their civil war. Churchill stoutly disagreed. He declared he had been against the Loyalists and on Generalissimo Franco's side until the 1940's, when Germany and Italy went into Spain to help Franco. But then Mrs.

Roosevelt never really liked Churchill anyway. She felt he was out of date in his political thinking about the British Empire. During his frequent long visits to the White House during the war, he kept Roosevelt up until 3:00 and 4:00 A.M. talking over strategy. Mrs. Roosevelt considered this thoughtless, because Churchill could nap every day while the President worked. After each Churchill visit, it took the President several days to catch up on his sleep.

In her unceasing efforts to keep the President on the straight and narrow moral path, she wrote this angry letter to him in 1940 about another State Department policy: "I've just read the State Department report to me on their attitude on trade with Japan and the figures on that trade. What you told me on scrap iron being only a small amount was incorrect and their whole attitude seems to me weak. We help China with one hand and we appease and help Japan with the other. Why can't we decide what is right and do it?"

Mrs. Roosevelt played a prominent role in her husband's four presidential campaigns; but her influence was most in evidence at the 1940 national convention. That year the nation was uneasy about the spreading war in Europe and the President's "measures short of war" to bolster England and Russia. The President was having a feud with Postmaster General James Farley, his previous campaign manager, and there was considerable resentment about his insistence upon a third term. Roosevelt did not want to attend the convention himself, so he sent his wife as his trouble-shooter. "Eleanor always makes people feel right. She has a fine way with her," he told Secretary Perkins. The President was easily nominated, but the delegates were sharply divided on a vice-presidential nominee. Farley wanted Jesse Jones, and Roosevelt's son, Elliot, as a Texas delegate, was prepared to nominate Jones. The President, in his anger at Farley, had neglected to pass along the word properly that he preferred Henry Wallace as a running mate. Mrs. Roosevelt, under instructions from her husband, managed to ward off her son at the last minute and took the convention platform herself to urge the delegates to approve Wallace. She made a spirited, high-toned speech stressing the need for party harmony. "The only way to accomplish my aim was to persuade the delegates in the convention to sink all personal interests in the interest of the country," she said. The speech saved the day and Wallace was nominated. "She did sweeten the convention," said Secretary Perkins. Mrs. Roosevelt received a call almost immediately from the President, who said he had listened to her speech on the radio and thought she had done a very good job. He later told others, "Her speech was just right."

By 1940 the President was concentrating on preparing the nation for war. He proposed that the United States become the "arsenal of democracy," and under the unprecedented powers of the Lend-Lease Act began a vast system of lending war materials to Europe. He proclaimed an unlimited national emergency, and ordered the strengthening of United States defenses. In August, 1941, Roosevelt and Churchill held a surprise meeting off the coast of Newfoundland to sign the Atlantic Charter, a declaration of democratic principles. Since September, 1939, Europe had been at war with the aggressor Germany; on December 7, 1941, "a day that will live in infamy," the Japanese attacked Pearl Harbor and the United States, too, was at war.

The President was plunged immediately into the military problem of mapping out the grand strategy. He created the Joint Chiefs of Staff, spent long hours in the map room, consulted again and again with Churchill. The White House was closed to the public. Blackout curtains were hung at every window. Troops guarded the entrances and manned machine guns on the roof. Employees at the White House had to show special identification passes to get past the heavily guarded gates. A gas mask was attached to the President's wheel chair. In a subterranean basement a bomb shelter was installed.

The President did not keep his wife very well informed about the military progress of the war. Anyway, she was more concerned about the individuals caught up in the war—the servicemen. She became the President's personal emissary to servicemen around the world, and she regularly conducted private tours of the White House for returned wounded veterans in Washington hospitals. She took a job as an assistant director of civilian defense, but she soon found she was being blamed for every mistake of the new organization, so she resigned.

The President asked his wife to tour Great Britain in 1942,

to bring American servicemen stationed there his greetings. "I did not know that one of the reasons my husband was eager to have me go over was that those men would shortly be leaving for North Africa for the invasion," she said later. She considered that the purpose of her trip was to bolster morale and to define the national purpose in simple terms that ordinary people could understand. She toured Britain's Spitfire factory; climbed into the defenses beneath the white cliffs of Dover; ate lunch in the Prime Minister's private car, parked in a railroad tunnel lest an air raid interrupt; spoke to 15,000 cheering shipyard workers. She met, of course, England's King and Queen, and other monarchs, like The Netherlands' Queen Wilhelmina, of governments-in-exile. But she was more interested in talking to the ordinary people who had to do the fighting. In pouring rain one day she walked the length of a parade ground between two rows of girls standing at attention, water dribbling down their necks. The commanding officer suggested that Eleanor ride past in a car, but she replied firmly, "I would much rather walk." She carefully took down the name and address of the family of each serviceman she met, and when she returned to Washington she wrote to all of them.

The President gave her the code name of "Rover," and the next year he sent her to the South Pacific. She insisted upon visiting actual battle areas, like Guadalcanal; the President merely made her promise not to interfere with the conduct of the war. She traveled alone, without attendants, to take up as little space as possible. She made long flights in uncomfortable planes, rode in jeeps, walked miles through camp kitchens, hospitals, and warehouses, inspected Red Cross installations, smiled upon thousands of military patients. She got up before 6:00 A.M. in order to eat breakfast with the enlisted men, because she did not want to spend all her time with officers. She showed up in such battle-scarred, unlikely spots throughout the Pacific, that at Espirtu Santo in the New Hebrides soldiers were ordered not to take showers naked in the rain on the chance Mrs. Roosevelt might appear. The order was half-joke, half-serious; but shortly thereafter, she did show up unannounced.

Mrs. Roosevelt was roundly criticized for her efforts, as usual; but as usual the President was satisfied, and the recipients of her attention were delighted. By 1944 the President wanted her to take a message to the soldiers stationed in the Caribbean. He mapped the trip himself, thirteen thousand miles long. "I was getting a little weary of the criticism heaped on me for taking these trips, but because my husband insisted . . ." she wrote. She told the servicemen that the President had not forgotten them, even though they weren't on the front line.

In August, 1943, news came of Italy's surrender. Three months later Churchill and Roosevelt met at Teheran with Soviet Marshal Joseph Stalin for the first time, and worked out the over-all strategy which was to result in Germany's unconditional surrender. Roosevelt felt he had to run for a fourth term in 1944 to see the war through, although his health was deteriorating rapidly. In February, 1945, he met with Stalin and Churchill at Yalta, where they decided to call a meeting at San Francisco to prepare the charter for an International Security Organization. The war in Europe was coming to an end; the Allies were preparing to shift their full effort to the Pacific front. Mrs. Roosevelt worried about her husband's failing health, asked to accompany him to Yalta, but he refused. "There won't be any other wives there," he said. It was one of the few times he treated her like "any other wife." She was greatly disappointed.

By April the President was so exhausted the doctors recommended he go to Warm Springs for a rest. Mrs. Roosevelt, who had a full schedule of social events and speaking engagements, stayed behind in Washington. On the morning of April 12 she announced at her press conference that she would go to San Francisco with the President for the conference to set up a United Nations. But in the afternoon, as she attended a benefit tea, she received a call to return to the White House at once. The President had had a massive cerebral hemorrhage as he sat for an artist who was sketching his portrait. Mrs. Roosevelt did not weep. She moved automatically, sending for Vice-President Harry Truman and making arrangements to go to Warm Springs. When Truman arrived, she told him the President was dead. "I could think of nothing to say except how sorry I was for him [Truman], how much we would all want to help him in any way we could, and how sorry I was for the people of the country to have lost their leader and friend before the war was really won," she later said. She tried not to think of her husband's death as a personal sorrow. "It was the sorrow of all those to whom this man who now lay dead and who happened to be my husband had been a symbol of strength and fortitude." The President was buried in a simple grave at Hyde Park, and after the funeral she returned alone to watch silently as the workmen filled the grave. On her black dress was pinned the pearl fleur-de-lis which her husband had given her forty years before as a wedding present.

And then, at sixty-two, Eleanor Roosevelt entered into a new productive phase of her already productive life. "It isn't that I have so much energy. It's just that I never waste any of it on regret," she had said, and now she lived up to her own words. When Democratic party officials came to her in 1946 to urge that she run for the Senate, she laughed at them: "No—after all, I only have about fifteen years of service left." President Truman appointed her a delegate to the United Nations. She became the chairman of the United Nations Commission on Human Rights, and was chiefly responsible for the covenant on human rights. She was dedicated to furthering world peace through the United Nations: she considered the organization a fitting memorial to her husband. As far back as 1939 Mrs. Roosevelt had urged the establishment of a new official international group to plan continuously for world peace. Secretary of State Sumner Wells said that she had pushed the concept of such a group with the President, although most of his advisers were against it. In 1942 Wells wrote that the United States had two clear-cut alternatives in postwar planning: "One was to create the official international planning commission that Mrs. R. had suggested. . . ."

When Republican Dwight Eisenhower was elected President, she resigned from the United Nations delegation. She was promptly appointed chairman of the board of the American Association for the United Nations, and continued her work on behalf of this organization. She was still traveling: she toured the war ruins of Germany, Hiroshima and all of Europe, to better understand the plight of the refugees. She went to Russia, where she talked to Premier Khrushchev, and she visited cities all over the globe. She wrote her column, did regular radio and television talks, wrote fourteen books, gave lectures across the country. At a Roosevelt University dinner in Chicago she said, "The way to

defeat Russia without a war is first to feed hungry people throughout the world, and second to show that this country believes
in freedom and human rights." She remained active in politics,
campaigning fervently for Adlai Stevenson in 1952, 1956, and
pre-convention 1960. After John F. Kennedy was nominated in
1960, she served as an honorary chairman of the Democratic
Citizens Committee of New York.

When she died, at the age of seventy-eight, Eleanor Roosevelt had fulfilled her life's basic objective: "To grasp every opportunity to live and experience life as deeply, as fully, and as
widely as I possibly could. It seemed to me stupid to have the
gift of life and not use it to the utmost of one's ability. . . . There
is such a big, muddled world, so much to be done, so much that
can be done."

Elizabeth Wallace

TRUMAN

❀ ❀

During Mrs. Truman's eight years in the White House, astonishingly little information had been recorded about her. There has been less since her departure. In selecting material for this chapter, it was necessary to rely almost entirely upon interviews with former associates and friends and an interview with President Truman conducted in his book-lined office at the library bearing his name in Independence, Missouri.

Former President Harry S Truman opened our conversation: "If you don't say nice things about the Madam, I will spank you." He was smiling, but the tone of his voice clearly indicated he was serious in implication if not in specific intent. Surprised, I protested that my avoirdupois would be too large for even a former President to spank. He winked mischievously, and said, "I've spanked bigger ones than you."

The former President demonstrated this same fiercely pro-

tective pride toward his wife throughout our talk. He stressed that Mrs. Truman had never sought public attention, and did not do so now. He explained, however, that he could not resist an opportunity to pay her the tribute he felt she deserves, since they were now many years removed from the White House limelight. Mr. Truman conveyed the distinct impression that had Mrs. Truman known her husband was discussing her for purposes of publication, she would have protested mightily.

The former President was obviously aware of the difficulties involved in researching the life and personality of his wife. After my interview I sat in the Library's research room, looking with disappointment at one skimpy folder on Mrs. Truman, containing a meager handful of repetitious and unrevealing magazine articles. Truman passed through the room with a companion and remarked, "She thinks she's going to write something about the Madam."

Despite his protectiveness and his respect for his wife's reticence, former President Truman was greatly interested in a study of twelve First Ladies and offered considerable encouragement. His office is filled with the records and memoirs of Presidents, Cabinet members, and government dignitaries; he says he has read every volume. Because of his exhaustive study of the presidency, Truman is well informed not only on Chief Executives but on their wives as well. He inquired as to which First Ladies were selected for my book and nodded agreement to most names. He was particularly enthusiastic about Abigail Adams, who he thought displayed more leadership ability than her husband. He was especially delighted that Mary Lincoln was to be included, because he believes her to be "the most unjustly maligned woman in American history," a comment which reflects in some degree his sensitivity.

Harry S Truman, who is already being ranked by historians as one of our nation's strongest Presidents, was possibly the most underrated man ever to occupy the White House. Similarly, the nation never realized the vast influence exerted by his wife Bess, whose passion for anonymity made her appear like a housewife with nothing more on her mind than how to get the stains out of the rug and what to fix for supper.

It is high time that Mrs. Truman, the least-known First Lady of modern times, received some of the credit she deserves.

Former President Truman says today that his wife was "a full partner in all my transactions—politically and otherwise." He acknowledges that he has consulted her about every decision of his life—including some of the great decisions of American history, such as whether to fight in Korea, whether to use the atom bomb, whether to initiate the Marshall Plan to rebuild a shattered Europe. The final decision was always the President's alone, of course. But first, "I discussed all of them with her," Truman says. Then, as an afterthought, he adds, "Why not?"

Now, ten years away from the White House, Truman contributes to a clearer understanding of the role of the First Lady during the difficult postwar years. "Her judgment was always good," he says. "She never made a suggestion that wasn't for the welfare and benefit of the country and what I was trying to do. She looks at things objectively, and I can't always. . . ."

During her nearly eight years in the White House, Bess Truman managed to remain quietly in the background. She refused to give interviews. She rarely spoke a word in public. She confined her conversation at official functions to pleasant small talk, carefully avoiding anything that smacked of politics. She dressed in simply tailored, inconspicuous clothes, and never did anything to attract attention or seek special favors. Although the President never liked to have her far from him, she generally preferred to stand on the sidelines rather than at his elbow in the full glare of the public limelight. She was so successful at remaining out of the public eye, in fact, that nine months after the inauguration she shopped for Christmas presents in Washington's big department stores without being recognized.

President Truman conspired willingly with the First Lady to protect her from public attention, because he did not want to see her unjustly criticized, as several other First Ladies have been. He believes that the biggest hardship a First Lady must bear is the constant limelight, "with everybody pointing a finger at her." He says, "It can hurt. Some bear it, and some can't. Mrs. Truman was able to take care of the situation" (by virtually hiding out).

Yet it was Truman who sounded the call for a better appreciation of First Ladies, who are too frequently judged on superficial aspects such as clothes and the photogenic quality of their smiles. In his book, *Mr. Citizen*, he wrote: "I hope some day someone will take time to evaluate the true role of the wife of a President, and to assess the many burdens she has to bear and the contributions she makes."

In Truman's estimation, "the proper role of a First Lady is to be the First Lady of the land." And, he adds proudly, "That's what Mrs. Truman did. And she'll always be the First Lady as far as I'm concerned." He gestures to the cluster of little photographs and mementos of his family that clutter the top of his big desk in his office in the Harry S Truman Library at Independence, Missouri. "You see all these pictures here on my desk to prove it."

Both Harry and Bess Truman have a deep sense of history, and they were highly conscious during their terms of the importance and dignity of the White House and the leadership it symbolized. Mrs. Truman considered it her responsibility to maintain every protocol precedent set by former occupants and every tradition of formality and hospitality. She was one of the hardest-working First Ladies, personally directing the plans for all social events and never avoiding any public appearance she regarded as her proper duty. Truman says, "One of the biggest contributions she made was to see that the feminine part of the White House was run properly. She made sure that the snooty women were well treated. That's something I wouldn't do . . . I wouldn't talk to them.

"Certain receptions were customary, certain programs necessary. She did them all. She planned the receptions herself, and she was always there to greet the guests."

The blunt Truman is the first to admit that at times the public aspect of being President, with its endless hours of handshaking, can get pretty tiresome. It was a particular chore to Mrs. Truman, who is so reticent that mobs of staring strangers make her nervous. But she is conscientious, and she has devoted her life to doing things for her husband. Some visitors detected that she did not seem to enjoy her job as the nation's hostess very much. But, according to Edith Helm, her social secretary, "All over Washington I heard from people—many of them no friends of the Truman administration or its ways—nothing but praise of Mrs. Truman, her dignity and her unfailing cordiality when hostess at the White House." Truman says, "It's part of the game. If you can't stand it, you shouldn't be in it."

But it is the role of the First Lady in the privacy of her family that matters more, in the long run, than her public performance. This is the side of Bess Truman that the nation has never understood. And the key is the truly extraordinary, deep-seated, mutual devotion of the Trumans. Few presidential couples, by the time they reach the White House in their later years, have displayed such closeness and total dependence upon each other.

Recently the former First Lady was asked by an old friend what she considered the most memorable aspect of her life. Her answer was prompt: "Harry and I have been sweethearts and married more than forty years—and no matter where I was, when I put out my hand Harry's was there to grasp it."

Truman, who says, "I've got a close family unit," has always regarded his career as a team effort. He threatens to reprimand anybody who says an unkind word about his wife, and he once banished Representative Adam Clayton Powell and Representative Clare Booth Luce from all White House social events because they criticized her. The White House servants fondly called the President, the First Lady, and daughter Margaret "The Three Musketeers." Margaret wrote about her mother: "She worked from morning until night. In addition, she was always being required to divide what little time was left between my father and me and her own mother, no one of whom seemed able to negotiate without her."

George Allen, a friend of the Trumans, said, "I think he has been helped more than most people can possibly realize by an understanding wife and a wonderful daughter." Old friends today in Independence say, "He put his womenfolk on a pedestal," and point out that "Bess was his first and only sweetheart." Columnist Leonard Lyons recalls driving past a big billboard advertising the Broadway musical *Gentlemen Prefer Blondes*, with the President. The President sniffed and said, "*Real* gentlemen prefer gray."

"She always helped me," Truman says, "In everything." In his memoirs, which Mrs. Truman edited and helped to organize, Truman pays tribute to his wife for her help and encouragement, suggestions and corrections and "on whose counsel and judgment

I frequently called." Truman never made a speech without showing it to her first for suggestions. She was observed in Independence one day, in fact, sitting calmly under the hair dryer in the
beauty parlor, going slowly over a typewritten speech with a
stubby yellow pencil. During all of Truman's campaigns his wife
was included in the private sessions of the inner advisory councils
which discussed the next day's activities; the President frequently
referred to her as "my chief adviser." A relative contends that in
the White House the President and Mrs. Truman discussed their
plans and problems for the day over the breakfast table, and she
acted as a sounding board and critic for all his proposed projects.

A former Secret Service agent who observed the Trumans
closely claims that "the President was henpecked." But most of
the President's friends and former associates firmly disagree. Mrs.
Truman was his chief confidante, companion, supporter, and adviser—but when the President made up his mind to do something,
she never stopped him.

It has been generally assumed that Bess Truman didn't
know much about politics, largely because she never expressed
herself publicly on the subject. And former associates like Jonathan Daniels felt that in 1920, when Truman first ran for county
judge, "Bess had no very high opinion of politics as a career
(sometimes she gives the impression of feeling that way still)."
But Mrs. Truman merely felt, in the traditional concept of fifty
years ago, that politics was man's business (and pretty grubby
business at that) and a lady had no proper place being "political-
minded." But the former President says that his wife discussed
politics with him, as well as every other subject. He points out
that she was surrounded by politics all her life. She was the oldest
child in the Wallace family, and her three younger brothers all
looked to her for guidance. They were involved in politics, so
she could hardly avoid becoming interested in politics too. And
friends say that in her private conversation she reveals a deep
knowledge and familiarity with the events, people, and theories
that make political background.

The former President also lists, as an important contribution
to his years in the White House, Mrs. Truman's constant struggle
(largely successful) to maintain the same kind of private, comfortable home life they had shared before they moved into 1600

Pennsylvania Avenue. She continued to address her own Christmas cards and chatter for hours long-distance to friends in Independence. She played table tennis in the basement with Margaret, and they laughed and joked like classmates. She hired a new housekeeper on the sole qualification that "she keeps her mouth shut." She once got so lonely for her bridge club in Independence that she had the "girls" flown to Washington for four days. "We never let anybody up on the second floor, where our private living quarters were, except our closet friends," Truman says.

"The White House is not a home, but a temporary residence, and it takes a good deal of talent and work on the part of the President's wife to make it livable," Truman has said. "Making it livable makes it possible for the President to carry out his heavy burdens."

On paper, the Trumans sound like unlikely candidates for the really capable White House occupants they turned out to be. Truman never went to college, and failed in the only business he ever tried to operate. They continually teetered on the brink of poverty. His career was undistinguished for years, in minor political posts obtained principally because he was in favor with the powerful but corrupt political machine of Tom Pendergast. Mrs. Truman was an immaculate housekeeper, but she had no hobbies, joined no clubs, participated in no community endeavors. When she appeared in public with her husband, she was frozen-faced and forbiddingly stiff. They did not come to Washington until they were fifty, and they never became a part of the inner group that dominates the capital's social and official life. Truman's incurable propensity for swearing and blunt language made most officials consider him coarse and unintelligent. Neither Truman nor his wife aspired to the White House; few men in history have made less effort to attain the presidency. There seemed to be nothing special about the Trumans—they were "just plain folks," and liked it that way.

And yet, in his lifetime, Harry S Truman has already been rated by a panel of seventy-five noted historians as the ninth greatest President in history. It was their judgment that Truman "discharged impressively the awesome obligations devolving on the United States as the leader of the free world in the cold war with Soviet imperialism. The Truman Doctrine for the protection

of Greece and Turkey, the Marshall Plan for the restoration of
Western Europe, the Berlin airlift, the Point Four program for
backward countries, N.A.T.O. (our first peacetime alliance), and
the intervention in Korea in support of the United Nations—all
these constituted landmarks in an assumption of global responsibilities undreamed of only a few years before."

The Trumans were handed the burdens of the presidency at
a terrible and dramatic moment. The great leader who had
brought the nation through its worst depression and directed the
allied effort that was winning the world's worst war was suddenly
dead. In Europe, World War II was at last staggering to a close;
but the possibility of a long war in the Pacific still stretched
ahead. After twelve years of the magnificent Roosevelt, millions
found it difficult to accept the fact that another man could take
his place. The country knew very little about the man who had
been Vice-President only two months, and who had been described unimpressively during the 1944 campaign as "plain as an
old shoe" and "an inconspicuous man with thin lips, steel-rimmed
glasses, flatly combed gray hair, and a flat, not unpleasant Missouri twang." The American people would have been far more
disturbed had they known what Harry Truman knew—that he
had seen Roosevelt privately only twice since the inauguration
and that Roosevelt had never discussed anything important with
him. Truman did not even know what oral commitments Roosevelt might have made six weeks before when he had consulted
with Stalin and Churchill in the Crimea, or of the existence of the
atom bomb.

On April 12, 1945, the United States Senate recessed at
5:10 P.M. Vice-President Truman, who had been presiding (one
of the few tasks allotted a Vice-President by the Constitution),
headed for Speaker Sam Rayburn's office in the House side of
the Capitol, where a small party was in progress. Three weeks
before, Truman had confided after seeing President Roosevelt,
"He seemed a spent man. I had a hollow feeling within me." And
the Secret Service, whose business it is to be realistic about Presidents and potential Presidents, had recently assigned an agent to
the Vice-President, not a customary procedure in those days.
When Truman arrived at Rayburn's office, a phone call from Steve
Early, the President's press secretary, was waiting for him. "Please

come right over. And come in through the main Pennsylvania Avenue entrance," Early said in a taut voice, and hung up without another word. "Holy General Jackson," Truman muttered. His face looked as if he had just been hit with a baseball bat. "I'll be back soon," he told the men in Rayburn's office, and set off at a trot. He stopped briefly to poke his head into his own office, where his aide, Harry Vaughn, was still working. "Early wants me to come to the White House . . . I have a hunch the President is seriously ill. Something is wrong," he grimly told Vaughn. Flippantly, Vaughn blurted, "Well, don't let them swear you in without me." But Truman didn't grin back, as he usually did at Vaughn's sallies. He was already racing down to the Capitol basement, and through the underground tunnel to the garage. He got his car so swiftly that he lost his Secret Service agent, and was unguarded all the way to the White House.

At 5:25 P.M., Truman was ushered upstairs to Mrs. Roosevelt's study. She embraced him gently, and said, "Harry, the President is dead." Stunned, Truman was speechless for a long moment. Finally he asked, "Is there anything I can do for you?" Mrs. Roosevelt looked at him sadly. "Is there anything we can do for *you?* For you are the one in trouble now," she said softly.

The nation was without a President. Calls were immediately put in to gather the legislative leaders, Chief Justice Harlan Stone, and the Cabinet. Truman called the small apartment at Tilden Gardens, 4701 Connecticut Avenue, where he and his family had lived since he came to Washington as a senator ten years before. Margaret, who was dashing about getting dressed for a date, answered the phone. "Hi, Dad," she bubbled. "Are you coming home to dinner?" "Let me speak to your mother," Truman said curtly. Somewhat offended, Margaret called to her mother and went back to her room.

Mrs. Truman listened at the phone without a word, and suddenly burst into tears. Margaret recalled: "I went into her room and Mother was standing there in an attitude of dejection with the tears running down her face." "President Roosevelt is dead," Mrs. Truman sobbed. The shaken mother and daughter looked at each other in silence. Margaret said later, "I did not analyze her emotions at the time. I was too busy with my own. My mother is a mature and serious and private person. Along with her grief for a great man and a good friend, she must have looked down the unknowable future and shuddered."

Mrs. Truman and Margaret hastily gathered up coats and hats, but by the time they left the apartment the nation had been told over the radio of Roosevelt's death. Secret Service men were waiting outside to escort them, and a crowd of curious strangers, reporters, and photographers filled the sidewalk. Mrs. Truman plunged forward, staring straight ahead. "Come on," she murmured. "Her face was grave and sad and also stoical," said Margaret.

Mrs. Truman and her daughter reached the White House at 6:00 P.M. In the Cabinet Room, several officials had already gathered. Secretary of Labor Frances Perkins was weeping. Truman looked grim, but he smiled weakly at his wife and patted her hand. Later he recalled vaguely that "everyone was crying and carrying on. None of us could believe that Roosevelt was gone." Secretary of Commerce Henry Wallace, who had been Vice-President until only two months before, was having a difficult time controlling his emotions. "He looked very strange," a man who was there that night says.

Harry S Truman was sworn in as President at 7:09 P.M. in the Cabinet Room. "Bess Truman beside him looked like a woman in pain," Jonathan Daniels said. Only the day before, the Vice-President had told reporters that the Senate "is where I've always wanted to be and the only place I ever wanted to be. The Senate—that's just my speed and my style." And now, as President, a humble and worried man said, "I feel as though the moon and all the stars and all the planets have fallen upon me. Please, boys, give me your prayers. I need them very much."

His first executive order was to announce that the United Nations charter conference would proceed on schedule at San Francisco in two weeks, and to name Eleanor Roosevelt as a delegate.

Old friends in Independence, and former associates in Washington, asked to describe Bess Truman, invariably begin with the phrase, "She was always a lady." They tell story after story of her unfailing courtesy, her quiet kindnesses to friends in trouble, her propriety and composure, and her no-nonsense attitude. She was neat, but not fussy. She had a sense of humor, but she did not approve of jokes in bad taste. She devoted her full time to her husband, her daughter, and her home, and she never pretended to be anything but herself. Part of her concept of being a lady was the complete acceptance of responsibility, wanted or unwanted. Says Vaughn, "The greatest thing about Mrs. Truman is the sincerity with which she approached her job, even though she didn't like it."

So, having always conducted herself as she thought a proper lady should, Bess Truman at sixty had no intention of changing simply because she had become the First Lady. She ran the White House as she ran her own home: she attended personally to details many First Ladies left to the ample staff, answered personal mail in longhand herself, took charge of the bookkeeping, and carefully guarded expenses (for the Trumans, unlike more fortunate Presidents, had no income but the presidential salary and were required to live within its bounds). When she returned to their big Victorian gingerbread house in Independence for the summers, she continued to do her own cooking and shopping as she had for twenty-five years, with only one maid to help with the cleaning of the fourteen-room house. She initiated a Spanish class in the White House, which won accolades throughout Latin America; and, according to her teacher, she prepared her homework faithfully, just as though she did not outrank the other women students.

During their first week in the White House the President's new secretary, Eddie McKim, found some stenographers working on the thousands of letters that had poured in to Mrs. Roosevelt after her husband's death. McKim angrily fired the girls and ordered the work dropped. "Mrs. Roosevelt is no longer riding the gravy train," he growled. When the new First Lady heard about it, she complained to the President. As a result, the next morning the girls were put back to work on Mrs. Roosevelt's mail and McKim was soon dispatched in disgrace to the hinterland of the Federal Loan Administration.

The First Lady, guests soon discovered, did not at all behave like the Midwestern nobody they had suspected she might be. She had a remarkable memory, and seldom failed to get a name or face straight. She was efficient at the details that mark the good hostess: for example, she once sent a note down the head table to the President to remind him that the shy dinner partner he was ignoring was Dr. Lise Meitner, the noted atomic scientist. She remained a stranger to most of the White House guests, even those who came frequently, because of her coolly imposing manner (which was due partially to her shyness)—but they all respected her. She was never discourteous. Once, when a particularly nasty Republican senator approached them in the receiving line, the President whispered that he dared her to trip So-and-so. "Shush," whispered back the First Lady. "Remember he is a guest in our house."

And with her family and her longtime friends, Bess Truman remained the same kindly, warm, quiet person. In 1960, after all the honors and privileges that had come her way, she could still tell Sue Gentry, an Independence newspaperwoman, excitedly that "I've just had an orchid named after me—and that's as big a thrill as I've ever had." When asked what she considered the most important assets for a President's wife, she replied "good health and a well-developed sense of humor." One day, showing Leonard and Sylvia Lyons through the White House, she pointed out the President's big chair to Jeffrey Lyons, eight years old. Jeffrey, enthralled, immediately plopped himself down in it to pretend he was President. Mrs. Lyons, embarrassed, shooed her son away with the admonition that he must not sit there "unless some day you have the right to." Mrs. Truman, looking fondly at Jeffrey, murmured, "Pray not, pray not."

The Trumans were friendly with a Washington hostess, Perle Mesta. So when *Call Me Madam,* a Broadway musical based upon Mrs. Mesta's life, was produced, the First Lady and her friend decided to go see it. They arrived at the theater unannounced with Leonard Lyons, and got in line at the ticket booth. An usher who recognized the First Lady frantically tried to escort her in ahead of the other waiting ticket-purchasers. Mrs. Truman smiled politely, but refused to budge. "We'll wait our turn," she said firmly. When the trio marched down the aisle to their seats, the startled theater audience began to clap. The applause continued after they were seated, so Perle Mesta got up and took a bow. The applause didn't stop. Embarrassed, the modest Mrs. Truman urged, "Stand up, Perle. They want you again."

This reluctance of the First Lady to put on airs was part, again, of her childhood training in how to be a lady. In the spring of 1962 a young Independence photographer, Ken White, took the former President and First Lady fishing at a special spot along the river. He arranged for some other fishermen to be on hand to assist Mrs. Truman with her catch. For Bess Truman is the fishing enthusiast in the family; the former President prefers to watch while his wife does the work with rod and reel. (During their courtship, young Truman often took her fishing and sat on the bank reading a book while she fished.) Mrs. Truman caught five big crappies, and had a wonderful time. The next day she called to thank White. "I had such fun that I'd like to go again, and bring some friends," she said. "But none of that special treatment the next time!"

Even though she conducted herself most circumspectly, Mrs. Truman did not escape public criticism entirely. She created some resentment among reporters for refusing to continue Mrs. Roosevelt's practice of holding press conferences. Her attitude, however, was merely: "I am not the one who is elected. I have nothing to say to the public." And in the fall of 1945 she aroused a storm of complaints because she attended a tea given by the Daughters of the American Revolution shortly after the organization refused to allow the Negro wife of Representative Adam Clayton Powell, noted pianist Hazel Scott, to play in Constitution Hall. Powell, in a fury, called her "the last lady." Others charged that because of a background steeped in Southern tradition she must be prejudiced. Mrs. Truman seemed astonished at the public furor. "I deplore any action which denies artistic talent an opportunity to express itself because of prejudice against race or origin," she said, but added that having accepted the invitation before the incident she had "no other idea than to keep this engagement."

Because of this attack, Truman never invited Powell to the White House, even for the annual reception for members of Congress. Congresswoman Luce was similarly banished. The President explained why to Henry Luce: "I have been in politics for thirty-five years and everything that could be said about a human being has been said about me. But my wife has never been in politics, and she has always conducted herself in a cir-

cumspect manner. No one has the right to make derogatory remarks about Mrs. T. Your wife has said many unkind and untrue
things about her. And as long as I am in residence here, she'll
never be a guest in the White House. . . ."

(Ironically, Truman himself was to be banished for eight
years from the White House guest list in 1953 by the new Republican President, Dwight Eisenhower, who had never been in
politics before and could not forgive the derogatory remarks
Truman made about him during the 1952 campaign.)

After three years as First Lady, Mrs. Truman was asked how
she liked living in the White House. "Oh, so-so," she replied. The
President, too, had considerable reason to be less than enthusiastic about the White House. Italy and Germany had surrendered
within a month after his inauguration; Japan bowed on August
14, after Truman ordered atom bombs dropped on Hiroshima and
Nagasaki. But the problems of peace were monumental. The
shift from wartime restrictions to a peacetime economy was painful and chaotic: rationing adjustments were boggled, Truman's
juggling of Cabinet and top government posts created mass confusion, a flood of labor disputes and paralyzing strikes stalled re-
conversion. On the popularity polls, Truman sank to thirty per-
cent support. And in 1946 the voters gave control of both houses
of Congress to the Republicans.

The Congress stubbornly refused to give Truman the far-
reaching domestic programs he wanted, programs that were said
to "out-new deal the New Deal." The Republicans squashed every
part of his anti-inflation program. But the President was building
an impressive record on the international front. On March 12,
1947, he proposed the Truman Doctrine, asking Congress for aid
to Greece and Turkey, to bolster them against the Communist
threat. In the Foreign Assistance Act, Truman's Marshall Plan
was approved, to pour unprecedented vast sums into Europe to
rebuild her shattered cities and restore her independent industrial
capacity. When the Russians cut off access between the divided
city of Berlin and the West, Truman ordered the Berlin airlift,
to keep the city supplied until the blockade was abandoned.

In 1948 Mrs. Truman was eager to retire to Independence,
but the President felt differently. Margaret recorded: "Mother
. . . acquiesced because she knew how profoundly my father

wished to finish the job he had started." Democrats and Republicans alike figured that Truman didn't have a chance of re-election, anyway. Republican nominee Thomas E. Dewey was so confident of victory that he embarked upon an easygoing, lofty campaign, in which he grandly ignored all Truman's attacks and declined to make specific promises about his future policies. But Truman waged a peppery whistle-stop campaign, vigorously denouncing at every town the "do-nothing Congress" and painting himself as the plain people's President pitted against the privileged people's Congress.

A key part of the campaign was the family act. The President wound up each speech by introducing "the boss" and "the boss that bosses the boss." Mrs. Truman and Margaret never said a word, but they were sensational. A campaign train worker reported, "You could almost hear what the crowds were thinking—they were thinking what a nice family, just like the folks next door." And nobody seemed to notice that wherever Dewey campaigned there were those in the audience who whispered, "He looks like the little man on the wedding cake."

A reporter traveling on the Truman train recorded that Mrs. Truman was "a one-woman Gallup Poll and audience-reaction tester, keeping a sharp watch on the crowds which listened to her husband's oratory. She was also the careful censor of the President's occasional lapses into humorous overexuberance." Another correspondent noted that Mrs. Truman was a member of the small advisory circle which gathered with the President every night. Another reporter spotted her sitting at the window in her compartment, carefully penciling comments on a speech. Mrs. Truman considered herself responsible for the care and feeding not only of the President but of every person on the campaign train. She gave aspirin to reporters with colds and sewed buttons on male staffers' coats. She clucked over the comfort of local dignitaries, secretaries, weary aides. She personally checked the preparation of all the President's meals, and she insisted that he take naps when she felt he acted sluggish or sounded hoarse. She managed to look neat and unrumpled at each stop, and never complained about her cramped quarters or the lack of a maid to help her. She frequently made suggestions about aspects of the President's off-the-cuff speeches which seemed to have particular impact upon the audience. She protested the impropriety of Truman's use of a joke kidding mothers-in-law, and he dropped it from his repertoire of anecdotes.

Truman drew large, enthusiastic crowds wherever he went, but still the experts and the pollsters were convinced that Dewey would win. Only the President himself seemed to think otherwise. A reporter who visited the President's suite on election night reported back to his friends that "The old boy still thinks he's going to win. He's standing there under the shower telling everybody that he'll sweep the country." The friends laughed.

The confident President went to bed early that night, instead of waiting for the returns. But Mrs. Truman and Margaret sat up all night, listening to the radio. The next morning the Chicago *Tribune* headlined "Dewey Defeats Truman," *Kiplinger* magazine mailed its issue entitled "What Dewey Will Do," and columnists all over the country expounded on the new Dewey Cabinet. But in one of the most incredible upsets in political history, the impossible had happened. Harry S Truman was not only re-elected: he carried into office with him a brand-new Democratic majority in both House and Senate.

Politicians later gave part of the credit for his victory to his family. The country certainly liked "the boss." Actually, Mrs. Truman didn't "boss" the President, any more than any wife who loves her husband enough to keep after him to carry an umbrella when it rains and avoid rich foods that he fancies but which make him sick. Calling Mrs. Truman "the boss," or "Madam," his other pet nickname for her, was part of Truman's little family joke. He liked to tease her, in an affectionate, strictly masculine way, about her efforts to curb his impulsive tongue and remind him to watch his manners.

"The boss" was an expression used frequently by husbands in semi-rural mid-America a quarter of a century ago, when strong-willed women of good upbringing had no careers but their husbands. It was generally a good-natured admission that while a man's wife rarely had an opinion in public, she didn't hesitate to push her point of view with her husband in private.

One of "the boss's" more successful expressions of opinion affecting the career of Harry Truman was her insistence that he exercise moderation. A highly sentimental and emotional man, the

President had a low boiling point which sometimes led him to do and say things for which he was later sorry. If the President discussed the situation with Mrs. Truman before he reacted, she usually tempered his response. Frequently the President confided to his military aide, Harry Vaughn, "Well, I was going to do such and such but 'the boss' talked me out of it." Once the President, furious at an insubordinate official, snapped to an aide, "I wrote a letter to X this morning, and sent it out by messenger right away before 'the boss' could see it and talk me out of it."

Another time, when the President gave full vent to his anger before Mrs. Truman could counsel restraint, he created one of the most widely publicized uproars of his administration. Margaret had made her singing debut in a concert in Constitution Hall. Her mother later told friends that she had sat nervously with her heart in her mouth the whole time Margaret was up there on the stage, alone. The next morning Paul Hume, music critic for the Washington *Post*, said that Margaret was flat a good deal of the time and didn't sing with professional finish. The father in Truman overwhelmed the President in him, and he sent a bitter letter warning that if he ever met Hume he would "need a new nose and plenty of beefsteak," for writing such a "lousy" review.

Mrs. Truman fought a lifelong battle to change the President's habit of swearing whenever he was annoyed. The servants recalled that her most frequent expression around the White House was "You didn't have to say that." But Truman has never stopped "giving 'em hell." During the 1960 campaign Truman told a San Antonio audience that any Texan who voted for Republican presidential candidate Richard Nixon ought to "go to hell." Later, Kennedy lieutenant Richard Donahue found Truman pacing his hotel room in a gloomy mood. "The Madam," Truman explained, had just seen his speech on television and called up to bawl him out. "If you can't talk politer than that in public, you come right home," she told him crisply.

Early in his term, the President was annoyed by attacks by several newspapers upon his close associates and persistent suggestions that he fire certain officials. One night during a dinner speech, he exploded: "Everyone is telling me who I should have on my staff and in my Cabinet. No s.o.b. is going to dictate to me who I'm going to have." When he got back to the White House, the First Lady was waiting up for him, with a severe lecture upon the need for dignity in the presidency. Several days later, while the controversy over the President's uncensored words still raged, an aide told Truman the rector of a large Washington church had remarked that under similar provocation he might have said the same thing. Truman grinned ruefully, and said, "I just wish that the rector would go talk to my wife."

After his retirement in 1952 the former President and Mrs. Truman made a trip to Europe. Truman paid a special visit to Salerno, where he had fought in World War I. The next day a newspaper quoted him as having complained about the "squirrel-headed generals" who directed the battle. Truman called aside the guilty reporter to protest, contending that he had been misquoted. But Mrs. Truman, listening to the conversation, pointed out spiritedly, "Well, it certainly *sounds* like something you'd say."

They also spent one night in Rome, but since the former President had not been there since World War I, and Mrs. Truman had never been there, they did not know where to dine. A reporter traveling with the Trumans suggested a famous restaurant which overlooked the city, and said that he would make all the arrangements. The Trumans were delighted. That evening the little group gathered in the Truman suite before dinner. The reporter, describing his plans for their grand evening, explained that the restaurant was actually the converted villa Mussolini had built for his mistress Clara Petacci.

Truman's protocol officer protested: "We can't possibly go to such a place. Think how it would look in the press if it got out that the President visited the villa of Mussolini's mistress his only night in Rome. . . ." Truman was obviously disappointed, but he agreed that it might look bad back home. Mrs. Truman, who generally kept her opinions to herself in public, cut in. "Well, after all," she said sweetly, "*she* won't be there." The Trumans went to the restaurant.

Teasing Mrs. Truman about being "the boss" was only part of the banter that went on in the Truman family. It helped the President unwind after a tense day to indulge in a little gentle ribbing of his wife, who had a droll sense of humor almost as robust as the President's own. Vaughn was the President's favorite gagster, but his jokes were sometimes bawdy or irreverent. So frequently, after the President roared with laughter at an obviously naughty joke, he would grin and insist gleefully, "Tell that one to Bess. But I want to be there to watch her reaction." One day Mrs. Truman came home with a tale of woe about her frustrating attempt to dedicate the first hospital plane. Somebody had forgotten to score the symbolic champagne bottle, and when she swung it against the plane, the bottle didn't break but instead put a healthy dent in the aluminum fusilage. Mrs. Truman swung again, and the dent got bigger. Fortunately, a quick-witted mechanic leaped on the platform at this embarrassing point, held the bottle against the plane, and smashed it with his wrench. The President, chuckling, suggested that the First Lady ought to have pushed back her hat, spat on her hands, and let fly with a mighty swing as she used to do when they played sandlot baseball as kids. The First Lady failed to see the humor of the situation. "I'm sorry I didn't swing that bottle at you," she retorted.

Recently an old friend in Washington called the President in Independence. "What are you doing?" he inquired. "I'm doing as I damn please—when the Madam will let me," chortled Truman over the phone.

After their second inauguration, the Trumans moved into Blair House, the official guest house for state visitors across the avenue from the White House. The executive mansion had been inspected and found to be unsafe for habitation: termites and the long years of wear and tear had weakened the structure so badly it was ready to collapse. A leg of Margaret's piano, in fact, had fallen through a hole in the floor. The Trumans lived in the smaller quarters of Blair House for nearly four years, until the mansion's reconstruction was finished.

But no matter how cramped the quarters, there was always room for a piano. The President is a capable pianist, and once remarked, "We ought to have been a vaudeville team. We would have had lots of fun. I could have played the piano, Margaret could have sung, and the Madam could have managed the act." The piano got him into still another public fuss over his lack of decorum, though. One night, as the President played the piano at a public gathering, actress Lauren Bacall hopped on the top of it, displaying an expanse of leg. The photographs of the President thus cavorting spread across the newspaper front pages the next day. An exasperated Mrs. Truman complained: "I think it's time you gave up playing the piano." (He didn't, of course.)

A President, however, is not judged by history on his decorum. He is judged by results. In his second inaugural address, Truman announced his Four Points of a major program to promote world peace, of which the most famous section is the plan for industrial and scientific help to underdeveloped countries. In 1949 he signed the North Atlantic Treaty for the mutual defense of Europe. He ordered construction of the H-bomb, to keep ahead of Russia in the increasing arms race. He resubmitted to Congress his ambitious welfare programs, but about all he got passed was legislation boosting the minimum wage in certain industries engaged in interstate commerce from forty cents to seventy-five cents an hour. Inflation was growing, but the administration's attempts to freeze prices and wages failed. When the steel union announced a strike in 1952, Truman seized the nation's ninety-two steel mills to keep them operating; but his action was declared unconstitutional by the Supreme Court, and the strike had to be settled finally by mediation after a fifty-four-day layoff.

In June, 1950, North Korean troops crossed the 38th parallel and invaded South Korea. President Truman ordered United States troops to the aid of South Korea, and the United Nations authorized an international "police action," enforced by United States soldiers, to end the hostilities. Within six months American dead reached 100,000, and President Truman had declared a state of national emergency. Chinese Communist troops began openly helping the North Koreans, and the United Nations formally accused Communist China of aggression. General Douglas MacArthur, commander of the United States troops in the Far East, pleaded for permission to bomb the Communist supply bases in Manchuria and to pursue enemy planes. But Truman believed that unless the war was contained within the borders of Korea, a third world war might begin: an attack upon positions in Manchuria would be tantamount to declaring war on China, which was linked by military alliance to Russia. MacArthur, who had recaptured all the invaded South Korean territory by March, 1951, defied his commander in chief to demand publicly that the

United States–United Nations troops attack Red China. Instead of negotiations through the United Nations for a cease-fire, MacArthur also demanded that North Korea be surrendered to him personally.

The President, rightfully predicting that his action would "cause the darndest furor you ever saw," fired MacArthur in April. The public, irritated by a war in Korea they didn't clearly understand, cast its sympathy with the war hero. MacArthur was greeted with a hero's welcome, including a ticker tape parade in New York City. Even Mrs. David Wallace, the First Lady's mother, didn't approve of the firing of MacArthur. She asked her daughter, "Why did Harry fire that nice man?" Mrs. Truman, always loyal, merely tossed her head and marched silently from the room.

Exactly three months after MacArthur's dismissal, the first Korean truce talks were held between the United Nations and the Communists at Kaesong. But the negotiations were to stagger along drearily, interrupted by light skirmishes, so long that 1952 Republican nominee Eisenhower made the promise of a prompt peace agreement in Korea his most effective campaign weapon.

The President was surrounded on all sides by controversy. Close aides were investigated for misdoings. He seemed to be continually arguing with labor, which was flexing its muscles on the national political scene with new impact. The threat of internal Communism panicked the nation, with Senator Joseph McCarthy leading a probe of alleged Red activity in the State Department. Attacks on supposed corruption within the Truman administration increased.

Bess Truman, at sixty-seven, had had enough. She had been terrified by an assassination attempt by two Puerto Ricans upon her husband. She was weary of the public staring at her short, 155-pound, size-eighteen "let out at the waist" figure. She worried about the President's health, and she wanted him to spend his last years in peaceful retirement. She longed to return to Independence, where her family had lived for five generations and where old friends called her "Bess" instead of "First Lady." She was tired of thinking up ways to dodge the limelight, such as the time she sat for half an hour in a car with her brother one block from a party Truman was attending, waiting until just a minute before she knew he had to leave. Only then did she drive up, just in time to wave from the car before driving off again—with Truman—and far too late to be the object of attention.

This time Harry Truman agreed with his wife, and he refused to run for re-election in 1952. They returned home to be met by a cheering crowd of about fifteen thousand that jammed the streets from the railroad station to their home at 219 Delaware Street. Mrs. Truman, as usual, received the public demonstration in nervous silence. But once inside the house, she said, "If this is what you get for all those years of hard work, I guess it was worth it."

The Trumans adjusted easily to the life of private citizens, although they had to put up a locked fence around their big white house to keep the tourists away.

It is a strange paradox of our system that a President entrusted with the limitless powers of the greatest office in the world's greatest republic is turned out at the end of his term, with no responsibilities, no authority, and no occupation in which to utilize his exceptional experience. Truman's solution to the problem of keeping himself busy has been to establish the Harry S. Truman Library, which contains mementos from his and other presidencies and the records of his eight-year administration. Now, healthy and energetic at seventy-nine, the former President goes to work at 7:30 A.M. five days a week in an office in the library. He has written several books, which Mrs. Truman has helped edit. He answers a volume of mail, loves to talk history with visitors, and keeps his hand in politics. Mrs. Truman keeps their big house so neat that at every window the cream-colored shade is pulled exactly three-quarters of the way down. A sandbox, swing, and jungle gym in the back yard indicate frequent visits from small grandsons, children of Margaret, who married Clifton Daniel in 1956. Mrs. Truman often shows up at the library in the mornings herself, in housedress and flat shoes, to open and answer the mail for a few hours.

Now, out of office, Harry Truman is growing steadily in the nation's esteem. And although it is still too early for final assessment, the people are forgetting his words that were often aggravating and remembering only his deeds. After all, there is something grand and inspiring about the all-American story of a poor country boy who marries his childhood sweetheart and goes on to become President.

Harry Truman was born May 8, 1884, at Lamar, Missouri, the son of a poor mule trader and farmer. A year later, on February 13, 1885, in Independence, Elizabeth Virginia Wallace was born. She was the granddaughter of Mr. and Mrs. George Gates, who lived in the biggest house in town, were among its leading citizens, operated one of the town's most prosperous businesses, a flour mill, and were descended from a long line of proud Independence aristocracy.

Harry first saw Bess at the age of six, when his parents moved to Independence. He attended the Episcopalian Sunday school, although his family was Baptist—because, he said later, "The Episcopalians gave the best parties and Bess was there." Because of diphtheria, young Harry missed some schooling and wound up in Bess's class. He and Bess were part of a small neighborhood group that grew up playing games and attending parties and poring over books together. They were good friends, but Bess never considered Harry her beau—after all, she could beat him at mumbledy-peg and tennis. They were graduated from the town high school in 1901, and their paths separated. Harry, whose family was too poor to send him to college, became a bank clerk and in a few years moved to his uncle's farm, where he labored for ten years. When Bess's father died in 1903, she and her mother moved into the big fashionable Gates mansion, and she was sent to Barstow School for Girls, a finishing school in Kansas City, to study literature and languages.

Approximately a decade later, Harry rode in from the farm, twenty miles away, to visit his Aunt Ella Noland. During his visit he returned a borrowed cake plate to the Gates house across the street. Bess answered the door—and their old friendship was suddenly renewed. Mrs. Wallace heartily disapproved of Harry, but the young couple began to see each other. One of his friends has explained, "Harry was about the most unpromising prospect for a husband we had around here then"—a dirt farmer with no money, no college education, and apparently no future. He came by horseback to see Bess, and he launched a voluminous correspondence with her. Eventually he scraped together enough money to buy a second-hand Stafford, which made him slightly more acceptable on North Delaware Street.

After a courtship that lasted for five years, Bess and Harry announced their engagement; shortly thereafter, Harry joined the Army and was shipped overseas in World War I. He told a friend later that they delayed their marriage because he did not want Mrs. Truman to be faced with the prospect of a crippled husband or widowhood after the war. But some friends believe that the powerful opposition of Bess's mother was the main reason the courtship was so protracted.

During the war Harry wrote a letter every day to Bess. And when he returned they were married, on June 28, 1919. Bess was thirty-four and Harry thirty-five.

The newlyweds moved into the big Gates house, and Harry opened a haberdashery business with a war buddy in Kansas City. The business failed in the slump of 1921; Harry's partner filed for bankruptcy, but Harry paid back the debts in small driblets the rest of his life. Harry had met one of the Pendergast brothers, who ran the Kansas City and Jackson County political machine during the war. So Harry sought the Pendergast blessing, and became a candidate for county judge (actually, in those days, it was not a judicial post but a job similar to county commissioner). The Pendergast brothers voted the graveyards and the weeds in the lawns to get their boys elected, if need be, and no Democratic politican in Jackson County could expect to win without their backing. Harry served as judge for two years, but was defeated for re-election by a Republican in 1924. For two years he dabbled aimlessly in minor unsuccessful business ventures. Mrs. Truman gave birth to Mary Margaret, and spent most of her time caring for her infant. In 1926 Truman was elected presiding judge of the county court, and in 1929 he was promoted to unofficial Pendergast lieutenant for Jackson County. But Truman was never a voice in the inner councils of the corrupt Pendergast machine: the big boss, Tom Pendergast, passed him over both for the Congressional and gubernatorial nominations. Then, in 1934, Pendergast mysteriously offered Truman his support for the senatorial nomination. It has never been clear exactly why Pendergast suddenly made Truman his choice. In any case, Truman was elected; and newspapers across the country expressed their contempt for the new "office boy" of the big boss who was being sent to sit in the Senate.

The middle-aged Trumans were virtually penniless when they moved to Washington, so they rented an inexpensive apartment, bought low-cost furniture, and borrowed money to rent a piano. They lived simply: Mrs. Truman did all the cooking and housework; her husband wiped the dishes after dinner at night. It was five months before the new senator met President Roosevelt. "It was quite an event for a country boy to go calling on the President of the United States," he recalled afterward. The Trumans socialized very little; Mrs. Truman never smoked or drank, and the senator's chief source of fun was occasional nights out playing poker with friends. Mrs. Truman dutifully attended the Senate wives' luncheons, but confided "they bore me." Truman was an ardent New Dealer, but relations with the White House were strained: Roosevelt ordered an investigation of Pendergast, and when Pendergast was convicted of election fraud, Truman refused to denounce him.

After the outbreak of World War II, Truman became chairman of a Senate committee investigating the operations of the defense program. In the year of 1941 alone, the committee held seventy hearings all over the country, probing for waste in shipyards, aircraft factories, mines, and plants. Back in his hotel room each night after a hearing, the senator's first move was to ask associate counsel Charles Patrick Clark to "get Bess on the phone." And when the committee wasn't traveling, Mrs. Truman served as secretary and researcher. Later, when Republicans complained because he had his wife on the payroll, Truman replied, "She earns every cent of it. I never make a speech without going over it with her, and I never make any decision unless she is in on it . . . not one of these reports [of the committee] has been issued without going through her hands."

The war investigating committee became the public guardian of the home-front effort, and its chairman, Truman, a nationally respected figure. The President suddenly became very friendly. "The happiest years of my life were my ten years in the Senate," Truman says. But Truman's new national prominence made him an inevitable possibility for the vice-presidential nomination in 1944. He was respected by labor, came from a border state, was popular, and one of his biggest supporters was Robert Hannegan, the Democratic National Chairman. Because of Roosevelt's obviously failing health, the Democratic party knew that it was probably picking a President, not a Vice-President, which added an exceptional intensity to the maneuvering for second place.

Truman, however, showed no inclination for the post of Vice-President. He promised to nominate James Byrnes at the convention instead. Mrs. Truman was, according to Margaret, "bitterly opposed" to the vice-presidency. But Roosevelt wanted to dump the present Vice-President, Henry Wallace; he vacillated between Truman and William Douglas as replacements. Strong, clever politicians pressured Roosevelt to make Truman the choice: and, during the convention, he did. On the second ballot, while he was peacefully eating a hot dog with his friends in the Missouri delegation, Truman was nominated. He was immediately surrounded by stomping, cheering delegates and newsmen; Mrs. Truman and Margaret, who had been sitting in a sideline box, were buffeted and mauled by the mob as they tried to reach him. When they finally joined Truman, his wife said piteously, "Are we going to have to go through this all the rest of our lives?" Truman did not answer her. And back in Missouri, his mother told reporters she wished her son would remain a senator where "he can do more good."

The morning after the nomination, Mrs. Truman held her one and only press conference. She said that she did not realize her husband had a chance for the nomination until two days before, and had not particularly wanted him to get it (an understatement). Asked for personal details, she said her husband "is the type of person who would be satisfied to eat beefsteak and fried potatoes every night." The homespun picture she painted was in sharp contrast with the public image of the prestigious, sophisticated Roosevelt.

Truman did the campaigning in 1944 for both himself and Roosevelt, because Roosevelt was too sick and too busy with the war to spend time away from the White House. Mrs. Truman, for her part, immediately learned the penalties of living in the limelight. Shopping in a Kansas City department store, she overheard one woman say to another, "Why, that's Mrs. Truman." The second woman stared. "She's wearing seersucker!" she sneered. Mrs. Truman looked vacantly ahead, her head high, but later she grumbled to Truman, "I wonder if they thought a vice-presidential candidate's wife should be dressed in royal purple?"

The Roosevelt-Truman ticket was victorious. After election day the Vice-President-elect called his mother. "Now you behave yourself up there, Harry," she admonished him. How Harry did behave is, of course, now a matter of record.

But there is yet one part of Harry Truman's life that will never be a matter for historical record. One day, after he had become President, Truman discovered his wife on her knees, burning a yellowed pile of papers in the fireplace. He asked what she was doing. "I'm burning your letters to me," she said, hastily shoveling in the rest. "Bess, you oughtn't to do that," Truman protested. "Why not? I've read them several times," she said.

"But think of history."

"I have," said Mrs. Truman.

Mary Geneva Doud

EISENHOWER

❀ ❀

*Former President Dwight D. Eisenhower scheduled our interview
for 8:00 A.M., which was already well into his regular working
day. He had returned the day before from a vacation in Augusta,
Georgia, and appeared to be brimming with energy and good
cheer. He rose immediately from the big chair behind his desk
as I entered his Gettysburg office, and strode across the room to
welcome me with the famous smile and a cordial handshake.
This greeting set the tone for an extraordinarily amiable and uninhibited interview.*

*Reporters, who are required to elicit information from the
best possible sources but who do not wish to be offensively pry-
ing, normally are fully aware of the need for delicacy in discussing with anyone such a subject as the achievements and personality of his spouse. If the person happens to be a former President
the task can be, obviously, a formidable one. But it was impos-*

sible to feel awkward or uncomfortable in the presence of Gen-
eral Eisenhower's friendly and relaxed manner.

His office is at the top of a winding staircase in a brick
federal-style building which was once a home. His secretaries, a
military aide, and his son Lieutenant Colonel John Eisenhower,
occupy converted bedrooms and sitting rooms visible from the
hallway. Eisenhower's office, once a corner bedroom, is furnished
simply with modern chairs and desk, two small bookcases, a pic-
ture of his West Point graduating class, two paintings of pastoral
scenes, and an American flag and his General's flag. On the
floor is the room's one dramatic touch—an impressive, colorful
oriental rug. The General apologized for the disarray of his desk
—a jumble of papers, letters, volumes of Crusade in Europe *to*
be autographed, and several tomes on international and national
problems.

The General enjoyed reminiscing about his long life with
Mrs. Eisenhower, and occasionally appeared to be musing to
himself rather than speaking to the stranger seated on the other
side of his desk. He offered affectionate little vignettes about his
wife—buying a coffee pot in a hardware store in Falls Church,
Virginia; trying to learn to play golf in the Philippines; strug-
gling to keep an orderly house in the cramped quarters of a se-
ries of Army bases. Above all, he cited frequent examples of
Mrs. Eisenhower's ability "to make people feel at home."

The name of Mamie Doud Eisenhower belongs in any com-
pilation of memorable First Ladies—not because of what she did,
but because of what she is.

Mamie Eisenhower was never a confidante and adviser to
her husband on affairs of state, as were Abigail Adams, Sarah
Polk, Bess Truman, and Edith Wilson. She did not influence
politics and public policy by her own words and actions, as did
Eleanor Roosevelt. She was not the chief motivating force behind her husband's rise to the White House, as were Florence
Harding and Helen Taft. She set no dramatic precedents as First
Lady, and she was one of the least active hostesses in the history
of the White House.

Yet Mrs. Eisenhower was one of the most popular and best-loved First Ladies to occupy the White House. The nation liked her just for herself. Former General Dwight David Eisenhower was elected President in 1952 on a wave of adoration from millions who saw in him the combination of hero-leader and sincere, kindly father. And the public found the same kind of instant identification with the friendly, matronly woman who was his wife.

Because of this nation-wide affinity, Mrs. Eisenhower was able to make a deeper impression upon American women than some more active First Ladies. Two years out of the White House, the Gallup Poll rated her as still the world's fourth most admired woman, although she now limits her activities to answering correspondence and making an occasional appearance with her husband.

Mrs. Eisenhower is the kind of woman with whom the average wife and mother can easily identify. Her tastes are simple and typically middle-class American: steak, potatoes, or fried chicken for dinner, popular tunes and ballads for listening, scrabble or canasta for relaxation, reading mystery stories, watching television or movie musicals for evening entertainment. Her informal geniality with people of all stations in life marks her as a natural, kind woman with no pretentious social mannerisms. Her spontaneous smile and enthusiasm for even the most boring public function indicates a sincere liking for people. Pictures of a sprightly Mrs. Eisenhower with her four grandchildren give the impression of a happy housewife just like the viewer's own grandmother. She is always neat, fashionable, and inclined toward fluffy, pink, and feminine clothes—and what woman doesn't want to be feminine though a grandmother?

Former President Eisenhower feels that his wife's charm and friendliness, her warm interest in other people, and her unaffected manner were her great assets in the White House. He said recently, in conversation at his office in Gettysburg, Pennsylvania, that "I personally think the great contribution of Mrs. Ike was to make the White House livable, comfortable, and meaningful for the people who came in."

And he stresses her help and comfort during his three major illnesses in the presidency as an important factor in his ability to carry on his duties through the eight years of his administration.

"She was always helpful and ready to do anything," Eisenhower says. "And she has given me a most satisfactory and happy life."

Since January 20, 1961, the Eisenhowers have lived quietly at their sprawling 189-acre farm bordering the Gettysburg Civil War battlefields. The former President, who asked for his old rank back and prefers to be called "General" these days, maintains an office in Gettysburg, where he answers a flood of mail, works on an occasional speech, and keeps in touch with Republican fortunes and current events. He complains good-naturedly that he is actually busier now than when he was President, because he doesn't have a large administrative staff any more. "When I was in the White House, I was able to keep my desk clean every night," the General says and grins. "But now I never get through all these papers to a clean desk." Mrs. Eisenhower also gets a daily stack of mail, which she conscientiously tries to answer.

But the Eisenhowers, now aged seventy-two and sixty-six, are mainly just enjoying themselves. Their farmhouse is completely secluded from the public road, for complete privacy. John Eisenhower, his pretty wife Barbara, and their four children live in a neat white frame house on the edge of the farm. General and Mrs. Eisenhower spend several months during each winter at sunny Palm Springs, California, and frequent shorter vacations at Augusta, Georgia. Eisenhower plays golf and paints; his wife looks after their home, plays cards, and lavishes time and attention on her grandchildren.

The former President has grown increasingly reflective since he turned over the demands of the White House to a much younger man; he speaks out frequently with his views on world problems and prospects. President Kennedy has arranged special intelligence briefings for Eisenhower on complicated international crises such as in Cuba, Laos, and Berlin; and Eisenhower's subsequent public support of Kennedy's policies in handling these crises contributed greatly to winning bipartisan national approval. But Eisenhower has also climbed on the platform occasionally to counter what he considered overzealous speeches by President Kennedy and New Frontier aides on the subject of how much better things are in 1962 than they were in the fifties.

The General is quick to defend the record of his administration, and he is also voluble on the First Lady's contributions. He takes a rather limited view of a First Lady's responsibilities, centering his opinions on Mrs. Eisenhower's role in the areas of hostess and wifely duties. "She exuded hospitality. She saw that as one of her functions and performed it, no matter how tired she was," the General says today, reflecting on the past as he absently chewed the gray plastic earpiece of his glasses. "In the White House, you need intelligence and charm—to make others glad to be around you. She had that ability."

The General points out that Mrs. Eisenhower adapted more easily to life in the White House than some First Ladies have. For a lifelong military career is actually better training for a First Lady than for a President. A military man accustomed to the concepts of rigid discipline and an orderly staff system is apt to be bewildered by the haphazard complexities of civilian politics—as President Eisenhower sometimes appeared to be. But the wife of an officer gets her training in protocol, in the art of meeting great numbers of distinguished people, in self-assurance in public with strangers and important dignitaries, and in self-control when her husband confers in whispers about secret matters.

Eisenhower says: "From 1945 on, Mrs. Ike and I had been moving in official circles all the time. In Europe there wasn't a royal family or head of government that she hadn't met and been entertained by. So that part of going into the White House limelight wasn't difficult."

In fact, there is every evidence that Mrs. Eisenhower enjoyed being First Lady. General Eisenhower says that his wife had been concerned about living in the White House, because she heard it had the impersonal atmosphere of an institution. "But she found the mansion very livable and liked it very much," he says. She appreciated the honor of being the President's wife, and was delighted when the servants called her "First Lady" instead of "Mrs. Eisenhower." But her health was not good, the responsibilities were wearing, and by the middle of their second term Mrs. Eisenhower was looking forward to retirement to Gettysburg.

As much as Mrs. Eisenhower liked being First Lady, she was never tempted to expand her role beyond the domestic duties

She was a careful housekeeper, and directed the White House domestic staff with a firm hand and a perfectionist's eye for detail. She campaigned with her husband and generally accompanied him on public appearances, although she never spoke more than to say "thank you." And she was generous about lending her name and sponsorship to help worthy causes and charities.

But Mrs. Eisenhower never took an interest in affairs of state or in politics. For that matter, neither Eisenhower had paid much attention to public affairs until the General became a candidate for the presidency. Mrs. Eisenhower had never voted. And there is no record of the General having voted, either. When New Hampshire Governor Sherman Adams wanted to enter the General's name in the New Hampshire primary, he found that he had to prove Eisenhower's party affiliation. He wrote to C. F. Moore, the county clerk of Dickenson County, Kansas. Mr. Moore replied: "Mr. Eisenhower has never voted in this city as far as I know. . . . Dwight's father was a Republican. However, that has nothing to do with the son as many differ from their fathers . . . I don't think he has any politics." Consequently, Republican party leaders told Eisenhower in desperation that he would have to declare his party preference formally if he intended to become a candidate. So on January 7, 1952, General Eisenhower declared that he was a Republican. He later told Adams: "When I declared myself a Republican in 1952 I did so upon the representation of some of my friends in whom I had the greatest confidence. I believe the more enlightened principles of the Republicans were closer to my own beliefs than those of the other party. But I could have been a conservative Democrat."

President Truman and a lot of other Democrats had hoped that the apolitical Eisenhower would turn out to be a Democrat. In 1945, shortly after the World War II victory in Europe, Truman offered to help his general get the presidential nomination in 1948. Eisenhower declined. Again, as 1952 approached, Truman sent messengers to Paris, where Eisenhower was then commander of N.A.T.O., to guarantee the nomination if he wanted it Again Eisenhower declined.

Shortly after the General's candidacy was announced, Mrs. Eisenhower lunched with an old friend, an ardent Democrat, who had been her next-door neighbor at the Wardman Park Hotel during the war and a close friend for some time. The woman expressed surprise at discovering the Eisenhowers were Republican. But Mamie Eisenhower just chuckled. "Actually," she explained, "when you are in the Army you don't have any politics."

The former President acknowledges today that he never discussed matters pertaining to the operation of the government or political issues with Mrs. Eisenhower. But he insists that "she is quite clear in her own mind on the differences of the Democratic stand and the Republican." And he adds, with an engaging grin, that Mrs. Eisenhower is always prejudiced on his side of an issue anyway—on the grounds that her husband has to be right, regardless of whether she is familiar with the issues herself.

He says that Mrs. Eisenhower did, however, frequently discuss various government personalities with him, and what each stood for. And sometimes in letters to old friends she would engage in a little spirited partisan argument about the big issue of the day. But the one instance he can remember when Mrs. Eisenhower made an intentional remark with a slight political flavor occurred recently at their farm. Their dinner guests, in the midst of amiable conversation, admitted that they were Democrats. Finally, as the contented guests prepared to leave, Mrs. Eisenhower wagged a finger at them and asked, "Well, are you still happy with your votes?"

Mrs. Eisenhower had no objection to public life for her husband, despite her own lack of interest in activities outside her domestic sphere. The first time she was asked to comment about her husband's candidacy, she replied matter-of-factly, "What American woman wouldn't want her husband to be President?" Says the former President, "Mrs. Ike refused to get involved in public life herself—she was helpful in worthy causes, such as muscular dystrophy or the heart fund; but she was very much against pushing forward into public view."

General Eisenhower believes that his wife's intuitive observations on the people and events around them were extremely helpful during his presidency, even though she had no political background. "She is a very shrewd observer," he notes. "I frequently asked her impression of someone, and found her intuition good. Women who know the same individual as a man do give a different slant. . . .

"She had an uncanny and accurate judgment of people with whom she was well acquainted," the General says in admiration. "I got it well into my head that I'd better listen when she talked about someone brought in close to me."

A former Eisenhower official expressed the same feeling. He believes that White House thinking is too masculine in judgments regarding public sentiment and the qualities of individuals, since it is staffed, in the higher-echelon jobs, by men only. This official's theory is that a feminine mind, such as Mrs. Eisenhower's, with its different emphasis on interests and different viewpoint, can add a needed element to decisions below the substantive policy level. He says that Mrs. Eisenhower often served this purpose for the General, acting as a sort of "balance wheel."

This official adds that Eisenhower often consulted his wife about economic problems and budget matters. Eisenhower viewed the national budget as an enlarged version of a household budget, so it seemed natural for him to turn to his own household budget expert. Mrs. Eisenhower had managed their budget and finances throughout their military life, just as she did in the White House. So, during a conference on price increases, the cost of living index, or marketing trends, the former President frequently said, "Let me try this out on Mamie. She's a pretty darn good judge of things."

Mrs. Eisenhower was indeed a good judge of household matters. She checked on the details of everything, from the number of electric bulbs purchased to the furniture arrangement for a reception. She was such a meticulous housekeeper that it disturbed her to see footprints on the carpets. A White House servant recalled that although Mrs. Eisenhower was generally "very jolly," she was also "very strict" about getting things just right. Each morning she consulted with her household staff, propped up in bed with pillows, in a pink bed jacket and with pink ribbons in her short hair. She also dictated to her social secretary during these morning sessions, and discussed the day's flower arrangements. The White House gardener, Robert Redmond, recalls that Mrs. Eisenhower specified which flowers she wanted each day, and insisted upon approving sample arrangements before each official function. She was more concerned with the floral decorations than the previous two First Ladies; she liked to see the whole house banked with masses of flowers. Each morning two little vials of pink sweetheart roses were placed in her bedroom. And after each official event Mrs. Eisenhower ordered the leftover floral arrangements to be sent to veterans' hospitals, rather than left to wither and die unseen.

The First Lady was greatly handicapped in carrying out her responsibilities, however, by a rheumatic heart which limited her activities. It was to conserve her strength and avoid unnecessary strain on her heart that Mrs. Eisenhower held her morning staff consultations from her bed. She required exceptional amounts of rest, and sometimes spent several days a week in bed. She remained in bed the entire day before a dinner or reception so that she would not grow overtired at the function. But her complexion was so rosy, her smile so sincere, and her chatter so vivacious in public that few people realized the extra effort it cost her.

Mrs. Eisenhower was perhaps more careful of her health than many other people might have been in her position, but she had ample reason to be concerned about her cardiac difficulties. Her sister Eleanor had died of a heart condition, and another sister, "Buster," was a diabetic semi-invalid. And during her life she had several serious illnesses, all of which taxed her reservoir of strength. She adhered to a strict diet, and carefully kept her weight below 140. A masseuse came to the White House three times a week to give her a tension-releasing rubdown.

Mrs. Eisenhower's heart was weakened by a valvular lesion (a heart murmur), attributed to an undiagnosed case of rheumatic fever when she was a child. She also suffered from a mysterious inner-ear ailment known as Ménière's Disease, which disturbs the victim's sense of balance. The ailment was partially cured by the time Mrs. Eisenhower entered the White House, but it sometimes recurred, making her dizzy and unsure of her steps. (Consequently the President always considerately helped her up and down stairs, out of cars, down plane ramps, etc., his arm on hers to steady her if she faltered.) She had frequent headaches and was bothered by asthma.

Twice Mrs. Eisenhower was so ill she was not expected to live. Shortly after the birth of their first baby, Dwight Doud (nicknamed Icky), in 1917, she contracted a lung infection and was in critical condition for a long period. When Icky died of scarlet fever three years later, she was in the hospital with another respiratory infection. Her physical weakness made Icky's death doubly hard; but Eisenhower says that his wife was courageous enough not to let herself be broken down by it. In the late thirties, while her husband was on duty in the Philippines, Mrs. Eisenhower developed a mysterious stomach complaint which resisted medical treatment and left her so ill she rarely moved out of her apartment for nearly two years. Eventually she had a stomach hemorrhage and went into a coma, and the doctors did not expect her to recover.

Because of her ill health, Mrs. Eisenhower has never led an active life. She avoids exercise, dislikes to be outdoors, and seldom walks if she can ride. Life, therefore, was particularly difficult during the long years of World War II, when General Eisenhower was in Europe. Mrs. Eisenhower, lonely, restless, worried, developed insomnia. Her health slipped; her weight sagged to 112; she looked ten years older. When Eisenhower returned after the war, her health improved. But then she had a bout with pneumonia after attending a rainy-day ceremony honoring her hero-husband.

By 1955 White House intimates were aware that the First Lady's health was not robust. *U.S. News and World Report,* a news magazine which highly endorsed the Eisenhower administration, commented that the First Lady frequently complained of dizziness going up and down steps, tired quickly, feared high places, and found her social obligations wearing. The health of both Eisenhowers became the biggest topic of campaign debate.

The President had suffered a heart attack, which kept him from full-time duties for four months, and a major ileitis operation, by the summer of 1956. Nevertheless, he appeared hearty and strong enough to run for re-election. Politicians began to fear that even if Eisenhower felt his own health was up to another term, he would reject it because of Mrs. Eisenhower's health. In Denver, Mrs. John Doud, Mrs. Eisenhower's mother, had been widely quoted as telling friends "Mamie can't stand another four years in the White House." *U.S. News and World Report* reported that top Republicans feared Mrs. Eisenhower might be the biggest deterrent to another race by her husband.

But Mrs. Eisenhower, being a good Army wife, left the decision of whether to run for re-election strictly up to her husband. She told James Hagerty, his press secretary, that although she personally was against another term, "the decision has to be made by only one person—Ike." A current magazine noted that Mrs. Eisenhower would not try to influence her husband on this matter because she "always has left such decisions to her husband—more indeed than did Mrs. F.D.R. or Mrs. Harry Truman."

Eisenhower's decision was to run again—but that during the second term he and his wife would cut drastically the social functions traditionally expected of them, in order to save their energy for more important things. So Mrs. Eisenhower eliminated all five of the large receptions customarily included in the winter social schedule and transformed state dinners into state luncheons where she could. The *grande dames* of Washington society were dismayed, but most Americans didn't mind the idea of a President and his wife preferring to spend their evenings reading or watching television, instead of entertaining at an official gala.

Eisenhower explains: "We reduced our schedule after my heart attack [September 24, 1955], because deep involvement in social activities makes the day too long. I don't think, however, that Mrs. Ike felt the demands on her as First Lady were overpowering. At times there were events we couldn't avoid, and then we got a little weary. Once in a while, after a round of ladies' teas and luncheons, and that sort of thing, she said, 'My goodness, I'm getting as busy as you are.'"

It is ironic that Mrs. Eisenhower, whose major offering to the nation was her ability as a hostess, her identification with average American womanhood, and the effect of her example on the millions with whom she was incredibly popular, should have been forced by health to do less in public than any of her contemporaries.

President Eisenhower feels that his wife makes an impact on those who come in contact with her through "her charm and skill as a woman devoted to family and friends." These qualities in Mrs. Eisenhower are exemplified by spontaneous, thoughtful gestures that demonstrate an interest in other people. "I don't know any wife of the White House staff who doesn't love her," a former presidential aide said recently. She befriended all the White House aides—"made them feel they weren't just statues," the General says. She gave parties for the staff, and once a Halloween party, complete with skeletons, witches flying across the tablecloth, black cats, and owls hanging from the chandeliers, for the wives of staff members. If the President mentioned to his wife that some aide had done a particularly good job that day, or complimented a friend in some casual way, she would dictate a note the next morning to the man's wife. "Just between us girls, the President told me your husband did a great job . . ." she'd write.

When Supreme Court Chief Justice Fred Vinson died, his widow Roberta was so shaken that she refused to see any visitors but her immediate family for several months afterward. But one afternoon she rushed to answer the doorbell, wrapped in a robe, thinking that the caller was probably the laundry man bringing fresh diapers for her grandchild. Mrs. Vinson found instead the First Lady on her doorstep. Mrs. Eisenhower apologized for not calling before she came, but said that she had heard Mrs. Vinson was refusing all calls, and was afraid she would be turned away. "I just had to come and see how you are," she said sympathetically.

Mrs. Eisenhower was extremely feminine, in a rather sweet, clinging-vine way. She adored flowered hats, colored gloves, full-skirted, fluffy dresses, and anything done up in pink. She was very sentimental about such momentous events as birthdays and anniversaries. She wore charm bracelets hung with charms that signified milestones in her life. The President sent her flowers every year on the birthday of the baby who died in 1921. She preferred to play canasta with "the girls" to almost any other occupation. During her two duty stretches in Paris, she so surrounded herself with tried-and-true American military friends that she never even visited the Louvre. She doted on her only son and fussed over his welfare so much that she once confessed she never learned to control her "smother love" instinct until he was married. She had married in her teens, never went to college, never developed a major interest or activity outside of her home, her family, and her friends. And, like many housewives, her one lifetime ambition was to own an ivy-covered cottage of her own.

The eight years the Eisenhowers lived in the White House was their longest period in any one home. Shuttled from city to city and house to house, Mamie Eisenhower was impatient to have a permanent home which she could furnish as she pleased. President Eisenhower recalls: "She was constantly saying, 'When am I ever going to have a home of my own?'" At the suggestion of their friend George Allen, the Eisenhowers had acquired a farm neighboring his at Gettysburg in 1950. But the house on the farm was too small for the Eisenhowers and parts of it were over two hundred years old; and by 1952, when Eisenhower was elected, they still had not remodeled the house. The former President recalls that his wife "was the most disappointed person" when a series of complications prevented restoration of the old house. After his election he felt that they ought to delay their plans for the house another few years, but Mrs. Eisenhower was so eager that he didn't have the heart to tell her. So early in his administration the house was remodeled and enlarged, and became a weekend retreat for the Eisenhowers. Friends and associates rushed to help, and donated at least $40,000 worth of gifts for the new ranch, from tractors to pure-bred Angus cattle.

By the time they settled in the White House, with its peculiar inbred isolation from new friends, the Eisenhowers, mellowed by age, were very dependent upon each other's company. He generally refused invitations to stag affairs or evening events with the remark, "You know, I have a wife—I'll have to see what Mamie is planning."

The Eisenhowers were the all-American couple, and he had been elected in a great outpouring of popular approval—in 1952 Eisenhower carried all but nine states, and in 1956 he increased his victory by three million. The General's campaign was based on the American desire for peace and prosperity; and he promised to bring a higher moral tone to the federal government. The Democratic candidate, the liberal intellectual Adlai Stevenson, projected nowhere near the personal warmth of the Eisenhower team. If he had ever had a chance, it vanished when the General promised to go personally to Korea to see if he could bring an end to the war.

Only one thing marred the Republican campaign of 1952:

the exposure of a special secret fund set up by businessmen to elect the vice-presidential nominee, Richard Nixon, to Congress a few years before. Eisenhower had left the selection of his running mate up to his professional political advisers, and had only met Nixon twice, to shake hands, before the campaign. Worried Republicans pressured Eisenhower to take Nixon off the ticket, but the General hesitated. In a dramatic personal television appeal, Nixon bared his financial affairs and defended his acceptance of the secret fund. And Eisenhower, watching the performance in Cleveland on a couch with his wife, surrounded by approximately thirty aides, was visibly moved. He murmured to Mrs. Eisenhower that he thought Nixon was a completely honest man. So Nixon stayed on the ticket.

During the campaign Mrs. Eisenhower's sunny smile and breezy informality struck exactly the right note. She traveled with her husband everywhere, and posed willingly for pictures— once even in big round hair curlers. The General introduced her from the train platform, taking a note from President Truman's campaign handbook. "I want you to meet my Mamie," he said.

President Eisenhower was inaugurated on January 20, 1953, by Chief Justice Vinson. As he repeated the solemn oath, the new First Lady began to slump in her chair, and suddenly burst into uncontrollable tears. The President, hearing the sound, strode swiftly across the platform, clasped her shoulders, bent and kissed her on the cheek. There is no record of any other President publicly kissing his wife during the inauguration ceremonies. And instead of riding back to the White House with the Vice-President to view the inaugural parade, as is customary, President Eisenhower rode with his wife.

President Eisenhower approached the White House with a textbook viewpoint of the separation of legislative and executive powers; but by 1959 he was saying "I am part of the legislative process" to a reluctant Democratic-controlled Congress. The presidential power is both the power to persuade and to command, and at persuasion the charming Eisenhower was at his best. He set out in his first term with one broad objective for his administration—to persuade the world that peace and a fundamental easing of the tensions which trigger war is the right course for mankind.

In 1956 the public had both peace and prosperity, and it wanted President Eisenhower for four more years. The nation did not seem unduly disturbed that the President had suffered two major illnesses and had warned he would have to limit his activities. Nor did it seem to blame the President for the Dixon-Yates conflict-of-interest scandal. The government had attempted to restore private utilities to the Tennessee Valley, but a Boston banker who had advised the government on the move was discovered to be simultaneously helping Dixon-Yates set up its new power operation.

But Eisenhower's second term was not as calm as his first. He was forced to send federal troops to Little Rock, Arkansas, to enforce integration of Negro students in an all-white high school. Despite the Supreme Court ruling that segregation is unconstitutional, Arkansas's Governor Orval Faubus had ordered the state's National Guardsmen to prevent nine Negro children from enrolling. Soviet troops brutally squashed the Hungarian revolt, and the United States offered to admit Hungarian refugees. The United States withdrew offers to finance construction of the big Aswan Dam in Egypt, precipitating Nasser's seizure of the Suez Canal. But when Anglo-French-Israeli forces attacked to gain control of the canal, Eisenhower deplored the action and said the United States would not be involved. On October 4, 1957, the Soviets orbited the first Sputnik satellite; American prestige sagged around the world and demands grew at home for a greater effort in defense and space exploration. The economy grew sluggish; unemployment rose to a sixteen-year high; farm incomes shrank while surpluses mounted. Two United States satellite attempts failed (although on January 31, 1958, Explorer I was successfully orbited). Vice-President Nixon, on a good-will tour of Latin America, was attacked by anti-United States demonstrators. Eisenhower dispatched troops to Lebanon at the request of the Lebanese government, which was threatened by the muscle-flexing of Egypt's pro-Communist Nasser. Eisenhower's "new moral tone" in government was tarnished by the discovery that his chief assistant, Sherman Adams, had accepted gifts of a vicuna coat and a rug from wealthy industrialist Bernard Goldfine. Goldfine was in trouble with the government, and Adams had placed three calls to federal agencies on his behalf.

The Communists appeared to be consolidating their power in the Middle East, Africa, and Cuba. Soviet Premier Khrushchev paid a good-will visit to the United States, but shortly afterward destroyed a planned summit meeting in fury because a U-2 reconnaissance plane had been downed over Soviet territory on the very eve of the meeting. The United States State Department, embarrassed by the incident, denied everything; but Khrushchev produced plane, pilot, and plenty of evidence. Americans began uncomfortably to wonder if the tide of history was not with the Communistic system after all.

In a last attempt to promote peace in the world, President Eisenhower embarked upon four good-will tours around the world. He talked personally with every ranking head of state except those in Red China and the Iron Curtain countries. Mrs. Eisenhower did not accompany him; the strain of travel was too much for her health. Their daughter-in-law, Barbara Eisenhower, went along instead.

Eisenhower could not shake the image of himself as above the battle. He tried to create an atmosphere for peace, in the role of moderator and unifier. But his greatest failing was that he faltered in carrying out bread-and-butter specifics to accomplish the broad objectives he set forth. It is too early to compare accurately the achievements of the Eisenhower administration with his predecessors; that must wait the perspective of history. But Dr. Richard Neustadt, in his definitive analysis, *Presidential Power,* notes: "The presidency is not a place for amateurs . . . the presidency is a place for men of politics. . . . There can be little doubt that he [Eisenhower] exchanged his hero's welcome for much less than its full value in the currency of power."

Throughout all these disturbing events, Mrs. Eisenhower quietly supervised the East Wing operations (the White House wing which holds the social and housekeeping offices). She rarely, if ever, appeared in the West Wing, which houses the President's office and his immediate staff. During the General's long military career she had grown accustomed to hushed conversations in which she was not expected to take part. She had learned not to be curious about serious faces, papers marked "top secret," and telephone calls at strange hours. Her function was to make the men who called upon her husband comfortable—

and then not to bother them while they discussed business. One Eisenhower aide recalled: "We frequently had to hold business conferences upstairs in the private living quarters. Mrs. Eisenhower made it a point to be on hand to greet each man as he came in and proffer coffee, cocktails, or other refreshments. As soon as somebody began, 'Mr. President, I have some secret material to discuss,' Mrs. Eisenhower tactfully said, 'Excuse me,' and left the room."

Mrs. Eisenhower was more concerned with people than with policies and political principles. The public liked Mrs. Eisenhower for herself; and she liked people on the same intuitive basis. This was a sizable part of her warmth and her charm. She told visitors, "Call me Mamie." She was fond of Margaret Truman, but did not protest when her husband removed Truman's picture from prominent White House display, despite the tradition that the immediate predecessor's picture be hung in a vantage spot. (Both she and the President resented Truman's attacks during the 1952 campaign.) Yet she displayed a picture of President Roosevelt on a small table in her Paris villa drawing room during their N.A.T.O. assignment, despite strong criticism from the General's associates, simply because she liked Eleanor Roosevelt. And she sincerely admired Woodrow Wilson's widow, inviting her to several White House functions, despite Mrs. Wilson's ardent Democratic views. Because she viewed life in such an intensely personal sense, Mrs. Eisenhower was deeply wounded by attacks made upon her husband's administration during campaign years. In at least one case she refused to speak to a formerly very close friend for years because the woman had campaigned for Stevenson—she considered her action a personal insult to Eisenhower, although the friend was deeply wed to Democratic party principles and had long been involved in Democratic politics. Yet, on the other hand, she frequently made an extra effort to boost a charity or attend another creamed-chicken luncheon just because an old Army friend had asked her.

Every once in a while a wife of a prominent man pretends to be something she isn't, in the hope that she will be better loved by the general public. The wife of an official not long ago, for instance, posed for a picture ironing her husband's shirts, indicating that she carried out the regular routine of household chores which occupy the time of most wives; whereas all Washington knew, and surely the nation suspected, she could afford to send the shirts to the laundry but could not afford the time, amidst her official occupations, to do the ironing. But the image America had of Mamie Eisenhower as the example of a typical, good-hearted grandmother was based on reality. The entire Eisenhower story, in fact, is the kind of American reality that could have happened to you or me.

Eisenhower was a poor boy, reared in a tiny house on the wrong side of the tracks in Abilene, Kansas. His father, David Eisenhower, was a mechanic for the Belle Springs Creamery, but there was never enough money to go around for a wife and six boys. So young Eisenhower did chores, peddled vegetables from their yard, and learned to beat up tormenting classmates who jeered at his shabby clothes. At the age of eleven he went to work in the creamery. He decided upon a military career because it was the only way he could get a college education; he won the West Point competitive examination in high school. At West Point he was interested in sports and cheerleading, but finished 61st in scholarship and 125th in conduct in his class of 164 cadets.

Mrs. Eisenhower's family was far more prosperous; her father, John Doud, made enough money in the meat-packing business to retire and move his family to Denver at the youthful age of thirty-six. She was born November 14, 1896, at Boone, Iowa, and named Mary Geneva, although she has always been called Mamie. Mamie was an average student, and was frankly bored with books; she preferred being surrounded by friends, dancing, playing the piano, or playing jacks. In 1915, when the family went to San Antonio, Texas, for a winter vacation in warm, dry climate, Mamie was a blue-eyed, sparkling, vivacious teen-ager. Just assigned to Fort Sam Houston that winter was a shavetail named Eisenhower.

They met in October, at the home of a mutual friend on the post. "He was the spiffiest-looking man I ever talked to in all my born life . . . big, blond, and masterful," Mrs. Eisenhower recalled later. Lieutenant Eisenhower was equally impressed; he called for a date the very next day. Mamie, who had plenty of other beaux, was dated up for three weeks; but she worked out time for Dwight Eisenhower before dates in the afternoons and after them late at night. The Douds were indulgent parents who tended to pamper Mamie—Mrs. Doud called her "baby"—and her sisters; but they were not snobs and they did not object to Mamie's dating a young man who came from plain people. In fact, Mr. Doud took a great liking to the young lieutenant. So after five months, on Valentine's Day, 1916, Mamie and Ike were engaged. They were married on July 1, in the music room of the Doud home in Denver. Mamie was just nineteen years old; she wore a white dress with a pale pink satin cummerbund and carried pink baby roses.

Mrs. Eisenhower said later, "I knew almost from the day I married Ike that he would be a great soldier. He was always dedicated, serious, and purposeful about his job. Nothing came before his duty. I was forced to match his spirit of personal sacrifice as best I could. Being his wife meant I must leave him free from personal worries to conduct his career as he saw fit."

The young Eisenhowers lived the transient life of the military, with twenty-seven homes in thirty-eight years. Mrs. Eisenhower has frequently been described as a "typical Army wife" —she adapted cheerfully to the society of other military officers' wives, life in one dreary post after another, loneliness when duty called her husband away, the need for self-reliance to establish a household in strange cities and strange countries. They struggled to maintain a budget on a junior officer's pay; life had been much more comfortable for Mamie in the Doud home, where there were servants and luxurious possessions. But Eisenhower indulged his young wife: once he had his appendix out without telling her until it was over, and he gave up smoking ready-made cigarettes in order to buy a small insurance policy. Later he noted, "It was easy to make little sacrifices because I was young and of course very much in love."

Mrs. Eisenhower influenced two crucial career decisions in those early days. Eisenhower decided to transfer to the Army Air Force because he felt the tank and the airplane were the weapons of the future—but Mrs. Eisenhower objected, because she had always feared flying and she was pregnant. So he remained where he was. And in 1928, when he had graduated from the War Col-

lege, Eisenhower was given the choice of general staff assignment
or a European trip to do research for a Battle Monuments Commission guidebook on World War I. Eisenhower was inclined
toward the general staff, which meant a chance at a field command, which he wanted. But Mrs. Eisenhower wanted to see
Europe; and so he chose the Commission.

At it turned out, the Commission assignment led to further
assignment at the Army's Industrial War College, where Major
Eisenhower's clear-cut reports and tactful relations with business-
men drew the attention of General Douglas MacArthur. Mac-
Arthur in 1932 was in dire need of some good public relations;
his reputation had been blackened when he led federal troops
against the veterans' Bonus Marchers, burning their shacks and
routing them with tear gas. So MacArthur selected Eisenhower
to restore his public image, by preparing his reports to Congress
and his public utterances.

Eisenhower did so well that MacArthur took him to Manila
as his aide when he was assigned chief of staff in the Philippines.
The Eisenhowers lived there for several years; but eventually
Eisenhower and MacArthur fell out for some as yet undisclosed
reason, and he requested a transfer back to the states. They returned in late 1939.

World War II, and Eisenhower's great role in history, was
on the horizon. On December 7, 1941, the Japanese bombed Pearl
Harbor. "Only when my little boy Icky died did I suffer more —
it was the most terrible night of my life," recalled Mrs. Eisenhower. An Army wife knows well what the horror of war means.
General of the Army George C. Marshall reached down, past
366 men senior in rank and tenure, to promote Eisenhower to
commanding general of the European theater of operations. In
June, 1942, Eisenhower departed for Europe, to direct the allied
invasions of Sicily, Italy, and Africa. Mrs. Eisenhower was left
alone in a Washington apartment with another war-separated
wife, Ruth Butcher. Their son John was away, a student at West
Point. Every week Mrs. Eisenhower received a report on the
General from his orderly and old friend, Sergeant Mickey Mc-
Keogh; and intermittently she got longhand letters from her husband. But the General never mentioned war strategy in his letters, and Mrs. Eisenhower had never paid particular attention to

military tactics in all their years together—so she relied upon
radio broadcasts and newspapers for news, just as did the rest of
the nation. She said later that she whiled away those war years
by just "living after sorts," playing cards, working in a U.S.O.
canteen, and waiting for word from her husband.

On D-Day, June 6, 1944, a reporter called Mrs. Eisenhower
and asked her what she thought of the invasion. It was the first
she had heard of it. "Invasion? What invasion?" she said.

The Nazis eventually surrendered; and General Eisenhower,
who had commanded the field victory, was a hero. He was immediately boomed for the presidency. But he consistently denied
any interest in the job. Instead he retired from military service in
1948 to become president of Columbia University, where his
chief function was to provide prestige and to raise money. The
Republicans made an attempt to draft him at their convention
in June, 1948, but he firmly resisted, just as he had resisted all
Democratic overtures.

In 1950 Eisenhower became supreme commander of the Allied Powers in Europe (N.A.T.O.). The boom for President was
growing louder. Finally, as Mrs. Eisenhower later recalled it, he
told her one evening that he felt he could no longer withhold himself in a time of national crisis without failing his duty to humanity. He said he felt the next election would be a critical turning point in American history, and that he should do it for his
grandchildren, and everybody else's grandchildren. Mrs. Eisenhower, who insists that up to that moment she had never heard
him hint he was interested in the presidency, told him that she
would do whatever he wanted.

The pressure on Eisenhower to run had been so great that
he didn't expect to fight for the nomination. But Senator Robert
Taft also wanted it, and his forces were so powerful that Eisenhower found it necessary to resign from N.A.T.O. to defend himself against Taft's attacks.

The Republican convention fight in 1952 was a bitter one.
Eisenhower's supporters conducted the battle in his name; the
General, a stranger to politics, watched the confused proceedings
on a television set in his Chicago hotel room. He was watching,
with his five brothers, as he won the nomination. Mrs. Eisenhower lay in a darkened adjacent room, attended solicitously by

her mother, who was keeping one eye on her daughter and another on a television set. Mrs. Eisenhower was suffering from a stabbing headache, brought on by her dismay at the attacks on the convention floor against her husband which she had seen on television the previous few days. The General poked his head in the bedroom door to see if his wife had heard the good news, and she nodded weakly at him.

But when, only a few hours later, the nation got its first look at the Republican nominee's smiling wife, no one suspected the suffering she had just endured. The public could not know that before she faced those 15,000 cheering conventioneers and the television cameras she had never set foot on a stage in her life. And it did not realize that this kindly-faced woman had mild claustrophobia, which made her so uncomfortable in large crowds she didn't even like to sit in a theater. But summoning her strength to go out into that convention hall, Mrs. Eisenhower recalled later, was the symbolic beginning of her new duties. "I was easy of mind and determined to do what Ike and everyone who believed in him expected of me," she said.

From that moment, Mrs. Eisenhower took her new responsibilities seriously. President Eisenhower says that his wife had "a great veneration for history." She was extremely conscious of the significance of her moral example upon the nation and of the symbolic importance of the White House. "She would say, 'This is in a way the home of the United States, and everybody that can do so ought to get some idea of it. It's not inspiring as architecture, but its history is inspiring.' She sensed that and made that idea live," former President Eisenhower says proudly.

Jacqueline Bouvier
KENNEDY

❀ ❀

In the daily drama of world events, Americans sometimes forget that President Kennedy is a Pulitzer Prize-winning historian. He has an appreciation for the personalities who make their entrance upon history's pages, be they men or women. His awareness of the unique problems of a First Lady—his wife's as well as her predecessors'—is clearly reflected in the thoughts he has expressed in this chapter.

I am a newspaperwoman, not a professional historian. President Kennedy, however, because he was interested in the concept of this book, expressed to me for the first time his personal views of the historical role of First Ladies in general and Mrs. Kennedy in particular.

President Kennedy spoke with me in Palm Beach, where each Christmas holiday the Kennedy family blends private life and public activity for two weeks. It was early evening. The

Secret Service agents gave me the clearance required to pass beyond the thick green hedges which border the street. As I drove up the crushed gravel driveway to the large white mansion, the sun was low on the horizon, just beneath the gently swaying tops of the palm trees. I climbed the elegant marble stairway which leads to the living room. Open French doors lead to a large patio, and there strolled the slender figure of Mrs. Kennedy's sister, Lee Radziwill. Through these doors came a pleasant mixture of sounds: the piping laughter of Caroline Kennedy and a playmate, and the barking of Caroline's dog Charlie, played against the pleasant monotony of ocean waves meeting the sea wall. A subtle odor of dinner cooking came from the direction of the kitchen.

President Kennedy, in a neat pin-striped blue suit, appeared shortly and settled back easily into a deep cushioned armchair. As we talked, it became apparent that he was especially interested in the widely varying ways past First Ladies have interpreted their roles. He firmly approves of this, believing that each President's wife, since she is not bound by Constitutionally defined duties, should fulfill her responsibiliites according to the dictates of her own temperament and capabilities. He was speaking, in a very real sense, for Mrs. Kennedy, whose views coincide with his on this subject.

Shortly before the 1960 presidential election, the entire Kennedy family accepted invitations to a big charity ball in New York City. They were all coming: Senator John F. Kennedy, the candidate, and his wife Jacqueline; his brother Robert, his campaign manager, and his wife Ethel; his sister Eunice and her husband Sargent Shriver; sister Patricia and her husband, actor Peter Lawford; sister Jean and her husband Steven Smith; brother Edward and his wife Joan.

Jacqueline Kennedy put in a call to Katherine DiMotezumelo, a magazine fashion editor who had reserved several tables for her guests at the ball. "Could we exchange half our tables at the ball?" Mrs. Kennedy pleaded. "Otherwise, all us Kennedys will be sitting together and we will be sure to end up arguing politics."

She had learned a great deal by then about the fine art of

getting along in a closely knit, competitive, and outspoken family. Six years before, while still a newlywed, she had approached an old friend, Jean Vanderbilt, at a party. "You come from a big family. How do you handle them?" she asked earnestly.

Since her marriage, in 1953, she has fought to keep from being overwhelmed not only by the forceful Kennedys but by the strange world of politics which surrounds her husband, a world in which she is not comfortable. During the summer of 1960 the Kennedys entertained a steady parade of visiting politicians at their summer home in Hyannisport, Massachusetts. One day a crowd of Ohio politicians sat around the living room, conferring with the candidate; Mrs. Kennedy, pregnant with their second child, was trying to be the good hostess and appear interested in the conversation of her guests. But she was clearly having a difficult time with the voting blocs of Ward Three and the size of the motor pool needed in Cleveland. Then she noticed a man standing slightly apart from the group and gazing absorbedly at a series of Segonzac drawings on the wall. She rushed over to him, her face lighting in a sudden smile. "You know Segonzac?" she asked delightedly, obviously relieved to find somebody in the room with more on his mind than politics. They chatted animatedly the rest of the visit; and that cultured politician has been her friend ever since.

By the time they were married, thirty-six-year-old Kennedy was already a senator, deeply immersed and thoroughly experienced in politics; twenty-four-year-old Jacqueline's sheltered, leisurely world had included no political acquaintances and she had not yet even bothered to vote. Her new husband never discussed political matters with her: her realm was their home and she had little sense of participation in his career. In 1956 Senator Kennedy lost the Democratic vice-presidential nomination to Estes Kefauver; virtually from that moment forward, he began campaigning for the presidential nomination in 1960. He accepted speaking engagements anywhere, any time; practically every weekend for four years he was away from home, crisscrossing the country, talking to politicians, addressing conventions, spreading his name and reputation. Yet as late as the spring of 1959, as she was escorted home from a dinner party by an old friend, Mrs.

Kennedy could ask him in bewilderment, "Do you think Jack *really* wants to be President?"

When the dream became, finally, reality, there were new problems. At thirty-one Jacqueline Kennedy was the third youngest First Lady in history. "It's frightening to lose your anonymity," she said. In late November, three weeks after the election, she sat pensively, alone, wrapped in a long black suede coat, on the roof of a Washington hospital where she had recently—after a difficult Caesarean operation—given birth to John Jr. Another woman patient wandered out onto the roof, noticed Mrs. Kennedy, and came toward her. "You're Mrs. Kennedy, aren't you?" she gushed. "I recognize you from your pictures." Mrs. Kennedy bowed her head and sighed resignedly. "I know. That's my problem now," she said, and soon got up to return to the privacy of her room.

At her husband's inauguration she murmured, "I feel as though I have just become a piece of public property." And there have been many times in the past two years when she has been dismayed—"livid" to use her own description—at the extent of the public's interest in her private life. But she has hideaways —behind the high fence at Hyannisport, deep in the private hunt country of middle Virginia, or behind the thick hedges of a Palm Beach estate—where she escapes curious eyes for weeks and months at a time. And in the spring of 1962, with her picture on every magazine cover and in every newspaper several times a week, she managed to take frequent strolls around the Washington Monument with her daughter Caroline's dog Charlie. Dressed casually in slacks, dark glasses, and headscarf, she was not once recognized by the hundreds of tourists around her, who were accustomed to seeing her pictured in more glamorous and formal clothes.

The beautiful First Lady looks like a fragile, exquisite Dresden doll; but she is also, as William Walton, an artist and close friend of the Kennedys, once bluntly put it, "a strong dame." She has steadfastly refused to be pressured into the mold of Organization Wife, Kennedy family version or traditional First Lady version. She means to keep her identity and her personal independence. As a bride she firmly withdrew from the Kennedy family football scrimmages after she broke an ankle; she remains today the only family member (besides the President, whose back might be re-injured by a good block) to defy the tradition. She has recalled the incident of her shock at the endless family competitiveness when she one day watched a five-year-old Kennedy push a four-year-old, and the four-year-old walk over to push a three-year-old. She also refused to take part in the huge nightly Hyannisport family dinners, when the brothers and sisters and their spouses gathered at Joseph Kennedy's big house, on the grounds that "once a week is great, but not every night!"

Similarly, when she became First Lady, Mrs. Kennedy determined to be her own kind of First Lady—to carry out her official responsibilities and to try to set an example for excellence in everything connected with the White House, but to change her private living habits as little as possible—despite the warnings of politicians who worried that average American families might not accept a President's wife who neither cooked nor sewed, who was especially fond of French cuisine and *haute couture*, who rode to the hounds and read Carlyle, and who wandered around in tight pants and flame-colored shirts.

Fortunately, the nation has approved of her because she dares to be different from the popular image of the average American housewife; paradoxically, just as it had approved of Mrs. Eisenhower because she was typical. President Kennedy is pleased by the impact his wife has made upon the country, and the world. "Any First Lady will do all right if she is herself," he says. He disagrees emphatically with former President Grover Cleveland, who once advised his wife that she would get along as First Lady if she did not try anything new. "It is up to each First Lady to do what best fits her temperament and personal inclinations," the President says.

"A woman's role is different from a man's," adds the President. Carrying this a step further, he believes that a First Lady's responsibilities are totally separate from those of the President. "First Ladies are not public officials. Their responsibility to their family is the same as any other woman's—efforts on behalf of charity, trips abroad, or special projects are extra. It is up to her to do what she can, within her own limitations.

"A First Lady must fulfill the responsibilities common to every woman who is a wife and mother. Her first duty is to her husband and her children—when her husband is also the President, that duty is considerably expanded."

Because she interprets her role in the same way as does the President, Mrs. Kennedy has made it very clear that her private obligation as a mother dominates her public life as the highest-ranking woman in the land. For this reason Mrs. Harry S Truman is her favorite First Lady. At first this might seem a peculiar choice, for Mrs. Truman was one of the most retiring and least-understood First Ladies in history, whereas Jacqueline Kennedy is an exciting young woman whose public ovations in a dozen countries abroad and dramatic innovations in the White House have made her the most highly publicized First Lady in history. President Kennedy explains his wife's—and his own—admiration of Mrs. Truman simply: "Mrs. Truman was always just Mrs. Truman. Her central responsibility was to be Mrs. Truman." Being Mrs. Truman meant being both well-mannered and warm-hearted: the President recalls the excitement of the White House servants when he invited the Trumans to dine one night, their eager anticipation of seeing Mrs. Truman after nearly nine years' absence, and her reciprocating delight in seeing them as she greeted each by name and inquired about their families and fortunes. The First Lady amplified the reasons for her affinity toward Bess Truman: "She brought a daughter to the White House at a most difficult age, and managed to keep her from being spoiled, so that she has made a happy marriage with lovely children of her own. Mrs. Truman kept her family close together in spite of White House demands, and that is the hardest thing to do."

President Kennedy explains: "If Jackie were older and our children older, she would have more time for public things. But she is concentrating on trying to live as normally as possible in abnormal circumstances, for the sake of our children."

Mrs. Kennedy has made a determined effort to shield her children, Caroline, five, and John Jr., two, from the head-turning publicity which is beamed upon every occupant of the White House. She is deeply concerned that her children develop healthy, unspoiled personalities; but today's massive radio, television, magazine, and newspaper coverage makes this a difficult task indeed. In the coming years, as the children grow older, the problem will grow worse, and the pending birth of a third Kennedy child would mean increased focus of interest for the curious public. Caroline is independent and precocious; she will soon have to be sent from the isolated White House world to an outside school, where other children and their parents will inevitably treat her with special deference.

Both Kennedys adore their children and seek to protect them; but upon Mrs. Kennedy falls the primary burden, and she does not hesitate to go to extreme lengths in her battle against the press. She has set up a special nursery school in the White House for Caroline and her friends. She planted rhododendron bushes around a play area on the back lawn, so that Caroline and her friends would not be visible to photographers' long-lens cameras poking through the iron grillework of the back fence. She once signed a picture to Press Secretary Pierre Salinger, "From the greatest cross he has to bear," because she protests so often to him about stories and pictures involving Caroline and John Jr. She hides from Caroline all magazines which contain her picture, or tears out the offending page if the magazine is to be left on a coffee table within Caroline's curious reach. Holding John Jr., she crouched behind some bushes during a ceremony on the back lawn welcoming Algeria's Premier Ben Bella, because she wanted him to see the colorful affair without being seen in turn; but when the cannon salute began, the baby cried, and photographers rushed over to take her picture crouched on the ground. Once she even donned a wig and nurse's uniform to take Caroline to Washington's Glen Echo amusement park—both had a wonderful day and were not recognized. "People must be as sick of hearing about Macaroni [Caroline's pony] and us as I am," she recently said. The gregarious Caroline has even absorbed her mother's attitude. Riding in an open convertible with her father one day, she turned and saw several photographers running toward the car. She held up her hand imperiously. "No photographs, please," she said.

Yet Mrs. Kennedy's problem of protecting her children from public scrutiny is compounded by her desire to let Caroline and John Jr. experience normal childhood pleasures. She allows Caroline free run of the White House, which is, after all, her home. But this also means she is constantly bumping into visiting officials who can't resist repeating their encounters with her. She has permitted Caroline to greet such dignitaries as India's Prime Minister Nehru, to whom she presented a rose for his buttonhole—an incident the press could hardly be expected to ignore. She permitted Caroline to observe a diplomatic reception from the stairway, but expressed surprise when Caroline's antics turned out to be the center of interest for the party and a topic of Washington conversation ever since. And in the winter of 1962 the First Lady not only let Caroline play on the back lawn, but imported Macaroni from their weekend retreat at Glen Ora, Virginia, to pull a sleigh filled with Caroline and her friends across the snowy lawn in full view of tourists on the street.

In her determination to rear her children well, the First Lady refuses to attend public luncheons and teas—something she has never liked to do anyway—on the grounds that she prefers to spend that time with her children. Similarly, she refuses to appear at most public dinners and political functions either with her husband or alone; generally her reason is given as her desire to be with her children. The President, for his part, does not think it necessary that she do these things. The First Lady explained recently that she did not accompany her husband on his frequent trips around the country because "the official side of my life takes me away from my children a great deal. If I were to add political duties, I would have practically no time with my children, and they are my first responsibility. My husband agrees with this. If he felt I should go on these trips, I would."

There is no doubt that Mrs. Kennedy is serious about her devotion to her children, and that she arranges her schedule to spend several hours of playtime with them every day. The results show: John Jr. has been observed screaming in dismay, "Mommie, Mommie," when she merely wanders into an adjoining room without him. But rearing a child in a family of great wealth, White House or no, is not so demanding a task as most American women know it. Caroline and John Jr. have had a nurse since the day they were born. The First Lady has never been tied to a daily routine of changing diapers, feeding her children (they eat separately from the adults), giving baths and wiping noses, mending torn jackets, and supervising unwanted nap times as, for instance, Mrs. Truman did when her daughter Margaret was a child. She has never been confined to the house for lack of a baby-sitter.

But the President and First Lady also believe that a President's wife cannot ignore her responsibility to the nation just because her family is more important. "The mere fact that she is First Lady, and the highest-ranking woman in the country, is a responsibility," says President Kennedy.

Asked to list his wife's greatest contributions as First Lady in her first two years, President Kennedy hesitated not a second. He cites: ". . . Her emphasis on creative fields, her concentration on giving historical meaning to the White House furnishings, and her success as an ambassador on the trips she has made with me abroad. And by carrying out her primary responsibility to support her husband and care for her children well, she is doing her real job as a woman."

The President is proud of his wife's popularity and her achievements. Perhaps he is even a bit envious that she maintains such steady high popularity while his own is so mercurial. Recently he told a group of students touring the White House that he hoped some day one would return as President—"or better yet, as a President's wife." During their 1961 state visit to Paris she received such public acclaim that he introduced himself to a press luncheon as "the man who brought Jacqueline Kennedy to Paris." And he has been overheard more than once telling a prospective host seeking his presence, "Does it matter if I can't come? After all, Jackie will be there."

Even the Soviet press, hardly an admirer of the Kennedys, has praised Mrs. Kennedy as "beautiful." The Polish magazine *Swiat* reported that she had given the West a new "tone and style" and lauded her for her interest in art, literature, and the theater, her independent mind, and her recognition of the long-neglected United States intelligentsia. The Latin American, French, Indian, Pakistan, and English press has waxed ecstatic over her chic and charm. Her fan mail, which comes from all over the world, ranges from 6,000 to 9,000 letters a week, and requires a staff of thirteen to process. A girl in Indonesia wrote: "I've seen pictures of you. I am studying English because I admire you so much." Another, in Japan, wrote: "My mother tells me not to slump so that I will grow up to be tall and queenly like you." Abroad, her beauty, her clothes, her brief speeches in flawless French or Spanish have made her a crowd favorite.

The American press is almost as blindly adoring, although she has no more direct communication with reporters than did close-mouthed Mrs. Truman. The public is so eager to copy her that even the stores in O'Neill, Nebraska, sell "Jackie-look" sleeveless two-piece sheaths; her effect upon fashion is so spectacular that Edith Head, the Hollywood designer, calls her the "greatest single influence in history." More than one hard-eyed female reporter has been rewritten by a male editor who thought her story about Mrs. Kennedy not enthusiastic enough. Said the late poet Robert Frost, who read a poem at the President's inaugural, "There have been some great wives in the White House —like Abigail Adams and Dolley Madison—so great that you can't think of their husbands, Presidents, without thinking of *them*. It looks as though we were having another one now."

Ironically, the very qualities in Mrs. Kennedy which keep her from an active private or public political role—the source of many First Ladies' influence—are those which make her uniquely suited for the contributions to the nation which have made her so popular. Her emphasis on creative fields, her restoration of White House furnishings, and the flair for the dramatic and tasteful are natural outgrowths of her personality and background.

Mrs. Kennedy grew up in an elegant, gilded world where servants, trips to Europe, stables, fine eighteenth-century French furniture, and morocco-bound classics in the bookcases were taken for granted. She had the leisure to pursue the rare and beautiful things of life; she was familiar with the ballet, opera, fine but relatively unknown art, expensive furniture and antiques to a degree impossible for Mrs. Eisenhower, growing up in Denver, or Mrs. Truman, in the small town of Independence. Her genteel life, unlike Eleanor Roosevelt's, never included exposure to poverty, hardship, or injustice, so she never developed a social consciousness which might have interfered with her interest in the finer things of life. Consequently, when she decided to restore the White House she knew exactly where to find expert help and was considerably knowledgeable in the field of fine furniture herself. And her enthusiasm for the arts is based not upon a feeling that patronage of the arts should be her solemn duty but upon her genuine appreciation of the need for art in the balanced lives of people who are interested in all the works of man. William

Walton once explained that the Kennedys were neither avid art experts nor self-conscious seekers of culture, nor were they doing something they merely thought politically expedient. "They are both susceptible to the comfort of the arts. They couldn't live without them—it is woven into the pattern of their lives," he said.

President Kennedy says, "A man marries a woman, not a First Lady. If he becomes President, she must fit her own personality into her own concept of a First Lady's role. People do best what comes naturally."

President Kennedy finds that one of his wife's chief attractions is her concentration on interests other than his own. "I don't have to fight the day's political battles over again at night," he says. He enjoys the "different kind of atmosphere" Jackie creates in his home life. Attorney General Robert Kennedy once explained, "What husband wants to come home at night and talk to another version of himself? Jack knows she'll never greet him with, 'What's new in Laos?'" The President sees her as "romantic by temperament in the old-fashioned sense of the word, fey even. Sensitive by contrast to my sisters, who are direct and energetic."

The First Lady decided shortly after the election that her contribution to the nation would be to inspire interest in history and the performing arts through the example of the White House. Says President Kennedy, "Her emphasis upon culture at White House functions is an expression of her feeling that the White House ought to be the center of excellence." Her first luncheon guest after the inauguration was George Ballanchine, the ballet master of the New York City Center. Her few public appearances are usually cultural affairs: a play, symphony, or ballet. She has invited the famed cellist Pablo Casals to play at the White House, given a dinner to honor Nobel Prize winners, added artists, actors, and writers to White House guest lists previously reserved for business tycoons and officials, scheduled a performance of Shakespeare, initiated dramatic readings. She enrolled Caroline in a junior ballet class. She created the new post of White House Cultural Co-ordinator, now held by August Heckscher.

David Finley, chairman of the Fine Arts Commission and a former director of the National Gallery of Art, says, "Mrs. Kennedy's interest has been very good for art. She has done a great deal to stimulate interest in visual and performing arts, by attending concerts, expressing her own appreciation of talent." Symphony conductor Leonard Bernstein, whom the First Lady recently kissed on the cheek and called "Lenny" in front of whirring television cameras, takes issue, however, with those who believe Mrs. Kennedy is purposefully striving to create a national cultural atmosphere. "She does not strive. It happens automatically because that's the way she lives," he contends.

Actually, the nation was developing an increasing awareness of the arts before the Kennedys came along. Since World War II, Americans have benefited from greater leisure hours, better educational facilities, and a higher standard of living. All these factors have encouraged Americans to explore new areas of interest, to the point where the nation now has more art galleries than baseball parks. The Kennedys, however, have given the trend a healthy stimulus. Mrs. Kennedy herself is modest about her efforts on behalf of culture. "I don't really like to call attention to anything. I think I'm more of a private person. I think everything in the White House should be the finest . . . just the best. But I don't want to be chauvinistic about it," she has said.

The First Lady's major project has been, however, not the encouragement of the performing arts but the restoration of the White House furnishings. Although the project has been carried out under her name, few people realize how much time and effort she has really put into it. President Kennedy says, "The restoration has been a more formidable operation than anyone realizes."

The First Lady conceived the project herself, and organized the several committees which have carried out the work. Not a scrap of material or a piece of furniture has been accepted for the White House without her approval. She has been deeply involved every step of the way, suggesting arrangements for newly furnished rooms, poring over old records and antique catalogues, double-checking with her experts for historical accuracy, sending memos to her committees, to antique dealers, to interested supporters. A guidebook to explain the historical significance of the furnishings was her suggestion, and she contributed to its development. She appointed a curator to keep records of everything in the White House; in the early days of her project she kept the records herself. She suggested a bill which would make the White House officially a museum and assure contributors their gifts would remain there permanently—and, with the President's approval, called congressmen personally to ask their support. "We couldn't have done this without her," a Fine Arts Commission member said recently.

During the first two years in the White House the restoration project consumed most of the First Lady's time. But now the major work has been done: only some third-floor private guest rooms remain to be overhauled. Mrs. Kennedy hopes that fine pieces will continue to be contributed through the years, but the major redecoration of the public rooms, from wallpaper to tables and chairs, has been completed. "Now we can relax and look for great paintings and objects of historical significance, and work on filling the library with appropriate books," she said recently. To these ends, she has appointed a committee to help her search for paintings by good American artists and a White House librarian to find rare volumes and presidential papers.

The First Lady is expanding her concern for the White House outdoors. She hopes to be able to landscape the grounds, following a plan proposed by a Park Service survey about thirty years ago. A rose garden outside the President's office was recently transformed into a formal garden with flowers planted to rotate blooms so that it never looks scrubby or barren. Another flower garden, on the east side of the mansion, is being similarly redesigned and replanted.

Her interest in preserving historical character may eventually embrace all of Washington. She is directly responsible, for instance, for preserving the old federal-style buildings which encircle Lafayette Park, the block-long square which faces the White House across Pennsylvania Avenue. During the Eisenhower administration it was decided to tear down these historic old buildings and replace them with badly needed modern government office buildings. When the new First Lady heard about this, she was appalled: she loved the peaceful, picturesque view the park afforded, and she thought it should be protected for future generations.

Mrs. Kennedy called David Finley, whose Fine Arts Commission is also charged with providing expert advice on the design of new buildings in Washington and proposed changes in such historic institutions as the White House and Congress. Together they went for a stroll in the square, and sat on a bench. They looked around them, at the brick houses to the east and west and the old Court of Claims building next to Blair House, the President's official guest house. "I want to preserve these wonderful old houses. How can I do it?" Mrs. Kennedy asked Finley. "Who is in charge of putting up these new office buildings?" Finley told her it was Bernard Boutin, administrator of the General Services Administration. That night she discussed the problem with the President, and the next morning she called Boutin. With the interest of the White House in the park brought so clearly to its attention, the General Services Administration hastily revised its blueprints and came up with a compromise plan to construct the offices in the rear of the old buildings, thus retaining them.

Mrs. Kennedy has explained her dedication to the restoration project this way: "I think the White House should show the wonderful heritage that this country has. We had such a wonderful flowering in the late eighteenth century. And the restoration is so fascinating—every day you see a letter that has come in from the great-great-grandson of a President. It was such a surprise to come there and find so little that had association and memory. I'd feel terribly if I had lived here for four years and hadn't done anything for the house."

Several factors have made the restoration such a success that it could be largely completed in two years. First, of course, is the First Lady's enthusiasm and personal attention to the project. For a woman who had never held a serious job, she turned out to have a keen sense of organization. President Kennedy says, "The organization of the committees was an impressive executive job. Mrs. Kennedy displayed more executive ability for organization than I had imagined she had." But the times in which we live helped, too. Historians believe that people these days have a new awareness of the importance of preserving American tradition and an interest in antiquity which was not present in less worldly days before World War II. (Mrs. Calvin Coolidge appealed for public donations to refurnish the White House, but failed to arouse any response and had to give up the idea.) Mrs. Kennedy has also had the advantage of mass communications, which have spread the word about her project into every home, and of mass transportation, which has brought more tourists to Washington to see the White House for themselves this year than ever before. The present heavy income-tax laws have assisted, too; wealthy couples are willing to contribute furniture or money to the White House restoration because it can be deducted for tax purposes as a charity donation.

The First Lady has always been fascinated by old houses, decoration, and antiques—particularly fine furniture. It is no secret that she was appalled at the department-store reproduction furnishings which she saw in December, 1960, when First Lady Mamie Eisenhower escorted her on her first tour of her new home. She had visited the White House as a child, aged eleven, but has admitted frankly that it made little impression upon her beyond annoyance at being shuttled through the rooms so rapidly. As a senator's wife, she had been in the White House several times for social events, but each time the rooms were crowded with guests and she had not paid much attention to the furniture. Mrs. Kennedy is not the only First Lady to be thus dismayed at the White House interior; Bess Truman suggested a Congressional appropriation to redecorate the White House, but got only $213,000 to furnish all 150 rooms—less than the cost of Mrs. Kennedy's restoration of the Green Room alone. And Mrs. Eisenhower, in her turn, often expressed the desire to see more priceless and beautiful objects in the White House, but she did not have the energy of Mrs. Kennedy, who is so much younger, and never found time to do something about it.

The new First Lady's practiced eye detected immediately that the White House furnishings were far inferior to those with which she had been surrounded in her own childhood home. She returned after her introductory tour of the White House to complain to her husband, the President-elect: "It looks like a house where nothing has ever taken place. There is no trace of the past." Shortly afterward she flew to Palm Beach, where the President's father Joseph P. Kennedy owns a mansion, to relax and recuperate from the birth of her son. She kept thinking about the White House, and what her contribution could be. She once expressed her philosophy this way: "Every First Lady should do something in this position to help the thing she cares about. People seem so interested in whatever the First Family likes. That is where I think one can lead. One doesn't know whether one leads in the right direction or not, but one hopes one does."

Mrs. Kennedy decided then, in Palm Beach, that her contribution would be to find things of historic association with the house or with former First Families. She spent long hours talking over the project with Mrs. Charles Wrightsman, wife of an oil millionaire, a close friend, and a self-taught expert on eighteenth-century furniture. They composed long lists of things to do and people to contact. They debated several approaches to the task, and finally decided to set up a committee of private citizens as the main advisory arm, which would assist in the national treasure hunt.

It frequently happens that prominent people in public life get credit for achievements which are merely done under their honorary sponsorship. But the First Lady once said, "If you want things to be right you have to do them yourself." So, wanting her project to be done right, she has done most of it herself. "No detail has been too small for her attention," says Jayne Wrightsman, who is now a member of the advisory committee, officially called "Mrs. Kennedy's Committee of the Fine Arts Commission for the White House." "She is so enthusiastic she is even interested in the proper Kleenex box for a third-floor bedroom."

Mrs. Kennedy's first move was to study White House history herself. She requested every reference to the White House that the Library of Congress could find. She was particularly intrigued by descriptions of purchases and belongings recorded by Thomas Jefferson, who decorated the newly built White House for the first time, and James Monroe, who had to decorate the White House all over again after it was rebuilt following the War of 1812, when it was burned down by the British. There was no trace of these furnishings in the White House. Through the years Presidents have sold furnishings they didn't like, carted away others, and just plain not paid much attention to preserving the possessions of the White House. Mrs. Kennedy is still continuing her study, not only of White House furnishings but of all pieces of the 1802 period forward: in 1962, for example, one of her Christmas presents was a rare volume on Victorian furniture.

Says one member of her committee, "The First Lady has acquired a terrific knowledge of the White House and period furniture. She has a mental filing system on it, and by now it is a passion with her."

Once Mrs. Kennedy was installed in the White House, the project was immediately under way. On January 24, only three days after the inauguration, she escorted David Finley and John Walker, director of the National Gallery of Art, on a special tour of the White House. She pointed out the lack of beautiful furniture and the need for systematic records to assist future First Ladies, and she said she would like to find ways to impress the history of the White House on visitors, particularly children. She spelled out, briefly, what she wanted to do; but at the end of the tour, William Walton, who had gone along, described it merely as "a general look-around to see what the joint is like."

Mrs. Kennedy scoured the White House for records of purchases through the years, but could find only a half-completed catalogue begun and subsequently abandoned some years ago by the National Park Service, which had been preserved by the White House head usher James West. She pored over ancient billing records from the National Archives and ancient photographs of White House rooms. It was time-consuming, difficult research; it became clear immediately that the White House would have to have a curator. "Everything in the White House must have a reason for being there," Mrs. Kennedy has explained. "It would be a sacrilege merely to 'redecorate' it—a word I hate. It must be restored—and that has nothing to do with decoration. That is a question of scholarship."

To assure the nation that she had no intention of tampering with history, Mrs. Kennedy appointed as the head of her committee Henry Du Pont, director of Winterthur, a museum of eighteenth-century American furniture and objects, and one of the most respected experts on Americana in this country. The incidental fact that Du Pont is a Republican helped to prove that she meant her project to be strictly bipartisan. She appointed eleven other people to the committee, all antiquarians with incomes permitting generosity to causes that interest them. The First Lady and Du Pont then set up an informal panel of experts across the country to authenticate gifts offered from their area.

Each gift is thus carefully authenticated, and approved by Du Pont and the First Lady, before it is accepted for the White House.

The Committee publicized its search for public donations for the White House—and everybody, including Mrs. Kennedy, was surprised at the eager response. Ordinary Americans cheered her project, although their homes do not contain, of course, museum-quality antiques in a quantity to fill up the cavernous rooms of the White House. The wealthy also provided enthusiastic support. The committee was quite successful in rounding up contributors who have been willing to purchase heirlooms approved by the White House from owners who are not wealthy enough to donate their possessions. Lists of approved furniture, available from private owners or from antique dealers, are sent out regularly to the committee, with prices attached. The First Lady does not contact potential donors herself, because she feels that it is more tactful and less demanding if her name is not directly involved. But she has been known to show acquaintances around the White House, subtly pointing out the pitiful lack of this or that—and the visitor has come away promising to donate his priceless old mirror or Baltimore ladies' table. One committee member said, "When the First Lady gets on the trail of something, she never gives up. If you have a bed that used to be in the White House, she'll have you sleeping on the floor before you know what happened."

The First Lady, like her husband, is very conscious of history "Since I am married to a historian I have such a feeling for that," she has said. That is why she has put such emphasis on historical accuracy in her project. She has checked personally with the Fine Arts Commission on such details as whether she would be setting a precedent to change the color of the dining-room walls or to hang pictures one on top of another in the high-ceilinged rooms. The President, too, has taken a great deal of interest in her project. He encouraged her to restore his reception room in the West Wing—with the one exception that a mounted fish he caught on their honeymoon in Mexico be allowed to remain, regardless how it might blend with the new decor. He has offered suggestions, generally along the lines of "When are we going to get rid of that awful chandelier?" or "Why don't you do something about the rug in the Green Room?" He sometimes looks over antique dealers' and auction-house catalogues with her in the evenings, taking particular interest in personal mementos and papers of the past Presidents: a sale of George Washington's papers and a portrait of Woodrow Wilson recently drew his eye.

Those involved with the First Lady in the restoration project say that she is always available for consultation on the subject, no matter how small the detail. Even when she is out of the White House, summering in Hyannisport, or vacationing elsewhere, the work goes on. She assigned various members of her staff to research projects before she left for her summer vacation last year. And she keeps up a long-distance exchange of memoranda on the work. She is helped in her efforts not only by her organizational abilities but by a good memory. One close friend described it as "the same kind of mind the President has, in a female way."

A side aspect of the restoration project, and another indication of the First Lady's dedication, is the formation of the White House Historical Association. The association was her idea, to assure that artistic and historic objects will continue to be purchased for the White House even if future First Ladies are not especially interested in furnishings. The association publishes the official White House guidebook; money from the sale of this booklet, priced at one dollar, will go toward future purchases for the White House. The First Lady felt from the beginning that the White House needed such a souvenir booklet. In the introduction to it, she wrote: "It seemed such a shame that they [children] should have nothing to take away with them, to help sort out the impressions received on an often crowded visit . . . its purpose was to stimulate their sense of history and their pride in their country." The guidebook was an instant best seller, with 350,000 copies sold in the first six months. A second booklet for sale to tourists is now being considered, which would contain pictures and word sketches of all the Presidents.

Mrs. Kennedy nursed the guidebook every step of the way, as she has the other facets of her project. She went over every word and picture in the book, as gathered and written by her curator, then Mrs. Lorraine Pierce. She composed much of the layout. She conducted the first meeting between the new association and the National Geographic Society, which donated its services to print the booklet. She approved its final draft one weekend at Hyannisport, but objected to the cover photograph as not dramatic enough. "She has a very good eye for that sort of thing," says an association member. The editors found a better picture of the White House, and substituted that just before the booklet went to press. As a further extension of her desire that Americans learn something about the history of the White House when they visit there, the First Lady proposed a printed panel showing the White House as it changed through the years, which tourists can read as they wait in line. She designed the panel layout and even selected most of the pictures herself.

To publicize her appeal for public support, the First Lady agreed to a rare television appearance, in February, 1962, for an hour-long tour of the newly furnished rooms. She proved to be an able performer and impressed the cameramen and producers by taping the program in one day, although she had previously given only one formal interview over television. She worked without a script even though one had been prepared in advance. She simply did not need it, since she knew each piece of furniture and its donor by memory and was thoroughly familiar with her subject. The program and the First Lady's performance were a great success; a book was made from the transcript and later the program was repeated.

The revived interest in the White House after the First Lady's televised tour is clearly illustrated by the increasing number of tourists who visit the White House daily. The month of the television broadcast, attendance reached 37,191 as compared to 21,361 the same month in the previous year. The yearly attendance continues to climb: in 1960 the recorded attendance was 977,142; in 1961 it passed one million, and in 1962 it increased to 1,562,467. The First Lady, remarking on the public response, said recently, "I have worked harder on this project than I ever have on anything, and so it has been especially gratifying."

Even the austere institution which is the United States Congress has felt the impact of Jacqueline Kennedy. She received permission from the Vice-President, and from the Majority and

Minority Leaders of the Senate, to move a magnificent chandelier from the Senate office of the Vice-President into her newly refurbished Treaty Room. The chandelier had once hung in the White House, but legend has it that its tinkling disturbed President Theodore Roosevelt, so he banished it to the Capitol, to keep the Vice-President awake. And Congress recently extended her idea of a curator to keep track of historic memorabilia. It passed a bill to provide a curator for the Capitol, to make an inventory of its furnishings and historical treasures—something that had not been done before.

The First Lady is a painstaking perfectionist. Some pieces of furniture have been moved from room to room before the First Lady and her expert advisers decided which spot was the absolutely perfect one. Some paintings have been up and down every wall. The First Lady moves furniture around, tacks pieces of sample cloth on chairs to be refurbished, and jots down sketches of how she would like to see things arranged. She keeps her own record book of the progress of the restoration—in addition to an almost daily pictorial record kept by the National Park Service. She keeps a long list of everything to be done; when an item is completed to satisfaction, she crosses it out. She sends notes to aides by the gross, with such remarks as: "Try such-and-such a painting on the left wall," or, "Contact so-and-so. I understand she has a rare table we have been searching for."

Often the First Lady uses the Treaty Room, on the second floor near Lincoln's bedroom and the President's sitting room, as her base of operations. It was refurbished to be a waiting room for the President's upstairs visitors, but the First Lady has gotten more use out of it herself. She sits at one end of the long table in the center of the room, working out of baskets piled high with items to be processed. When she is pondering some aspect of the restoration, she spreads out material samples, or sketches, or catalogues on the table. Often she sketches what she wants—in the way of a chair, or flower arrangement, and the like.

A large share of the First Lady's working hours, however, is taken up by unavoidable social planning. The problems of White House entertaining have grown so much since the days of Mrs. Madison's famous "squeezes" that each official affair is a massive production. The Washington diplomatic corps chiefs of mission, for example, now number one hundred and four, plus wives; the White House dining room seats only ninety people comfortably. And the White House pantry is so small that the serving for official dinners must be done from the family dining room. The First Lady, of course, does not get involved in the details of setting up a formal dinner—that is the responsibility of her social secretary, now Nancy Tuckerman. But because she feels the White House social functions ought to meet the same high standards she has set for its furnishings, the First Lady supervises the social planning much more closely than she would actually have to.

The Kennedys give approximately a dozen more formal receptions a year than did the Eisenhowers, and have entertained about twice as many state visitors at formal dinners. In January of 1963 the First Lady was already discussing with Letitia Baldrige, her former social secretary, the details of events for spring—menus, flowers, entertainment, guests, protocol (such dull but necessary points as whether a march and formal entrance would be appropriate at a particular affair, or which of the dinner guests should also rate an invitation upstairs for cocktails beforehand). Sometimes Mrs. Kennedy suggests a certain performer, or a certain kind of menu; sometimes she approves suggestions submitted by others.

The possibility of inviting Pablo Casals to entertain at a White House dinner, for example, was suggested by Pierre Salinger, who had once met Casals. The First Lady was delighted with the idea. It was the First Lady herself who thought of inviting Frederic March to read excerpts from Nobel Prize author Ernest Hemingway's works at her dinner honoring Nobel Prize winners. But when the White House contacted his widow for permission to read some excerpts, Mrs. Hemingway volunteered that she had some unpublished writings which she would be happy to have read at the White House. Mr. March was dispatched to see Mrs. Hemingway, selected several excerpts he considered appropriate, and sent them to Mrs. Kennedy for her approval.

The First Lady paid extra attention to the details of a dinner honoring French Minister of Culture André Malraux, who had been a host to the Kennedys during their state visit in Paris the year before. The dinner went off flawlessly, and it resulted in two unusual benefits for America. Before the dinner, Mrs. Kennedy discussed with Malraux the possibility of a loan of paintings from the Louvre to Atlanta, Georgia, as a memorial to the one hundred and twenty-two art lovers from that city killed in a Paris plane crash after a pilgrimage to the Louvre. (When Malraux returned home he took up the matter with the French government, which later shipped some priceless masterpieces, among them Whistler's "Mother" and Georges de la Tour's "Mary Magdalene," for exhibit in the Atlanta museum.) Then, after the dinner, the Washington *Post* White House veteran correspondent Edward Folliard broached with Malraux the idea of loaning the "Mona Lisa" for exhibition in Washington's National Gallery. Malraux was intrigued by the possibility, and discussed it later at great length with the First Lady, who pressed Folliard's plea. And eventually, after some trepidations on the part of the French government, the deed was done: da Vinci's masterpiece was put on exhibit in Washington—its first public display outside the Louvre—under heavy guard. The "Mona Lisa" proved to be the biggest attraction in the Gallery's history, with as many as 23,702 visitors a day.

Just as she has dared to be different in her private life, the First Lady has dared to be different in her official entertaining, making more social innovations than any other modern-day First Lady. She has sought, with the President's approval, to reduce the starch and stodginess of White House dinners. She wants very much to have guests come to the White House to enjoy themselves, not just because they feel a White House invitation is a command performance. She abandoned the formal receiving line; instead, she and the President circulate among their guests, chatting and shaking hands. She put ash trays on the tables, to indicate that smoking was no longer disapproved. She lit fires in the fireplaces, which had been unused so long they filled the rooms with black smoke during the first reception. Guests are now ushered directly in the front door, instead of through the north portico, where they used to wait in uncomfortable silence until the President and First Lady arrived in the East Room or Blue Room to begin the receiving line.

The First Lady has also launched some new special events for children—the one area in which she has shown an interest outside her home and family. The White House has given a Christmas party for children of the staff, a series of youth concerts, and a musicale for two hundred embassy children, who heard excerpts from Mozart's comic opera *Cosi Fan Tutte*. She attended the musicale, and even brought along Caroline, who sat enraptured on her lap throughout. Mrs. Kennedy attended three of the first five concerts given for crippled children on the White House lawn by young musical groups.

Likewise, the First Lady's rare visits to charities have been to those which benefit children. She has visited Children's Hospital in Washington, and Junior Village for homeless children— at the latter, she became so absorbed in the children that she overstayed her planned visit by one hour. Generally, however, Mrs. Kennedy feels that her time and energy can be better spent behind the scenes working on her central projects, rather than making appearances, trailed by dozens of reporters and cameramen, at charity institutions.

The public appearances which the First Lady does seem to enjoy, however, are the trips abroad, where she has scored her greatest triumphs. At first she was startled at the cheers from the crowds. But now she recognizes that she has a personal attraction all her own, unrelated to the fact that she is the wife of the President, and she has warmed to her role. She also realizes that her beauty and her chic have a great deal to do with it, and she prepares her wardrobe carefully for each trip, even though she claims she does not want people interested in her for her clothes. One newswoman who has followed her in recent years calculates that she wore four hundred different outfits in public in 1962 alone. She is the first First Lady to appoint a personal designer. But of course the First Lady's world popularity is due not only to her youth and her fashions. There is something regal and dignified in her bearing, her shy wave, her smile. She impresses officials with her knowledge of the arts and foreign countries, and by her unpredictable witticisms and frequent disarming naïveté.

Her greatest asset, however, has been her ability to speak French and Spanish effortlessly and well. In Paris she melted even the imperious President Charles De Gaulle by conversing animatedly with him in French, to the extent that at the formal dinners and luncheons he barely bothered to speak to any of the other guests, including the President. In a dusty farm field outside Caracas, Venezuela, she literally mesmerized a crowd of wizened, bent peasants by appearing like a vision in a lime-colored sheath, stepping her way delicately through the dung-filled field, and greeting the group with a warm, simple speech in Spanish. American officials, including the President, have called her "the Number One Lady Good Will Ambassador." The press, delighted to have something to write about the traveling First Lady besides her wardrobe, has given her brief foreign language talks almost as much attention as the infinitely more serious and important words of the President.

The First Lady, in fact, often appears more at ease when abroad than at public appearances in the United States. For instance, although she speaks frequently in French or Spanish abroad, she rarely speaks in public in English. Part of this is due to her own retiring nature, which the President understands— and consequently does not expect her to do more in public than she feels she can handle. Part of this reticence, however, is also due to her inability to get used to mobs of reporters and photographers trailing her everywhere. She does not seem to mind reporters so much if she is on foreign soil, for she knows that she is there strictly as a public personage. But in this country, she is constantly torn between her public role and her desire for absolute privacy. She cannot accept the fact that the First Family, as well as the President, is an object of total interest to the nation. She has been stung by press criticism, although it has been relatively mild and infrequent and generally on such unimportant subjects as whether her bathing suits are dignified enough for her position or whether she should abandon her preference for dresses from French designers. The First Lady's press office, directed by Pamela Turnure, absolutely will not give out personal information except basic statistics and the content of menus to clamoring reporters; yet the First Lady herself has granted exclusive pictures and a few interviews to reporters and photographers who happen to be personal, and therefore trusted, friends. She works hard at being a success in the type of official role she has chosen; yet because of this very success she cannot ignore public interest whenever she wants. Her attitude was probably half-serious when she replied flippantly to a note from a reporter handed her on a plane trip from Hyannisport to Washington. "What does Clipper [her German Shepherd pup] eat?" was the query. "Reporters," was her reply.

In small groups, however, with visiting dignitaries, officials, friends, and just plain interesting people, the First Lady is at her best. Here her apolitical nature is a definite asset, for officials find it easy to relax with her and discuss something other than business. She is briefed before each dinner for a foreign head of state—as is the President—on the visitor's likes, dislikes, his family, his background, his achievements. And she invariably remembers, say her associates, the kind of little personal details which frequently make the biggest impression. "She may not remember what the visitor's job encompasses, but she remembers that he has a daughter, aged nine, who recently toured Italy," one acquaintance says.

The President fits very well into the atmosphere of elegance which his wife has created for the White House social life, despite the fact he is usually depicted in the press as one whose extracurricular interests are limited to such things as swimming, sailing, golf, and a fondness for naval paintings (all of which he enjoys, but they reflect only a minor facet of his personality). He shifts easily from his own world of politics and national affairs into the First Lady's preferred world of the gentle and beautiful. British Prime Minister Harold Macmillan, after his second meeting with the new President, told a fellow Englishman, "One of the most reassuring things about him is his capacity to change pace. He always does his homework and is always on his toes during our discussions. But in the evening there will be music and fine food and good company. There is something very eighteenth-century about this young man. I imagine it's quite a new note in the White House."

The President goes over proposed guest lists for functions, and usually stops to taste the wine on his way from the office to dress for a dinner. But all other aspects of the White House social life are Mrs. Kennedy's responsibility. When a staff member or acquaintance proffers a suggestion for an unusual entertainment or reception theme, the President refers him to his wife with "Go sell it to Jackie. She's the one who will decide." The running of the household, likewise, is totally her job. The First Lady once protested, "When I start to ask him silly little insignificant questions . . . about whether Caroline should appear at some reception, or whether I should wear a short or long dress, he just snaps his fingers and says, 'That's your province.' And I say, 'Yes, but you're the great decision-maker. Why should everyone but me get the benefit of your decisions?' "

Actually, benefit of decisions or no, Mrs. Kennedy runs her East Wing operation as though she had borrowed the President's textbook for efficiency. While she prefers a memorandum system to dealing directly on the phone as the President does, her principles are the same: brevity and action. If a job will be accomplished faster if done in an unorthodox fashion, she's all for doing it that way. She doesn't rely on a formal procedure of letters and orders, with carbons to appropriate persons involved. In fact, she seems to keep her chief records in her head. Her former social secretary Letitia Baldrige greatly admired her and found her talents for getting things done "amazing."

According to Mrs. Kennedy's staff, she does not have a set routine. In the first place, she has been away from the White House a great deal—three months in the summers at Hyannisport and Newport, Rhode Island, Friday through Monday weekends at their Virginia horse-country retreat, Christmas and Easter weeks in Palm Beach, trips abroad with the President, occasional jaunts to New York City, four weeks in Italy and two in Greece vacationing, and a three-week semiofficial trip to India and Pakistan with her sister, Lee Radziwill. At such times she keeps track of the continuing White House projects through work folders which shuttle back and forth between her and her staff. When she is present in the White House, life takes on a certain pattern, if not a rigid routine. Generally she rises at 8:00 A.M., in order to spend an hour or so playing with her children before Caroline's classmates arrive at 9:30 A.M. It is not unusual for one of her staff to get a call about some pending matter as early as 8:15 A.M.—and also not unusual for that person to be caught at home, still having breakfast. Likewise, Mrs. Kennedy frequently works in the evenings, and has been known to call as late as 10:00 P.M. During the first months of her restoration project, she spent many evenings writing long, detailed letters to her new committee members or to antique experts she hoped to interest in the project.

When Caroline's classmates arrive, they file in prim order upstairs to the third-floor playroom, now converted into a classroom, for a morning of play and instruction under the supervision of two paid teachers, Miss Alice Grimes and Miss Elizabeth Boyd. The classmates are kept a dark secret, but they are drawn from families close to the Kennedys personally or officially. In its second year the son of Associate Press Secretary Andrew Hatcher, a Negro, was added to the group, making Caroline's class an integrated one. The first year, when the children were only three years old, Mrs. Kennedy and the other mothers took turns supervising their sessions. But now the children are old enough to be left alone under the control of their teachers.

While Caroline is at nursery school, Mrs. Kennedy goes to work on her projects. She discusses social problems with Miss Tuckerman, reviews housekeeping details with the housekeeper, Anne Lincoln, dictates personal and official correspondence three times a week to her secretary, Mary Gallagher. According to her staff, she makes decisions quickly. Generally her staff dealings fall into three categories. There is the strict business, requiring prompt answers, such as approval of a menu or a decision on a request to attend some event. There are briefings, in which she is kept informed of upcoming events, protocol requirements she is expected to meet, personal background on future visitors. And there are the more pleasant things—articles clipped by Miss Tuckerman or Miss Turnure or sent to them by people who thought they might interest the First Lady. These deal with subjects in which she has expressed concern, such as the effort to save the temples of the Nile from being flooded by a massive dam project; art magazines and new catalogues. People the world over send things to the First Lady; most of them, of course, get no further than her staff. All gifts from well-wishers valued above five dollars, for example, are forwarded directly to hospitals or other institutions. Recently, however, she was fascinated by a catalogue sent to her from an exhibition of contemporary Near Eastern art in Beirut.

Caroline's school is finished at noon, when the First Lady frequently lunches with her. More often she will continue working as she lunches from a tray, or shares an intimate lunch with a friend or associate in her fine arts project. The President prefers to utilize the lunch hour with what the White House refers to as "eating and working" luncheons in the family dining room with aides, out-of-town politicians, or officials.

After the children's post-luncheon nap, Mrs. Kennedy usually takes them outdoors to play. Sometimes other children are invited to play with Caroline, since John Jr. is still too uncommunicative to be much company for an energetic older sister. A jungle gym, sandbox, swing and slide have been set up behind the rhododendron bushes. Macaroni, who is ordinarily bedded at the Kennedy's Virginia retreat, is sometimes transported to the White House, where he trots around the lawn with Caroline on his back. Mrs. Kennedy, a keen sportswoman of good co-ordination and considerable muscular control, was once observed playing tennis, in white slacks and turtle-neck sweater on the White House courts with a Secret Service agent, while snow flurries filled the air and the temperature registered a chilly thirty-two degrees. Nearby, Caroline's head was visible above the foliage, bobbing up and down as she jumped on a trampoline. The President can see his family at the play area from his window, and has sometimes briefly interrupted a conversation to watch them. One day, in a mischievous mood, Mrs. Kennedy led Macaroni, holding Caroline and John Jr. on his back, up the shallow portico steps to the President's open office door. Macaroni poked his nose inside the office, decided it was not for him, and refused to put a single hoof inside.

About 5:00 P.M. Mrs. Kennedy and the children return to the mansion for the evening. She has frequently remarked that one of the best aspects of living in the White House is that she and her husband now are able to spend more evenings together than ever before, because the isolation of their high position means people come to them, and her husband, the ever-active politician, does not find it necessary to travel as much as when he was campaigning.

There is much evidence to suggest that Jacqueline Kennedy was not eager to be the First Lady; but, having married a man who wished to be President, she was given no choice in the matter. She said that the first months in the White House she felt like a moth banging against a windowpane. But there was ample evidence at the end of her first two years that she enjoyed her role, for the most part. She had been tested and had proven herself. This could not help but deepen her self-assurance and her interest in accomplishing even more during the remainder of her husband's administration. Those close to her detected a growing confidence and maturity, reflected in her manner, her determination, and her attitudes. When she entered the White House she was a rather shy young woman who knew very little about life outside a small private family circle and inbred social world. By 1963 she had shown herself to be a true asset to her husband, and had developed her own area of competence and contribution. Intimates said this even affected the Kennedys' marriage, brought them closer together and added a new, deeper dimension. She has now become a full partner in the marriage, something she had not been when she played no important role in his pre-presidential career.

The President professes to notice no change in his wife since the election, but it is in his nature to be restrained, even detached, in comments about his family and those closest to him. His attitude is simply that Mrs. Kennedy is still Mrs. Kennedy. And what Mrs. Kennedy is is a complex, many-sided individualist, as are all highly intelligent and sensitive people—and as the President is himself. The President once described his own temperament as steady and relatively consistent through both pain and pleasure, and his wife's by contrast as intense and mercurial, vibrating continually through the whole range of emotions. Her mother, Mrs. Hugh Auchincloss, has said that her daughter always "felt strongly about things." Ethel Kennedy, her sister-in-law, described her: "The wheels go round constantly in her head —you can't pigeonhole her. You have a hard time getting to the bottom of *that* barrel, which is great for Jack, who's so inquisitive." Robert Kennedy put it this way: "She's poetic, whimsical, provocative, independent, and yet very feminine. Jackie has always kept her own identity and been different. That's important in a woman." The President gracefully acknowledges her independence, just as she from time to time has openly acknowledged his. Recently he greeted a delegation of twenty-five cultural leaders from North and South America touring the White House. One of them asked the President if he would invite Mrs. Kennedy to attend a South American art show at the Pan American Union. "I don't know how much influence I have with her, but I'll ask her anyway," said the President, smiling. The First Lady appeared the very next evening for the exhibition's formal opening.

President Kennedy is one of the most intellectual Presidents we have had in the White House. Mrs. Kennedy has always admitted she stands in awe of his brain power, and said if she were to draw a picture of him she would draw a figure with an enormous head and a small body. "After I got to know him, I went out and took a course in American history," she said. But Mrs. Kennedy herself has a formidable intellect. A longtime friend, Mrs. Earl E. T. Smith, wrote to Mrs. Kennedy from Cuba in 1958, while her husband was assigned there as United States Ambassador, to request the favor of mailing some books. She explained that she had never gone to college and had lots of time on her hands in Cuba, but couldn't buy books in English there. Would Mrs. Kennedy please send some classics that she should read to get a solid education in literature? Mrs. Kennedy compiled a long list and soon mailed one hundred and fifty books to Florence Smith. Mrs. Smith says now that she has the best collection of English literature of anyone she knows—outside of Mrs. Kennedy herself, perhaps.

The First Lady is often very thoughtful, too, in little personal ways. In 1961, for example, she noticed that the Secret Service agents who accompanied the First Family to Palm Beach for the holidays were forced to spend Christmas without their families. So the following Christmas she insisted that the Secret Service men be allowed to bring along their wives. Just before the family left for Palm Beach, she walked through the East Wing offices, with John Jr. and Clipper, to wish a Merry Christmas to every member of her personal staff. On her own, she sent a brightly decorated Christmas tree last year to Saudi Arabia's King Saud, who lay ill in an American hospital. She said in her note that she knew his religion did not recognize Christmas as Christians do, but she thought he might like to share a bit of the joyful celebration spirit, since he was a visitor here.

The same growth that is evident to intimates in the First Lady is evident in the President. He is a sure-handed executive, a more positive and forceful leader than during the first half of his administration. He has faced down the challenge of Big Steel, rioters at the University of Mississippi, the Cuban missiles of Soviet Premier Khrushchev. After election by the narrowest of margins in 1960, he has proven himself a leader, and a President.

Although President Kennedy sometimes says, "I can't remember what it was like not to be President," he did have some considerable adjustments to make when he was catapulted literally overnight from a seat in the Senate to the most powerful position of leadership that the Western world has yet devised. He had grown up in a Boston Irish Catholic family steeped in politics; since 1946, when he was first elected to Congress, he devoted his life to it; since 1956, he had been running for the presidency. Yet he has said, out of his own experience, that there can be no real training for the presidency, that no man can understand what it is like to be President who is not himself President.

Although the responsibilities which devolved upon Jacqueline Kennedy when she became First Lady were in no way comparable to the burdens the President assumed, the adjustment in her personal life was far greater. She had not prepared for that sort of life at all. She was born July 28, 1929, to John and Janet Lee Bouvier, both rich, Republican, socially very Old Guard, and very good-looking. Three and a half years later, Caroline Lee, her sister, was born; as they grew up, they became each other's closest friend, and remain so today. Mrs. Kennedy's sister is now married to Prince Stanislas Radziwill, who is a real estate dealer in London. Jacqueline Bouvier attended fashionable girls' schools —Miss Chapin's in New York, Holton Arms in Washington, and Miss Porter's in Farmington, Connecticut—where the emphasis is on training students to be little ladies. As a student, Jacqueline was rather a solitary soul, contrary at times but bright. She enjoyed reading and wrote little poems to her family. But her chief interest was horses: since the age of one, when she was lifted astride a pony, she has been riding with her mother in horse shows and hunts.

When she was in her teens, her parents divorced; two years later her mother married Hugh Auchincloss, a wealthy Washington broker. Jacqueline then spent her summers on a seventy-five-acre waterfront estate at Newport and her winters at Merrywood, an estate in Virginia overlooking the Potomac River. Playwright Gore Vidal, who with Mrs. Kennedy shares Auchincloss as a stepfather, once described life at Merrywood as "a life that gave total security, but not much preparation for the real world." When she was graduated from Miss Porter's school, Jacqueline's yearbook profile noted: "Ambition—not to be a housewife." In 1948, when she was eighteen, Jacqueline was presented to society at debutante parties in New York and Newport, and was dubbed "deb of the year" for her beauty by the New York *Journal-American*'s society columnist.

Jacqueline attended Vassar for two years, then spent a year studying at the Sorbonne in Paris. She extended her stay with an extra summer vacation in Europe, then returned home to finish her studies at George Washington University. Her flair for sketching, fashion, and composition won her a *Vogue* magazine fashion contest, which included a job in Paris; but the Auchinclosses felt she had been gone from the United States long enough, so she turned down the job. Instead, she secured a job through a friend as a $42.50-a-week inquiring photographer for the Washington *Times-Herald*. It was not much of a challenge, and it lasted only a few months: it consisted of asking a question of some stranger, scribbling the answer, and snapping the picture of the interviewee.

While still a student, in 1951, Mrs. Kennedy met young Representative Kennedy, then thirty-five, at a dinner party given by Charles and Martha Bartlett, who are still close friends of both. Kennedy was already campaigning for the Senate, and he spent nearly every weekend and sometimes the greater part of weekdays in Massachusetts. It was a spasmodic courtship; twice a period of six months went by when they did not see each other. But in January, 1953, John Kennedy returned to Washington as a senator—and he began to court Jacqueline, who was by then working as an inquiring photographer. They were married September 12, 1953, in a lavish wedding at Newport; three thousand uninvited spectators crashed through the police cordon around the church, trying to glimpse the handsome senator and his society bride. The reception was an extravaganza for nine hundred; there were twenty-six ushers and bridesmaids in the bridal party. During the wedding toasts the bride noted wryly that her mother had always told her to judge a man by his correspondence. She held up a postcard from Bermuda tenderly inscribed: "Wish you were here. Cheers. Jack." That, she said, was her only written communication from her groom.

The newlyweds bought a large home at McLean, Virginia. It was a mistake; the senator did not like the long traffic-snarled ride to the Capitol, and Mrs. Kennedy felt lonely and stranded way out in the country when he was away speaking or politiking. There were other adjustments: her arty friends bored him, his political ones bored her. Their tastes, in almost everything from reading to eating habits, did not mesh. But by the summer of 1954 there was a bigger complication to worry them—the senator's back, injured playing football in college and re-injured during the war, was so painful he was spending much of his time on crutches. In October surgeons performed a double fusion of spinal discs; but the months slipped by and Kennedy was still flat on his back, in almost constant pain. In mid-February a second operation on his spine was performed. This time the operation was successful, and the senator was able to fly to Palm Beach to recover. Finally out of danger, he utilized his recuperation period, when he had plenty of undisturbed time to think, to write his Pulitzer Prize-winning study of political courage, *Profiles in Courage.* Legislative Assistant Theodore Sorensen did much of the research for the book in Washington, and other scholarly friends helped; but Kennedy himself, lying on his back in Palm Beach, did the bulk of the writing, scrawling in laborious longhand. Mrs. Kennedy helped to co-ordinate material and check facts, and the senator dedicated his book to her.

In May, 1955, after a seven-month absence, Kennedy returned to the Capitol and to politics, limping slightly but otherwise recovered. Within a year Jackie was pregnant, and Kennedy had launched a Kennedy-for-Vice-President boom. But Kennedy lost the vice-presidential nomination, and Mrs. Kennedy lost the baby by miscarriage. Shortly afterward they moved to a more convenient location, purchasing a row house in fashionable Georgetown. There, in 1957, Caroline was born, and her birth gave Mrs. Kennedy a sense of purpose which she had lacked. "It's terribly creative to make a house a happy place to live in," she has said. She concentrated on doing just that, and playing with her baby daughter. She has never been a "joiner," and always avoided women's clubs and similar organized activities.

During the campaign for the nomination and then the presidency in 1960, Mrs. Kennedy was again pregnant, and her public appearances were rare. Her most notable public expression was a tart, no-nonsense remark to a claim by *Women's Wear Daily*, an influential trade publication, that she and her mother-in-law spent $30,000 a year on French clothes. Mrs. Kennedy replied that she couldn't spend that much even if she wore sable underwear.

On election night, November 8, the exhausting campaign at last finished, the candidate and his family waited at Hyannisport for the returns. The candidate, Mrs. Kennedy, and William Walton had a quiet dinner; at first they talked about painting, instead of politics, then they changed to a series of reminiscences, vignettes from the campaign. After dinner they settled in the living room to watch the returns slowly come in on a small portable television set; Sorensen joined them. Next door, at his brother's house, the rest of the family and aides were manning a "command post," gathering reports by phone from workers across the country before they were registered by the television news commentators. There was little conversation in the living room. At 10:30 P.M., when early returns showed a big lead for Kennedy, Jacqueline whispered, "Oh, bunny, you're President now." He replied quietly, "No . . . no . . . it's too early yet." It was indeed too early; the Republican candidate, Richard Nixon, pulled ahead steadily for the rest of the evening. At eleven-thirty, because she was expecting her baby in three weeks, Mrs. Kennedy was sent to bed. The candidate followed at 3:00 A.M., when he had not yet won. But at 5:45 A.M., the Secret Service moved to establish security and surround the house. When he awoke, John Kennedy was President-elect. His victory margin—a mere 112,881 votes— was so narrow that Robert Kennedy, standing on his sofa in his stocking feet, told reporters it was a "miracle."

When Nixon's press secretary, Herbert Klein, read Nixon's concession over television at 11:00 A.M. that morning, Mrs. Kennedy did not watch. She was walking along the beach alone. Later that afternoon she met a small group of Washington reporters in Robert Kennedy's house, her one and only direct exchange with them collectively to this day. She appeared shy but straightforward: she said she believed her first duty as First Lady was to take care of the President so he could best serve the people, that she would do whatever her husband wanted her to do, and that her chief interests would be in the area of programs dealing with children or foreign students. And she stressed her intention to try to rear her children in a normal fashion.

She seemed to find it difficult to believe that she was about to become the partner to the President.

ABOUT THE AUTHOR

MARIANNE MEANS is the White House correspondent for the Hearst newspapers. Since 1960 the author has observed President and Mrs. John F. Kennedy closely, both in the White House and during their travels abroad.

Miss Means was a member of the Washington bureau of the Hearst newspapers before her assignment to the White House. She had previously been the women's editor of the *Northern Virginia Sun* in Arlington, Virginia, and a copyeditor on the Lincoln, Nebraska, *Journal*.

A native of Sioux City, Iowa, Miss Means is a Phi Beta Kappa graduate of the University of Nebraska. In 1962 the author won the New York Newspaperwomen's Club Front Page Award for the best feature writing.

DATE DUE

GAYLORD			PRINTED IN U.S.A.